# THE "LOST"
# SAM SPADE
## Scripts

Edited by Martin Grams, Jr.

Published in the USA by:
BearManor Media
P O Box 71426
Albany, Georgia 31708
www.bearmanormedia.com

ISBN 978-1-59393-717-1

Printed in the United States of America.

Book and cover design by Darlene Swanson of Van-garde Imagery, Inc.

# INTRODUCTION

When Dashiell Hammett's *The Adventures of Sam Spade* made its debut over ABC in August of 1946, personable Howard Duff, a comparative unknown in Hollywood circles, was assigned the title role. The selection of young Duff for the hard-hitting detective was perfect casting, his success was immediate, and Hollywood began predicting important things to come for this new personality.

Just one year after his "Sam Spade" debut, Howard Duff found himself under personal contract to Mark Hellinger, movie producer. His first screen role as "Soldier" in Hellinger's production of *Brute Force*, had rated him star material from critics throughout the country. He received on-screen credit as "radio's Sam Spade." Even when Duff was given offers for movie roles, he never gave up the radio gig, often making long trips to multiple studios so he could juggle both acting forms.

The enormous success of the Sam Spade radio program spawned a comic strip series, magazine articles and radio crossovers, and at one time Universal Studios even considered the possibility of making a Sam Spade movie with Duff in the lead.

All this and much more because of a single radio program, based on a fictional detective glamorized in one novel, three short stories, and three films, including the impressive 1941 motion picture, *The Maltese Falcon*. Dashiell Hammett, the creator of the fictional private eye, received royalty checks for the use of his character, but had no direct involvement with the series except the lending of his name in the opening and closing credits.

About the time the radio program gained popularity, Hammett joined the New York Civil Rights Congress, a leftist organization that was considered by some to be a Communist front. When four Communists related to the organization were arrested, Hammett raised money for their bail bond. When the accused fled, he was subpoenaed about their whereabouts, and investigated by Congress.

Although Hammett testified to his own activities, he refused to divulge the identities of known American Communists, resulting in a five-month imprisonment sentence for contempt of court, and he was promptly blacklisted.

In June of 1951, Howard Duff's name appeared in the Anti-Communist publication known as *Red Channels*, and both the networks and the sponsor attempted to evade the program altogether, resulting in Steve Dunne taking over the lead role, and soon after, the radio program's cancellation.

Before the series was cancelled, 245 episodes were broadcast. According to which reference guide you prefer, between 60 and 70 episodes are presently available from collectors across the country. The reason for this is simple: the networks never made it a policy to record the broadcasts. It was very expensive to do so, and no one at the broadcasting studios had any notion that a commercial value could be placed on the recordings. The few that survive today are courtesy of collectors who sought out the wire recordings and transcription discs, and took the time to transfer the sound to a medium such as compact discs and audio cassettes. All that remains now of the lost episodes are the scripts.

This book contains a total of 13 radio scripts from *The Adventures of Sam Spade*. To select which scripts was not a difficult task. It was merely a process of elimination. First, I chose only scripts to episodes not known to exist in circulation, so that fans of the program could enjoy "new" and "further" adventures, rather than relive what they already have heard. Second, I eliminated the mysteries that were below average for the series. Even today's television programs have their occasional "stinkers." Third, I chose scripts that were of importance, such as the September 29, 1946 broadcast (the premiere episode of the series) and the only episode from the Steve Dunne season that does not exist in recorded form (which was also a holiday offering).

In the premiere episode, "Sam and the Guinea Sovereign," there were a few lines scratched out of the script, including one where Sam takes Lina's money to exchange for helping return the coin to her, even though he was hired by Tonescu to do the same. Another deleted scene was when Effie asks about the thousand dollars he earned on the case, and Sam explains that he lost it all on a horse race. I did not include the deleted lines, since they were never broadcast. The scriptwriters wrote more than was needed, knowing it was easier for producer/director William Spier and the cast to delete lines rather than add lines. Hence, this and the other twelve scripts are *as they aired over the network.*

"The Jane Doe Caper" (broadcast May 29, 1949) was a magnificent episode, and was chosen for this book solely because it reveals an emotional side of Spade that was not captured in any of the other 244 episodes.

"The Judas Caper" (broadcast April 11, 1948) reveals another side of Sam, in which he purposely hides a woman - possibly a murderess - in his apartment solely for the affections of a woman. Keeping a woman in his apartment for said reasons was implied in Hammett's *The Maltese Falcon* (1929), but this was the only time on the radio program that Sam restaged this scene.

"Inside Story of Kid Spade" (broadcast February 16, 1947) reveals Sam's past as a prizefighter before going into the private detective business. The plot is actually a script rewrite of the July 20, 1944 broadcast of *Suspense,* also produced and directed by William Spier, entitled "Of Maestro and Man." Richard Conte played the lead role of the boxer, with Peter Lorre as The Maestro. A love interest was added to the *Sam Spade* version, offering radio listeners the one and only time Spade ever considered settling down with a woman by marriage. A character in this episode, "Pretty Boy Gluskin," was a tip of the hat (or a pull of the leg) to Lud Gluskin, the show's musical director. This inside joke was repeated often throughout the series, and this script reveals one such example.

"The Short Life Caper" (broadcast January 11, 1948) offers another inside joke. Sam questions a woman who claims to have been with her roommate, Peggy Rea. Peggy Rea was, in reality, William Spier's secretary. In "Jury Duty" (broadcast May 25, 1947), the character of "Big Louie Havoc" was a tip-of-the-hat to actress June Havoc, William Spier's wife. Juror number three was Mr. R. Crossley Hooper, described by Sam as a little man. Crossley and Hooper were the names of two official rating systems for radio programs.

Sam's methods also tested the network's censorship board that had to review each and every script and approve of the contents before broadcast. In these scripts, you'll read Sam stealing money from a dead man's wallet, slap a sobbing woman, and other tactics not applied by other radio detectives on other networks.

Without giving away any fun scenes or surprises, I have to refrain from revealing the other scripts' importance (the reason they are included) except to say that you should have a fun time reading. Some episodes were so poorly written and poorly conceived that they would never have made it in this book. If I personally made a list of the ten best episodes of the series, they are included among the 13 in this book. Since the "lost" recordings will probably never see the light, thanks to Ben Ohmart of BearManor Media we are offering the next best thing.

Goodnight, Sweetheart,
Martin Grams, Jr.

# "THE ADVENTURES OF SAM SPADE"

PROGRAM #1
5:00-5:30 PM

9:00-9:30 PM
1946
SUNDAY, SEPTEMBER 29

# CBS

| | |
|---|---|
| ANNCR: | The hair-raising adventures of Sam Spade, detective brought to you by the makers of Wildroot Cream-Oil for the hair. |
| MUSIC: | PUNCTUATION . . . UP ONTO TRILL . . . INTO PHONE BELL |
| SOUND: | PHONE BELL |
| SOUND: | TELEPHONE ON FILTER MIKE:     LIFT RECEIVER: |
| EFFIE: | Sam Spade, Detective Agency. |

SPADE:      (ON FILTER) Hello, Sweetheart, it's me. Sammy the Spade.

EFFIE:      Sam, is it over? Who was behind the battle of Montgomery Street?

SPADE:      I'll tell you all about it when I get there. What a day! I even had a fight with a—I guess you'd call it a woman.

EFFIE:      Why, everyone knows you can lick any woman your weight.

SPADE:      Not this one. Sharpen a couple of pencils, Sweetheart, I'll be right over to dictate my report on the Blood Money caper.

MUSIC:      THEME AND TO B.G.

ANNCR:      Dashiell Hammett, America's leading detective fiction writer and creator of Sam Spade, the hard-boiled private eye, and William Spier, radio's outstanding producer-director of mystery and crime drama, join their talents to make your hair stand on end with the *Adventures of Sam Spade* . . .

MUSIC:      (ACCENT)

ANNCR:      . . . presented each Sunday by Wildroot Cream-Oil, the non-alcoholic hair tonic that will put your hair back in place again, grooming it neatly, naturally, the way you want it. Why does a girl turn thumbs down on a man? Here's one very important reason why: According to a recent survey, 97 out of 100 girls dislike a man whose hair is either unkempt or too slicked-down. So don't look that way. Spruce up with Wildroot Cream-Oil. It grooms your hair neatly and naturally. And as our survey shows, that's exactly how girls like to see it. Non-alcoholic Wildroot

Cream-Oil contains LANOLIN, the soothing oil that's so much like the oil of your own skin. Four out of five users, in a nation-wide test, preferred Wildroot Cream-Oil! You'll like it, too!

MUSIC:     SNEAK UNDER

ANNCR:     And now, Wildroot brings to the air the greatest private detective of 'em all . . . in . . . *The Adventures of Sam Spade*!

MUSIC:     UP TO OVERTURE

MUSIC:     OVERTURE

SOUND:     DOOR . . . FOOTSTEPS

EFFIE:     (FADING ON) Oh, Sam! Your eye! She did hurt you!

SAM:       Nuts! I just ran into a closed fist! Get your book. Let's get started!

EFFIE:     Get any of the ten million dollars, dear?

SOUND:     STEPS; CHAIR; DRAWER; BOTTLES; POURING;

SPADE:     Yeah, All of it. But there's a hole in my pants pocket! Come on! Shake the lead out of your pencil!

EFFIE:     (FADING ON) Look what I got, Sam. It writes under water!

SPADE:     For this report, you'll need one that writes under Humphrey Bogart! Put it on our best stationary. It's going to the President of the Golden Gate Trust Company—what's left of it. . . . Ready?

EFFIE:     (SOFTLY) I'm always ready, Sam . . .

MUSIC:     SNEAK

SPADE:     Dear Mr. Newhall; You may consider this my final report.

There's nothing more I can do – or want to do. From here out, your daughter Ann is your problem. Two weeks ago, you retained me to check on her movements. You suspected she was seeing a man known as Red O'Leary. You also said you feared he was a–quote-"disreputable character." You were right on both counts. On the night of September 16, I picked up the subject, your daughter, at the Blue Bottle Bar and Grille. She and Mr. O'Leary were seated in a booth in the rear, punishing the phony scotch. I kept a plant on them, and during the next ten days, they met regularly at the Blue Bottle. They never went anywhere else – just sat and talked. That is, Ann talked. Red listened. This routine continued until last night. I tailed them to a joint called Big Flora's on Telegraph Hill. I cooled my heels outside for a while – then went in after them.

SOUND:     SALOON NOISES:

SPADE:     Big Flora's was a new gin mill on the hill. It'd been going less than a month – but it was going strong. I drifted over to the bar, and threw a fast case around the place. No local guns, strictly an out-of-state mob. O'Leary and your daughter were in a side booth – Big Flora herself pinned me with a look when I entered. She stood at least five-ten in my stocking feet, broad-shouldered, deep-bosomed, thick-armed, a pink, accordion-pleated throat – a handsome, brutal face.

FLORA:     Just get in town, dearie? Or are you the local talent?

SPADE:     I'm from K.C. That makes you happy?

FLORA:     K.C. eh? Pobey?

SPADE:     Pobey Pushkin? He's still eatin' jude.

FLORA:     Know him, eh? What's your name?

SPADE:     I got a dozen. You like Little Morphy?

FLORA:     (HARD) Little Morphy's dead!

SPADE:     (SOFTLY) I know. I was with him in the busted caper that croaked him. He gave me his name before he died.

FLORA:     Well! If that's so, you must be a right guy. Shake!

SOUND:     BARSTOOL CLATTER:      STEPS AROUND THE BAR:

SPADE:     Ow!

FLORA:     What's the matter, kid, you soft? Come on, this calls for one on the house. Out of my way, Pappadopolos. Big Flora's mixing these herself. This boy's from Kansas City. Meet my bartender, Pappadopolos.

SPADE:     Papa who?

PAPP:      Pappadopolos. Pleased to make your acquaintance . . .

FLORA:     Was there anyone here in particular you wanted to meet?

SPADE:     How about that gold-plated mouse over there?

FLORA:     Her? Un uh, that's Red O'Leary's property. Miss Ann Newhall. She came in here . . . slumming, I think they call it. Her and Red looked at each other, and dearie that was a look. Love, I think they call it.

PAPP:      Yes. To talk to her might encourage trouble.

FLORA:     You shut up! (SOCK)

PAPP:      (YELP) Please, I did not mean anything. No, Flora, no – don't strike me again.

FLORA:     (LAUGHS) Stop shaking, Pappadopolos. I'm not mad at you. I'm not mad at anyone tonight.

PAPPADOPOLOS:     I am so glad, Flora. It is so nice to see you so happy.

BLUEPOINT:        (FADING ON) Flora. I got to see you. In private.

FLORA:            Sure. Take over, honey. I got to talk to this boy. (FADE) Come in the back room, Bluepoint.

PAPPADOPOLOS:     Yes, Flora dear.

SPADE:            Why do you let her knock you around like that, Pap? Ain't you got a union?

PAPPADOPOLOS:     What can I do?

SPADE:            Who's the gun she took in the back room?

PAPPADOPOLOS:     Some gangster, I think. Vance is his name. Bluepoint Vance.

SPADE:            Quite a few guns here this evening. There's Paddy the Mex. Haven't seen him since the days of the old beer mob. Fat Boy Clarke, Cokey Harmon. That frizzy blonde dame is Angel Grace Cardigan, isn't it?

PAPPADOPOLOS:     Believe me, everyone here is a criminal. They've been drifting in here ever since that Red O'Leary came to San Francisco.

SPADE:            A new mob! Red O'Leary the big gun?

PAPPADOPOLOS:     Please . . . I know nothing of such matters.

SPADE:            Any idea what's the caper?

PAPPADOPOLOS:     I have no idea.

SPADE:            Flora know?

| | |
|---|---|
| PAPPADOPOLOS: | Flora don't know. She likes anybody that brings money into the place. |
| SPADE: | Smart gal, Flora. |
| PAPPADOPOLOS: | Yes. (NERVOUSLY) I must wait on a customer (FADE) Excuse me. |
| SPADE: | (MUSIC SIMULTANEOUS) I looked up. Big Flora was coming out of the back room with Bluepoint Vance – they laughed about something – and he walked away. Then Flora went over and whispered to Ann Newhall. Looking a little frightened, Ann got up and followed her into the back room. Red gave her a reassuring smile as she disappeared through curtains. I went over to Red's table. |
| RED: | What do you want, Shamus? |
| SPADE: | Mind if I sit down? |
| RED: | Yeah, I mind. But it looks like you don't. |
| SPADE: | Red, why don't you leave the girl be? This isn't her crowd. |
| RED: | Look, Spade, I don't mind your tailing us. That's the way you make your living. But let's keep it formal, shall we? |
| SPADE: | Okay, Mr. O'Leary, let's. Who's the boss-gun of this mob? |
| RED: | Mob? What mob? |
| SPADE: | Don't be coy. There's not a face in this room that doesn't have a picture of it, front view and profile, with a number under it. |

RED:      Why are you telling me?

SPADE:    My job is to look after Ann Newhall.

RED:      Go ahead, if you think she needs it.

SPADE:    She needs it. She's drinking too much, and it's beginning to show.

RED:      You're not a snob, are you, Sammy?

SPADE:    Why should a kid that's got everything throw it away for what you've got, which is nothing?

RED:      You sound like you wish she'd throw it away in your direction.

SPADE:    I do indeed, Red, I do indeed.

RED:      Now, look, Sam. I've been walking the straight – and . . . ever since I left Chicago.

SPADE:    That what you told her?

RED:      That's what I told her, and that's what I'm telling you.

SPADE:    It couldn't be that you're rushing Ann Newhall because she knows her way around the Golden Gate Bank?

RED:      Use your head, Sammy. You couldn't blow the Golden Gate with A-bombs.

SPADE:    Ann might know what day the time-locks are sprung. Or she might find out from her Daddy.

RED:      Use your head, Sammy. Montgomery Street is crawling with cops, bank guards, who can lay their hands on more heavy artillery in thirty seconds than this mob ever saw in their lives.

SPADE:      Guys have been crazy enough to try it.

RED:        Not this guy.

SPADE:      Good. Now what about Ann Newhall?

ANN:        What about Ann Newhall, Mr. Spade?

SPADE:      Oh, hello, Miss Newhall.

RED:        Sammy doesn't believe I've gone straight, Ann.

ANN:        Why do you waste time talking to a sneaky gumshoe like him, anyway, Red?

RED:        I felt like talking to him. You got any objections?

ANN:        Of course not, Red darling. I just thought – maybe you thought you had to be nice to him because he's working for Father.

RED:        He thinks he's working for you.

ANN:        Well, he's not. Mr. Spade, I'm sick and tired of being followed around. Red is very well qualified to protect me. And if you don't leave us alone I'm going to ask him to protect me from you. Do I make myself clear?

SPADE:      Okay, Sweetheart. I'll call your old man in the morning and tell him I'm through. And I'm going to tell him why I'm through.

ANN:        Because Red threatened you, I suppose.

SPADE:      No, Sweetheart, that's not why. The why is because you aren't worth protecting!

MUSIC:      (BRIDGE: TO B.G.)

SPADE:      I went home and tried to forget Ann Newhall. I did –

pretty nearly. But I couldn't shake the hunch I had about the mob in Big Flora's place. I kept thinking about them and about your bank, Mr. Newhall. Your bank and the bank that faced it across the street on Montgomery contained a good part of the cash money in the City of San Francisco. For a mob of cheap gunsels to knock over every one of those banks would be like splitting Gibraltar with a B.B. gun. But supposing the cops were really master-minded. A hundred really tough guns might crack both of them at once. I'd counted thirty in Big Flora's alone, and they were still coming in when I left. It was a cute hunch. But wild. I decided to sleep on it. Next morning I was reaching for the phone to call you –

SOUND:      PHONE DIAL

SPADE:      When it rang.

SOUND:      PHONE PICKED UP

SPADE:      Yes?

NEWHALL:    (FILTER) Mr. Spade, this is Taylor Newhall.

SPADE:      Yes, Mr. Newhall. I was just going to call you. About your daughter . . .

NEWHALL:    Yes, Mr. Spade. About my daughter . . . there's no point in your continuing on that job. I've decided that Mr. O'Leary is all right.

SPADE:      You feeling alright this morning, Mr. Newhall?

NEWHALL:    Yes, Mr. Spade . . . I've met O'Leary and . . .

SOUND:      POLICE SIREN OFF

SPADE:      Just a minute, Newhall . . .

SOUND:      STEPS:    WINDOW RAISED

SOUND:      MACHINE GUN FIRE – GRENADES EXPLODING . . .
            BUILD BATTLE SOUND UNDER

SPADE:      Mr. Newhall! Where are you calling from, the bank?

NEWHALL:    No, I'm at home. I decided not to go into the bank today.

SPADE:      You're a lucky man, Mr. Newhall.

NEWHALL:    What do you mean by that?

SPADE:      I'm looking out my window toward Montgomery Street,
            Mr. Newhall, and I can barely see your bank for the gun
            smoke.

NEWHALL:    What's that? I can't hear you!

SPADE:      I can't hear myself! I'll call you back, Mr. Newhall!

MUSIC:      IN AND UNDER

SPADE:      I couldn't see the bank buildings distinctly, but the block
            between Kearny and Montgomery told me enough. Ten
            police squad cars were piled up near the corner and the
            cops had been moved down as they crawled out of the
            wreckage. The bandits had started the caper by knock-
            ing over the garage where the banks kept their armored
            trucks and they mowed down the law as fast as it could
            come in. A police grenade blew one of the trucks sky high
            and the cops moved in another few yards, but the gunsels
            had thrown up a barricade behind it and held their lines.
            Guns chattering, grenades exploding, sirens screaming,
            and the yells of the battling men, it was like the sound
            track of "All Quiet on the Western Front." The Battle of
            Montgomery Street had begun.

SOUND:      BATTLE UP INTO

MUSIC:      FIRST ACT CURTAIN

ANNCR:      The makers of Wildroot Cream-Oil are presenting "Blood Money," an adventure of Dashiell Hammett's famous private detective . . . . SAM SPADE!

MUSIC:      UP AND RESOLVES OUT

ANNCR:      In just twenty-one words I can sum up for you the reason why more and more men are using Wildroot Cream-Oil all the time. Here they are . . .  "Mainly because Wildroot Cream-Oil has the advantages that men expect from a fine hair tonic – without the disadvantages they sometimes find!" Yes . . . that's the gist of it. Now, what real man wants a tonic that plasters his hair and gives it a greasy, sissified look? Wildroot Cream-Oil never does that! It grooms your hair naturally, without a trace of that slicked-down appearance. Or, what man wants a hair tonic that makes him smell like a perfume factory? Wildroot Cream-Oil never does that either! This grand non-alcoholic product has just a slight, masculine fragrance. Besides it does a really thorough job of grooming – keeps your hair handsomely in trim . . . relieves annoying dryness . . . and removes loose ugly dandruff. And remember – there's not a single drop of alcohol in Wildroot Cream-Oil. What's more, it contains soothing LANOLIN. So get the big economy size at your drug or toilet goods container. And next time you visit your barber, ask him to use Wildroot Cream-Oil on your hair.

MUSIC:      ACCENT AND HOLD

ANNCR:      And now back to "Blood Money," tonight's adventure with . . . SAM SPADE.

| | |
|---|---|
| MUSIC: | (SECOND OVERTURE AND TO B.G.) |
| SPADE: | By twelve o'clock the Battle of Montgomery Street was over. On the desk in my office the afternoon papers screamed the news of the Seamen's National and Golden Gate Trust double-looting in five colors. The returns weren't all in yet, but the score stood at sixteen coppers knocked off, three times that many wounded, and twelve innocent spectators, bank clerks and the like killed. The bandits had lost seven known dead and thirty-one prisoners. The others, a hundred-odd, had made a clean getaway, using ordinary cars that were easily lost in traffic. I was reading the newspaper guesses as to the size of the loot – around ten million dollars— |
| SOUND: | DOOR OPENS |
| EFFIE: | Sam – there's a man outside. I think he's been shot. There's blood all – |
| SPADE: | Stay in here. |
| SOUND: | CHAIR PUSHED BACK: STEPS |
| SPADE: | I'll see him in the outside office. |
| SOUND: | DOOR CLOSES: STEPS |
| SPADE: | (FURIOUS) What do you mean coming in here, messing up my carpets? |
| BLUEPOINT: | (HOARSELY) They jumped me. It's started. |
| SPADE: | What's started? You need a doctor. |
| BLUEPOINT: | (BREATHING HARD) You got to listen to me, Spade. I don't think I got much more time. I got five slugs in me. I'm Bluepoint Vance. |

SPADE:        Yeah, you're a pal of Big Flora's – one of the mob that in the Montgomery Street push. What else?

MUSIC:        SNEAK IN

SPADE:        He talked. The way he told it, the mob was split up into ten groups. Each group had a leader. Each leader received a map and a detailed plan of his part of the operation. But none of them knew who made the plans. Each one took his orders from the group leader just ahead of him, like a chain letter scheme. Bluepoint was the top link in the chain. I asked him who was the Eisenhower.

BLUEPOINT:    Don't . . . know. Every man's cut . . . a hundred grand. Every one of us knocked off . . . ups the divvy for the others . . . .see? . . . That's what I mean . . . it's started . . . see?

SPADE:        Yeah, who'd you get your orders from?

VANCE:        (TRIES TO SPEAK AND CAN'T)

SPADE:        Come on, Bluepoint, try. Who was it?

VANCE:        It was . . . Red . . . .O'Leary . . .

SPADE:        Red, huh? I was afraid of that.

SOUND:        DROP OF BODY

SPADE:        Effie!

SOUND:        DOOR OPENS

EFFIE:        Yes, Sam. (A BEAT, THEN) Dead?

SPADE:        Yeah. Call homicide. Tell him to get the boys up here with the basket. Take the rest of the day off.

EFFIE:     Did he tell you anything?

SPADE:     Some, Effie. Some.

MUSIC:     BRIDGE AND TO B.G.

SPADE:     Bluepoint Vance said it had started. It had. They were dropping all day long – in alleys, singly at first, Happy Jim Hacker and Rat Face – and then in twos and threes, and finally two dozen mowed down there they were lined up against a wall in a house on Fillmore Street. And for every mobster killed, there was a bigger chunk of blood money per man among the survivors. Around six in the evening I walked up Telegraph Hill to Big Flora's . . . the neon sign was dark, curtains drawn tight over the windows, and a sign on the door said "closed for alterations." I climbed a flight of stairs to Big Flora's rooms over the saloon . . .

SOUND:     KNOCK ON DOOR

SPADE:     . . . and pounded on the door.

SOUND:     DOOR OPENED

FLORA:     Well?

SPADE:     Wacky Washburn sent me.

FLORA:     Step inside.

SOUND:     DOOR SLAMMED

FLORA:     We'll talk in here, the parlor's in use.

SOUND:     STEPS

PAPP:      (FADING ON) So it's you, Flora . . . Oh, I thought I heard the door be . . . ..oh, excuse me!

FLORA:      (SOUND: SLAP, PAPP YELPS) I told you to keep your trap shut in front of our guests!

PAPP:       No, please, Flora, I will be good, don't strike me again.

SPADE:      So you and Pappadopolos are at it again. He your husband?

FLORA:      (HEARTY LAUGH) Him? Does lidde man love his big Flora?

PAPP:       No . . . Flora . . . please, not that.

FLORA:      What's the matter, honey, don't you like to be hugged?

PAPP:       Yes, Flora, yes. But remember last time. My ribs – and they had to tape me up.

FLORA:      (LAUGHS) You should have heard him squeal when I pulled off the adhesive. Sit down, honey, before you fall down. You too.

SPADE:      Thanks.

FLORA:      All right, you, talk. Who, what and why?

SPADE:      I'm Percy Maguire. I'm Percy Maguire and I want my hundred and fifty grand.

FLORA:      Listen, Percy. You got a bill you got to give it to the big gun.

SPADE:      I don't even know who he is.

FLORA:      That makes two of us.

PAPP:       But, Flora, that is not true. He is coming here this evening.

FLORA:      What was that you said, dearie?

PAPP:       Now, Flora, darling . . .

| | |
|---|---|
| SOUND: | SLAP |
| PAPP: | (IN TERROR) No, Flora! No! I did not mean to say any-thing wrong. I swear I did not. |
| FLORA: | I'll kill you. So help me, this time I'll kill you. |
| SOUND: | BEATING |
| SPADE: | That's enough of that. |
| FLORA: | Who says so? |
| SPADE: | I say so. Pick on someone your own size. |
| FLORA: | You look about my weight. |
| SPADE: | Better not, Flora. You might get hurt. |
| SOUND: | SOCK IN JAW:     DANCING AROUND |
| FLORA: | Defend yourself, man! Defend yourself! |
| SPADE: | Okay, sister, you asked for it. |
| SOUND: | BOXING |
| SPADE: | (MUSIC: SIMULTANEOUS) I got the worst of it from the beginning. She led with her right like a woman, but what I didn't know was that she was a southpaw. I got in a couple where they should have counted. But where most women are soft, she had muscle. I was punchy before the round was over . . . |
| SOUND: | DOORBELL OFFSTAGE |
| SPADE: | . . . and when somebody rang the doorbell I was on the carpet. Saved by the bell. |
| FLORA: | Pardon me while I answer that door, Mr. Maguire. We'll finish this later. Oh, let me just take your gun. (WHEEZES |

– THUMPS HER CHEST) Getting old – out of condition! But we had fun, didn't we? (FADE) Help him up, Pappadopolos, get him some water.

SOUND:      FLORA'S STEPS FADING

PAPP:       You are all right? . . . you are not badly hurt?

SPADE:      Jaw's not broken.

PAPP:       Stay close by me this evening. We will help each other against that she-devil.

SPADE:      That wouldn't be the big gun she's letting in now?

PAPP:       Yes . . . yes . . . it is time.

BIG FLORA:  (FADING ON) Step in here, kids. You know Pappadopolos, Mr. Maguire . . . Red O'Leary and Miss Newhall.

RED:        Maguire, eh?

ANN:        Miss Flora, Red is badly hurt.

FLORA:      Hurt? Why didn't you say so? What happened, Red, they jump you?

RED:        Slug in my neck – can't move my arm.

ANN:        Red thought you might know of a doctor we could trust.

FLORA:      Only Doc I know got knocked off with that bunch on Fillmore Street.

SPADE:      Lemme have a look at that, Red.

FLORA:      You a doc, Mr. Maguire?

SPADE:      I don't think he'd last to the hospital and through the questioning they'd give him there before they'd touch this.

ANN:        No. No, don't say that.

SPADE:      He's lost a lot of blood, but he's tough. The slug's stuck in the neck muscle. I can dig it out; you got any disinfectant in the house?

FLORA:      Nothin' but a little bottle tincture of iodine, but it's mostly dried up.

SPADE:      You – listen carefully, Miss Newhall.

ANN:        Yes?

SPADE:      Go down to the corner drugstore, get some alcohol, swabs, iodine, cotton, gauze, (DELIBERATELY) The kind with the blue cross on it. If he doesn't have that kind, tell him to phone out for some.

FLORA:      I don't know why, she don't look right to me. I don't know as I—

SPADE:      Shut up. Go out in the kitchen and boil some water. Get some towels and clean rags. Hurry up. (MUSIC: SIMULTANEOUS) I started digging the slug out of Red O'Leary's neck. It took about an hour. He was out most of the time. Then I put a bandage on it, using Flora's iodine for disinfectant. He was still running a fever when he got to his feet wearing his lips in a grin. His right arm hung useless. He reached out with his left to pick up his shoulder holster, and the gun wasn't in it anymore. The other empty holster was mine.

RED:        Where's Flora?

SPADE:      I sent her out to boil some more water. Shall we talk?

PAPP:       Listen, there is no time to talk. I know that you sent that girl to phone the police, Mr. Spade. Yes, I also know that you are Sam Spade.

RED:       Anne's no stool pigeon, she wouldn't rat on me.

SPADE:     She would if she thought it was the only way of saving your life. If she got what I was trying to tell her, that's what she thinks.

RED:       Why, you-

PAPP:       No, no, he is right, Mr. O'Leary. That she-devil will kill us all. Better the police. Spade, listen to me. Let me get out past the police and I will give you everything.

SPADE:     Go on out, who's stopping you?

PAPP:       Look out the window. Plain-clothes men watching the door, waiting for a squad car. I am old. I am sick. What have I to do with robberies? You have seen it here. I am a slave- I, who am near the end of my life. Abuse, cursing, beatings, and those are not enough, and now I must go to prison because of that she-devil! You will let me go out; I will give you that she-devil. I will give you the money they stole.

SPADE:     How can I get you out?

PAPP:       How not? You are a friend of the police; you can take me out past your friends, the police. Do what I ask and I will give you the monies. Ten Million Dollars! Make no mistake, when that she-devil comes back into this room, you will die . . . both of you! She will kill you certainly!

SOUND:    FLORA'S FOOTSTEPS POUNDING DOWN THE HALL-WAY

| | |
|---|---|
| FLORA: | (OFF) Pappadopolos! |
| SPADE: | Sounds like it's too late. |
| FLORA: | (BELLOWING CLOSER) Where are you, you old hound? |
| PAPP: | In . . . .in here, Flora. |
| FLORA | (COMING ON) Where is that stool pigeon? Ha! There you are! Put the police on me, will you? |
| SPADE: | Who, me? I tipped the police? |
| FLORA: | You or that dame that came here with Red. You're done, both of you, you hear me, done. |
| PAPP: | No. Wait . . . .wait, Flora. Not here like this, please! Don't give the police such evidence. Let me take them into the cellar. |
| FLORA: | Okay, but make it quick, dearie. Soon's that squad car gets here, they'll be pounding at the door. Call me when you're finished, and I'll help you haul 'em out of sight. |
| PAPP: | (TRYING TO BE TOUGH) You will march ahead of me. If either one of you makes one move I will shoot you. I am holding two guns on you. |
| SPADE: | (MUSIC: SIMULTANEOUS) Red and I walked ahead of Pappadopolos into the hall. |
| SOUND: | TO SUIT OF ACTION |
| SPADE: | I opened the door he indicated, switched on the basement light, and helped Red down the uneven flight of steps. |
| PAPP: | (HOARSE WHISPER) Listen to me. I will first show you the monies, and then I will give you that she-devil. You will not forget your promise? I shall go out through the police? |

SPADE:        Sure, sure.

RED:          How about me?

SPADE:        You think Big Flora would let a rabbit like him change her plans?

RED:          So Big Flora was the boss? That's a laugh.

SOUND:        STEPS LEAVE STAIRS ECHO ON CONCRETE FLOOR AND OUT

PAPP:         Now turn around, both of you. Here, take these.

SPADE:        What kind of a joke is this supposed to be?

PAPP:         I give you these guns to show you I keep my promise. (SLIGHT FADE) Now quickly, follow me, I show you where the monies are hidden.

SPADE:        (MUSIC: SIMULTANEOUS) I followed him and Red O'Leary to the end of a low passageway. Pappadopolos got down on his knees and started clawing at the wall like a rat. With trembling hands he lifted out a section of lose bricks. And then we saw it . . .

MUSIC:        ACCENT

SPADE:        . . . It was still in the boxes and bags the way it came carried from the banks. He insisted on opening some of them to show me the money – hundreds of bundles of green stacked in a metal-lined cell that was as dry and airless as the bank vault they'd lived in before.

SOUND:        STEPS FROM UNDER NARR:        MUSIC OUT

PAPP:         (ECHO) That, as you see, is the money. Now for that she-devil. You will stand hiding behind these boxes. When I bring her down the stairs you will know what to do.

RED:        Yeah, Pappy, we'll know what to do.

MUSIC:      BRIDGE AND B.G.

SPADE:      He wasn't long in coming back. Flora came down the steps ahead of him. She had a gun in each hand. Her grey eyes were everywhere. Her head was down, like an animal's coming to a fight. Her nostrils quivered. Her body, coming down, not fast, not slow, was balanced like a dancer's. She was a beautiful fight-bred animal.

FLORA:      (OFFSTAGE) Come out! Come out or I'll come and get you!

RED:        Stay here, Spade, I want the first crack at the old witch.

SPADE:      Red! Come back here, you fool! Red!

SOUND:      TWO SHOTS ON ECHO, ONE NEAR, ONE FARTHER AWAY . . . RED YELLS . . . DROP OF BODY

SPADE:      (MUSIC: SIMULTANEOUS) She dropped Red without moving a muscle that I could see. I guess the poor guy must have been a little feverish from his wound, running out in the open like that firing wildly with his wobbly left hand. I didn't feel heroic myself. I just aimed the best way I knew how from my ambush and squeezed the trigger.

SOUND:      ONSTAGE SHOT ON ECHO . . . BODY TUMBLES DOWN STAIRS

PAPP:       (SCREAMING) You bungling idiot! You shot the wrong one! You shot the . . . wrong . . . one!

MUSIC:      (SLAMS IN AND UNDER)

SPADE:      My aim had been bad. I'd aimed for his leg, but got him in the side. After that last scream he didn't make any more noise. Then he didn't move anymore. Big Flora let the guns fall from her hands and knelt down beside his body.

FLORA:    (SOBS) What did you do that for? I was the one with a gun on you. Why didn't you shoot me instead?

SPADE:    I figured who he was when you let him bring me down here where the money was without squawking your head off.

FLORA:    He was the smartest, kindest man that ever lived.

SPADE:    Smart enough and kind enough to put about three hundred people out of their misery. Listen, Flora, don't you know he gave us guns and brought us down here so we'd knock you off, and he'd have all the loot to himself?

FLORA:    He wasn't much of a man for muscle. But he had brains, see? He was smarter than you or any copper that ever lived. You killed a great man. I hope you feel good about it.

SPADE:    Yeah, you and he were quite a team. Nobody would have suspected that the arch-gun of the biggest mob in history was Big Flora's whipping boy.

FLORA:    I never wanted to bat him around like I had to. I never really hurt him; we used to laugh about it afterwards.

VOICE:    (CALLING DOWNSTAIRS) All right, down there. All your exits are covered. Come out with your hands clasped behind your necks. This is the police.

FLORA:    (WEARILY) All right! All right! Keep your shirt on! (TO SPADE) Come on, let's get it over. No use fighting anymore.

SPADE:    You really loved him, didn't you, Flora?

FLORA:    So what? Who are you to laugh at us?

SPADE:      Yeah, you're right, Flora. Who am I to laugh at you?

MUSIC:      BRIDGE AND TO B.G.

SPADE:      After the cops had cleaned up at Big Flora's, I took your loving daughter on home in a taxi, Mr. Newhall. (See itemized account enclosed.) She was pretty broken up about Red O'Leary's death. But I think she'll recover. Please don't leave either your ten million dollars or your daughter lying around loose again, as the entire incident has caused me a great deal of trouble, and I will therefore have to charge you my regular fee of twenty-five dollars a day and expenses, instead of the usual fee for tailing. Period. End of Report.

EFFIE:      Oh, Sam, I wish you'd just taken one little package of that money. They'd never have missed it.

SPADE:      Effie, I'm surprised at you. That wouldn't be ethical.

EFFIE:      I don't know why you have to get ethical every time the installment is due on the office furniture.

SPADE:      Hey, what's this?

EFFIE:      Oh. Letter for you. Came this morning.

SPADE:      Why didn't you tell me? It's from the Golden Gate Trust. A reward for my services. Well, hurry up, open it. (PAUSE) Ah ha! A check!

EFFIE:      It's a check all right.

SPADE:      How much?

EFFIE:      Three dollars and eighty-three cents.

SPADE:      What's that for?

EFFIE:      I don't know. It's made out to Big Flora's Bar and Grill, signed by you, and stamped "returned for lack of funds."

SPADE:      How do you like that?

EFFIE:      I'll get used to it, I suppose in time . . . Goodnight, Sam.

SPADE:      Goodnight, Sweetheart.

MUSIC:      CURTAIN

# The Adventures of Sam Spade
## "SAM AND THE CORPORATION MURDERS"

PROGRAM #9
4:00-4:30 PM
FRIDAY, SEPT. 6, 1946

# KCEA

ANNCR:     The hair-raising adventures of Sam Spade, detective, brought to you by the makers of Wildroot Cream-Oil for the hair.

MUSIC:     PUNCTUATION . . . UP INTO TRILL . . . .INTO PHONE BELL

SOUND:     PHONE BELL

SOUND:     TELEPHONE ON FILTER MIKE:     LIFT RECEIVER:

EFFIE:     Sam Spade Detective Agency.

SPADE:     (FILTER) This is Convict Number 137596.

EFFIE:     SAM! I was just packing a lunch to bring you.

SPADE:      Forget it, Sweetheart.

EFFIE:      Sam, you must eat and keep up your strength. I know that prison food can't be very wholesome. Mother fixed some chicken especially – you know, it's the kind she calls chicken a la Sam Spade, because it has capers in the dressing.

SPADE:      Save some for me. The governor just gave me a last minute reprieve; I'll be right down to dictate my report.

MUSIC:      THEME AND TO B.G.

ANNCR:      Dashiell Hammett, America's leading detective fiction writer and of Sam Spade, the hard-boiled private eye, and William Spier, Radio's outstanding producer-director of mystery and crime drama, join their talents to make your hair stand on end with the Adventures of Sam Spade . . . (MUSIC:   ACCENT) . . . presented each week by Wildroot Cream-Oil, the non-alcoholic hair tonic that will put your hair back in place again, grooming it neatly, naturally, the way you want it. Right now the youngsters are going back to school. And folks, you'll want that boy of yours to make a neat, handsome impression. So why not have him spruce up with Dad's bottle of Wildroot Cream-Oil? Just like the man of the house, he'll find that Wildroot Cream-Oil grooms his hair neatly and naturally. There's not a drop of alcohol in Wildroot Cream-Oil. Remember, though, that Wildroot Cream-Oil contains LANOLIN, the soothing oil that's so much like the natural oil of the skin. So to make sure that boy of yours gets a head start in his class be sure he uses Wildroot Cream-Oil.

MUSIC:      SNEAK UNDER

ANNCR:      And now, Wildroot brings to the air the greatest private detective of 'em all . . . *Adventures of Sam Spade!*

| | |
|---|---|
| MUSIC: | UP TO OVERTURE |
| SOUND: | OPEN SLAM SHUT DOOR:        RAPID STEPS IN: |
| EFFIE: | Oh, Sam! You're so pale. Did they have you in solitary? |
| SPADE: | (FADING ON) Get your book! Quick! Come into my office! |
| EFFIE: | Y-yes . . . Sam . . . |
| SPADE: | (CALLING) Shake it, Effie! The underworld is seething . . . crime is rife . . . people are being . . . |
| SOUND: | OPEN DESK DRAWER: BOTTLES: FOOTSTEPS IN: |
| EFFIE: | (FADING ON) Here I am. R-ready, Sam . . . |
| SPADE: | Did that letter come from the commissioner's office? |
| EFFIE: | Yes, Sam. |
| SPADE: | Okay. Then we'll give him his. Subject:        The Corporation Murders . . . (SNEAK MUSIC B.G.) . . . Dear Mr. Commissioner: The aforementioned caper started when I was retained by Mrs. Anita Desmond to keep a plant on her restless husband, Harold Desmond, President of the stock-brokerage firm of Desmond, Sterling, Pine and Phelps. It was a dull, routine gumshoe job, of a type I don't ordinarily handle, but it came at a time when my landlord, too, was beginning to show signs of restlessness. After a week of tailing said Desmond, I had Mrs. Desmond come to my office and I told her I was through. |
| MUSIC: | PUNCTUATE |
| ANITA: | I don't understand, Mr. Spade. |
| SPADE: | I can't make it any plainer. There's nothing more I can do. |

I've given you my dope:    quote: on dates you find specified in report, your husband visited woman named Lela Cornell at her home in Oakland. Unquote. You probably knew all that before you hired me.

ANITA:    No . . . no, Mr. Spade. This is a great shock to me. I didn't know where to turn. I have confidence in you. I'm begging you, Mr. Spade, to see me through this thing.

SPADE:    If by that you mean you want me to testify to this in court, Mrs. Desmond-no dice. I don't do that kind of work. Besides, when a husband makes up his mind to be friendly with another woman, what the wife needs is not a private eye but a mother to go home to!

ANITA:    (VENOMOUSLY) I don't deserve this kind of treatment from him! He should be killed for it!

SPADE:    That's always a possibility. Plenty of gunsels around who'd do the job for ceiling price. Want the address of one?

ANITA:    Mr. Spade! You-you can't be serious!

SPADE:    I wasn't. But were you?

ANITA:    Sam, well, I'd like to tell you that confidentially you-

SPADE:    Yeah, I know. Bye, bye, Mrs. Desmond.

EFFIE:    (COMING ON) Sam-no, no, please, Mrs. Desmond-don't go out that way. Use the private door, please.

SPADE:    Why should she? What's the matter with-

EFFIE:    Mr. Spade . . . You have apparently forgotten that the King of Bohemia is here incognito.

SPADE:    Yeah, apparently I did.

SOUND:      DOOR SLAMS OFF

EFFIE:      Oh, Sam . . . it's her husband . . . he's . . .

SPADE:      What-the guy I've been tailing?

SOUND:      CLOSE DOOR FOOTSTEPS

DESMOND:   Ah, Mr. Spade. I'm Harold Desmond.

SPADE:      Yeah, my secretary told me. What's your problem, Mr. Desmond?

DESMOND:   Well, perhaps you'll think it's all in my imagination, Mr. Spade, but I have a feeling, I've had a feeling for the past two weeks that I'm being followed.

SPADE:      (CHOKING A BIT) Do you ah . . . have any idea . . . uh . . . who it could be?

DESMOND:   I haven't the slightest idea who it could be.

SPADE:      (SIGHS IN RELIEF) Oh, well that's goo . . . I mean . . .

DESMOND:   I am willing to pay a most generous fee, Mr. Spade. If you can find out who this man is that has been dogging my footsteps.

SPADE:      Uh hummm. That might be difficult, he's apparently a very clever man, you really haven't any idea who it might be? . . .

DESMOND:   No, I haven't. Something happened to me about three months ago, you may have read about it in the papers. I was held up and robbed by a pair of hoodlums. Although I made no move to resist them they assaulted me brutally, fractured my skull.

SPADE:      And you figured they had something else on their minds besides robbery?

DESMOND: Yes. The conviction has grown upon me that someone wants to take my life. (AGITATED) I've no enemies that I know of, no reason why anyone should want to take my life, why anyone should-

SPADE: Now, wait a minute, Mr. Desmond. Don't go jumping to conclusions. The fact is, the guy that's been following you is me.

DESMOND: You? You must be joking, Mr. Spade.

SPADE: How'd you happen to come to me?

DESMOND: Why I . . . I happened to run across a card of yours. I found it in my car, as a matter of fact.

SPADE: Uh huh. Your wife probably dropped it there.

DESMOND: My wife?

SPADE: Yeah. She hired me to keep a plant on you. Oh, but you can stop worrying. I quit the job this morning. I don't think you'll be bothered anymore by people following you.

DESMOND: I must say it's very decent of you to tell me this.

SPADE: Not at all. Anytime you have a job where I can make a dollar honestly, I'd be glad to help you, Mr. Desmond.

DESMOND: Well, you've taken a great load off my mind. Goodbye, Mr. Spade.

SPADE: Goodbye.

SOUND: STEPS TO DOOR. DOOR OPENS. GUN SHOTS. DES-MOND SCREAMS, FALLS

| | |
|---|---|
| MUSIC: | PUNCTUATE |
| SOUND: | DOOR BURSTS OPEN WOMAN'S FOOTSTEPS RUNNING ON |
| EFFIE: | Sam! Sam! Oh, thank . . . I thought he'd (SHE SEES THE BODY) Oh! |
| SPADE: | Close that door. Call a doctor. |
| SOUND: | DOOR CLOSE STEPS TELEPHONE DIALED. |
| EFFIE: | What happened, Sam? |
| SPADE: | He was on the way out. He opened the door. There were two mugs standing there. They let him have it, threw the gun on top of him and scrammed. |
| MUSIC: | BRIDGE AND TO B.G. |
| SPADE: | While we were waiting I frisked Desmond. There was nothing on him that I could use for a lead. There was a thousand bucks in his wallet. I put it in my pocket. I had a hunch I might be needing it. One hour later, Mr. Commissioner, I was in your private office with Lieutenant Dundy and Anita Desmond. You were hot, and Mrs. Desmond acted like I was Hitler. |
| SOUND: | OPEN CLOSE DOOR |
| ANITA: | (HYSTERICALLY) That's him, that's the man! |
| THOMPSON: | Now, now, Mrs. Desmond, You must calm yourself. |
| ANITA: | He'd been following my husband, knew he carried large amounts of cash . . . |
| THOMPSON: | One thing at a time, Mrs. Desmond. |
| ANITA: | He offered to hire a man to kill my husband only this |

|  |  |
|---|---|
| | morning! But he did it himself, himself! (SCREAM-ING LAST) |
| THOMPSON: | Dundy! Take her outside. Get a matron to help her. |
| DUNDY: | Please come with me, Mrs. Desmond, (FADE) Every-thing will be all right . . . |
| SOUND: | FOOTSTEPS: SHE WEEPS: OPEN CLOSE DOOR: |
| THOMPSON: | Mr. Spade, you know that story of two assassins is untenable! |
| SPADE: | Your boys found the gun in my office. It isn't mine. |
| SOUND: | DOOR OPENS AND CLOSES |
| THOMPSON: | Or anybody else's! Numbers filed off! Why couldn't it be yours! |
| DUNDY: | (COMING ON) Commissioner, I have a suggestion. |
| THOMPSON: | You keep out of this, Dundy! Now, Spade . . . this is what happened, and I'll make it stick:   You   called Desmond to your office, told him you had some in-formation to sell, that his wife was having him fol-lowed by you-he at once reached for the phone to call the police, you were trying a reverse blackmail on him, you scuffled to stop him, and shot him! What do you think of that? |
| SPADE: | I can't tell you. My mother taught me respect to my elders! |
| DUNDY | (CONCILIATORY) Mr. Commissioner – may I make a suggestion? |
| THOMPSON: | (TESTILY) What is it, Dundy? |

DUNDY:    I suggest that Mr. Desmond learned that Spade was tailing him, came to his office for a showdown, one word led to another, and Desmond pulled the gun. It's unregistered. It could be his. Spade tussled with him, the gun went off. That, Mr. Commissioner, is an open and shut self-defense.

THOMPSON:    Ummm . . . ..I see what you mean . . .

DUNDY:    What do you have to say, Sam?

SPADE:    I've said all I care to say. Now book me or let me go!

THOMPSON:    (FURIOUS) All right! You asked for it! First, Mr. Spade, your license as a private detective is revoked as of this minute! And make up your mind that you'll never get it back! I'll see to that personally! And second – Lieutenant Dundy, you will take this man downstairs! Book Him! First degree murder!

MUSIC:    BRIDGE AND TO B.G.

SPADE:    I ought to tell you about here, Mr. Commissioner, that if you think you can use such high handed methods as that on Sam Spade . . . you are perfectly right. But I didn't love you for it. I like my license and I like my reputation. Well, I called my mouthpiece, Sid Weiss. Fifteen minutes later my bail was set at a grand. The dough in the late Harold Desmond's wallet sprung me. A little after one o'clock I jumped on a ferry boat and went across to Oakland, to see Lela Cornell the dame Desmond's wife had hired me to find out about – the "other woman" as they say.

LELA:    Harold . . . killed? I can't believe it. Who-?

SPADE:    That's what I'm trying to find out. The police are trying to hang it on me. I'm out on bail now.

LELA:      Did you – see it happen?

SPADE:     Yeah. The job was done by a couple of cheap gunsels named Jack Corbett and Probey Larson. That's not the point. They'd knock over anybody for the price of a couple of weeds.

LELA:      Somebody else hired them to kill Harold?

SPADE:     Yeah. Tell me, Miss Cornell, how long has Desmond been visiting you here?

LELA:      Why ever since we were divorced.

SPADE:     Ever since . . . ? Let's get this straight. You and Desmond were married?

LELA:      Why yes, of course. Harold Junior will be six years old next month.

SPADE:     I see. Why didn't she tell me that?

LELA:      Anita? Oh, she never knew about it. Her religion wouldn't allow her to marry a divorced man.

SPADE:     And you kept quiet for the money that was in it?

LELA:      That's a crude way of putting it. Harold and I haven't lived together for some time. He was dead broke when he met her. She had a good deal of money, and set him up in this brokerage firm. Harold and I never quarreled . . .

SPADE:     How did you and Anita get along?

LELA:      I've never met her. All I knew is what Harold told me about her. That she was a very suspicious kind of woman . . . violent-tempered at times. But that doesn't prove anything. Who isn't? Are you going to try to prove she did it?

SPADE:      Sweetheart, it's this way. As long as I don't take the rap. I don't care whose nose I lay it on.

MUSIC:      BRIDGE AND TO B.G.

SPADE:      Back in the city I phoned the Desmond residence. Anita Desmond wasn't at home, but the maid told me I could find her at the offices of her husband's business firm – the brokerage house of Desmond, Sterling, Pine and Phelps on Sansome Street where she was attending a Board of Directors meeting. The outfit occupied the entire tenth floor.

SOUND:      BABBLE OF VOICES TICKERS TELETYPES TELEPHONES RING

            INTERMITTENTLY VOICES SHOUT AND LIB

VOICES:     (AD LIB) Well, how long does it take to get through to New York? I told you I wanted to drop those airlines and put it in AT & T! Where's Mr. Sterling? He always covers me! He can't be disturbed. He's in a Board of Director's Meeting.

VOICES:     (AD LIB) (OFF) Five hundred Allied Chemical offered and a hundred and twelve and a half. I'll give a hundred and ten!

            HUB BUB FADES UNDER

MUSIC:      UNDER

SPADE:      Telephones rang without stopping. Men were buying and selling wheat and steel and copper they couldn't possibly use. I elbowed through the crowd to a door that was marked "Board of Directors, Private." (DOOR OPEN) I opened it and went in.

SOUND:      CLOSE DOOR HUB BUB OUT

ANITA:      I don't care what my husband told you about those insurance policies! That money was mine. He had no right . . . .

STERLING:   Mrs. Desmond. As Harold's widow you will participate in the profits of the corporation to the same extent he did. Since your husband chose to withdraw his securities and convert them into life insurance, we are only making a reasonable request that you allow them to remain as collateral against the loan.

ANITA:      I don't understand anything about financial matters. All I know is that that money was my money in the first place, and now that Harold is dead I have a right to have it.

PINE:       Perhaps Mrs. Desmond would listen to a proposition such as this- (STOP ABRUPTLY) I say, Sterling, who's that chap over by the door eavesdropping?

STERLING:   What?

ANITA:      That's the man who shot Harold!

STERLING:   (COMING ON) What are you doing here? Get out!

SPADE:      Now cool off, Mr. Sterling. I wasn't trying to eavesdrop. I came here to see Mrs. Desmond.

STERLING:   You want to talk to him, Mrs. Desmond?

ANITA:      I never want to see him again.

STERLING:   All right, you. Outside.

SPADE:      I'm on my way, shoulders. Tell Mrs. Desmond I'll wait for her downstairs in the bar. If she's smart, she'll meet me there.

MUSIC:    BRIDGE AND B.G.

SPADE:    I was trying ginger ale and gin, which I'd always wanted to try, when she came over to me.

ANITA:    Mr. Spade, I'll give you one minute to talk and then I'm going to call the first policeman I see.

SPADE:    If you want to collect your late husband's insurance we'd better take a little longer than that.

ANITA:    I – what do you know about the insurance?

SPADE:    I figure it this way. A few months back you found out that your husband had been turning all his assets into life insurance. Maybe you knew that before, but what you found out recently was that he was planning to cash them in and leave the country. Probably settle in Brazil or some nice warm place with cheap money. Anyway he didn't plan to take you with him.

ANITA:    Did Harold tell you that?

SPADE:    He might have. The important thing is this: That money was mostly yours, that is he came into it when he married you. There was only one way you could get that money back.

ANITA:    Look here, Mr. Spade, you and I are both after the same thing. Money. If you'll keep quiet until I can collect I'll make it worth your while.

SPADE:    After you collect isn't good enough. A widow can get too far too fast these days on one of those clippers.

ANITA:    Give me until the bank opens tomorrow. I think I can raise some money on one of those policies. Ah – would a thousand dollars on account make you happy for a while?

SPADE:      Well, it'll keep me in Benzedrine.

ANITA:      Then it's settled. (GETTING UP) Order a drink, will you, Sam? I have to make a phone call.

SPADE:      (MUSIC SIMULTANEOUS) There were phone booths at both entrances. The street entrance was farther away, and that was the way she headed. I waited until she disappeared around the corner of the bar before I started after her. She edged into one of the phone booths without looking back, and I edged into the booth next to it, glued my ear to the partition and listened.

SOUND:      PHONE DIALING

ANITA:      (OFF MUFFLED) Police Headquarters? Homicide, Please. I'd like to speak to Lieutenant Dundy, my name is Mrs. Harold Desmond. Hello? Hello? Lieutenant? Yes, this is Mrs. Desmond. I want you to listen closely to what I have to tell you. I may not have time to finish, so I'm going to talk fast. Samuel Spade, the man who is under indictment for the murder of my husband, broke into a business meeting at my husband's firm this afternoon, behaved in a violent manner and was ejected from the room by Mr. Lloyd Sterling. There were five witnesses to this besides myself. He met me when I came out of there, forced me to come here with him, to the place I'm calling you from now, and made me promise him a thousand dollars before he would let me go. I want that man arrested immediately, do you understand? I feel that my life is endangered by-

SOUND:      BURST OF REVOLVER SHOTS FIRE BODY SLUMPS IN BOOTH THUD

MUSIC:      PUNCTUATE AND HOLD AGITATO UNDER FOLLOWING:

SOUND:     DOOR OF PHONE BOOTH OPENED

EXCITED AD LIBS FROM CROWD:     "I don't know, she was drinking with a man at a table by the lobby door, and she" "It was two men – one of them had a tommy gun, they didn't get out of the car." "He must have been one of them, he followed her from the table." (FADING) . . . " Well, don't stand there staring at it...go and get a cop . . . call a doctor. (MUSIC: FAST SWELL AND UNDER)

SPADE:     I walked past, nobody looked at me, they were all looking at Anita Desmond's body where it had fallen head first out of the booth. Her eyes were wide open and she was still looking at me in the same accusing way.

MUSIC:     FIRST ACT CURTAIN

ANNCR:     The makers of Wildroot Cream-Oil are presenting the ninth in a new series of programs bringing to the air for the first time, the adventures of Dashiell Hammett's famous private detective....SAM SPADE!

MUSIC:     UP AND RESOLVES OUT

MIDDLE COMMERCIAL

ANNCR:     Isn't it true that some men seem to get all the "breaks." They make a "big hit" with the girls – and they make "big money," too. Of course, there's no single rule for that kind of success. But, frankly, it helps a lot to watch your appearance – especially the appearance of your hair. That's why I'm so eager for all of you to try Wildroot Cream-Oil. It gives you everything you want in good grooming. In fact, Wildroot Cream-Oil is the one hair tonic that has all five advantages voted most important by an impartial consumer jury of hundreds of men in Metropolitan New York.

One-Wildroot Cream-Oil grooms your hair neatly and naturally – never leaves it sticky or greasy.

Two-Wildroot Cream-Oil relieves annoying dryness.

Three-It removes lose dandruff.

Four-There's not a drop of alcohol in Wildroot Cream-Oil.

And Five-It contains LANOLIN, the soothing oil that's so much like the natural oil of your skin.

No wonder four out of five users, in a nation-wide test, liked Wildroot Cream-Oil better than any other hair tonic they'd tried before. So next time you visit your barber, ask for Wildroot Cream-Oil . . . and get the big economy size bottle at your drug or toilet goods counter.

MUSIC:        ACCENT AND HOLD

ANNCR:        And now back to "Sam and the Corporation Murders" tonight's adventure with . . . . .SAM SPADE.

SPADE:        About here I thought I better have legal advice. I called my lawyer, Sid Weiss, and asked him if a man is divorced from one woman and marries another, and the second wife is beneficiary of an insurance policy, would the child of the first wife be in line for the dough in case anything happened to the second wife? He said, if there were no children, by the second marriage, the kid would probably get it. I hung up and went for another ferry ride back to Oakland.

SOUND:        DOOR BELL. DOOR OPENS

LELA:         Oh . . . Mr. Spade. Come in.

| | |
|---|---|
| SOUND: | STEPS INSIDE. DOOR CLOSE |
| SPADE: | Thanks. |
| LELA: | I was just listening to the news on the radio. About poor Anita. |
| SPADE: | You're a pretty good gal, Lela. |
| LELA: | What do you mean by that? |
| SPADE: | Well, you must know the cops are after me for a murder rap. Maybe two of 'em. |
| LELA: | That's ridiculous. What possible motive could you have had? |
| SPADE: | Yeah, that's the puzzler of this whole caper. Motive. By the way, I found out a couple of things today about insurance. It's all yours now that Anita is out of the way, isn't it? |
| LELA: | You mean you have an idea I might have wanted Anita dead? Because of Harold's money? |
| SPADE: | It spells motive, and it doesn't spell it backwards. |
| LELA: | Mr. Spade. Neither Anita, nor I, nor my son stands to gain one penny through Harold Desmond's death. I didn't know that when I talked to you before. I did Anita a great injustice. I only found it out this morning from Harold's lawyers. |
| SPADE: | Found out what? |
| LELA: | That Harold had been forced three months ago to gut up all of his insurance policies as collateral to keep the firm of Desmond, Sterling, Pine and Phelps from going on the rocks. |
| SPADE: | Oh. |

LELA:    Every penny reverts to the business. So you see, Mr. Spade you'd better start looking for another motive. You can't very well indict a corporation for murder.

SPADE:    No, you ca – (STOPS) You're a good gal, Lela. Thanks. Well, I'll be going.

SOUND:    DOOR OPEN DISTANT TRAFFIC

LELA:    Oh a car just drove up. Somebody calling for you?

SPADE:    Yeah. Kinda looks like it. Bye, Sweetheart.

SOUND:    DOOR PULLED SHUT. STEPS.

POBEY:    Hello, We was in the neighborhood, so we thought we'd give you a lift home, Spade.

SPADE:    That was mighty considerate of you.

POBEY:    Go on, get in the car. Don't try any moves.

SPADE:    Take that clumsy rod out of my ribs.

POBEY:    You're cute, Sammy. We're gonna get along fine.

SPADE:    That's better. Come on.

SOUND:    REGISTER STEP CAR DOOR OPEN

POBEY:    You ride in the middle, Sammy.

SPADE:    Thanks.

SOUND:    CAR DOOR CLOSES CAR STARTS UP

SPADE:    Well, this is cozy. I never did like riding the ferry boats on a foggy night.

JACK:    Let's talk, Sammy.

SPADE:    Sure, what about?

JACK:       Desmond's wife hired you to keep a plant on her hus-
            band, didn't she?

SPADE:      Yeah.

JACK:       Okay, let's talk about that. Who had it in for him?

SPADE:      The treatment you guys gave him wasn't exactly chummy.

POBEY:      We didn't have nothing against him. It was a job.

SPADE:      Who hired you?

JACK:       That's what we want to know.

POBEY:      Yeah. We ain't collected yet.

SPADE:      (LAUGHS) That's good. That's very good. You want me
            to tell you who hired you to bump off Desmond!

JACK:       Explain to him, Pobey.

POBEY:      Yeah. You see we took the job like on a sub-contract. This
            friend of ours was to get five grand, keep two and pay us
            three.

SPADE:      Why don't you ask him who hired you?

JACK:       He's dead.

POBEY:      Yeah. Now he is. We figured he was holding out on us,
            kept stalling telling us he hadn't been paid yet.

SPADE:      So you knocked him off too?

JACK:       Yeah. And can you imagine, he was tellin' the truth alla
            time? Just a shame.

POBEY:      Wasn't nothing on him but a couple of five-dollar bills.

SPADE:      Boys, I think I know who owes you that money, but I've got a little something personal to settle there first. After I've finished, it's all yours.

POBEY:     You see, Jack. I told you he was the right guy.

JACK:      I don't like it. If we give him the first shake, there may be nothing left for us.

SPADE:     You guys work too cheap. There was seven hundred and fifty grand in the caper. That ought to be plenty for the three of us.

POBEY:     Seven hundred and fifty-

SPADE:     Here's what we'll do. When we get across the bay, drop me off at the Marguerite Hotel on Kearny Street. I'm picking up a guy there and taking him across town. You can keep a close plant on me if you don't trust me. Follow us where we go, but don't come on in until I'm finished with my business. If you'll play it like that, I'll let you in on the seven fifty G's. If you don't play like that, I won't play. And if I don't play, you'll never collect a penny.

JACK:      Okay, Sammy, we'll play it like that.

MUSIC:     BRIDGE AND TO B.G.

SPADE:     From the Marguerite house dick I learned that Sterling occupied a seven-room duplex and lived there with just one servant. It was Thursday night, so he was really alone. I had to move fast to get inside before he could slam the door in my face.

SOUND:     DOOR KICKED SHUT

STERLING:  It was very foolish of you to come here, Spade.

SPADE:     It wouldn't be the first foolish thing I've done.

STERLING:     I can't make you out. A man who keeps asking for trouble.

SPADE:     Trouble? What kind of trouble?

STERLING:     All I have to do is pick up that phone and the police would be here before you could get out of the building.

SPADE:     You're going to pick up the phone all right, Sterling. But you're not going to call the police.

STERLING:     Holding a gun on me doesn't give you such an advantage as you imagine it does. Any intelligent man knows that the man with the gun leaves himself no alternative but to shoot his adversary in which case . . .

SPADE:     All right, let's try another way. Any intelligent man knows, that if a desperate character lets him have it across the muzzle like this . . . (SOUND: WHAM)

STERLING:     (WINCHES)

SPADE:     . . . and the adversary still doesn't do what he's told to, he's going to get it again, like this . . . (WHAM)

STERLING:     You're crazy, what do you want?

SOUND:     SOCKS INTERSPERSED WITH THE FOLLOWING

SPADE:     I told you (SOCK) Pick up the phone! . . . . (SOCK) . . . Call your secretary . . . . (SOCK)

STERLING:     Stop it! Stop it! I'll do as you say!

SPADE:     That's more like it.

SOUND:     PHONE PICKS UP

STERLING:     (BREATHING HARD) Douglas five one seven oh four. (TO SPADE) What . . . what do you want me to say to her?

SPADE:    Tell her to call every member of the board of directors of Desmond, Sterling, Pine and Phelps. An emergency meeting – tonight. Lay it on heavy, they gotta be there. Matter of life and death.

STERLING:    No . . . no . . . please. (INTO PHONE) Miss Driscoll? This is Mr. Sterling. I'm sorry to disturb you at home, but a serious crisis has arisen. I want you to reach all the directors of the company by telephone immediately for a special emergency Board Meeting. The time of the meeting is eleven o'clock tonight.

MUSIC:    BRIDGE AND TO B.G.

SPADE:    For the next couple of hours I made myself comfortable with a bottle of Sterling's scotch. Sterling didn't talk much. Just sat with an ice pack on his jaw and looked grim. At ten minutes of eleven I helped him into his hat and coat. At the offices of Desmond, Sterling, Pine and Phelps, the lights were on and the Board members were at their places around the long table in the Board room when Sterling and I walked in.

STERLING:    Good evening, Gentlemen.

AD LIBS:    BOARD MEMBERS MURMURED "GOOD EVENING L.B."

PINE:    I say, Sterling, what's up??

STERLING:    Gentlemen . . . er . . . .I owe you an apology. You have been brought here under false pretenses.

AD LIBS:    SURPRISE FROM MEMBERS:    "What    a    deuce" "But I thought probably" . . . ..

SPADE:    I'll take over now, Sterling.

STERLING:    Er . . . .very well, Mr. Spade.

SPADE:         I didn't have time to explain to Mr. Sterling why I wanted
               to have this talk with you guys. You all know who I am, and
               you all know I'm mixed up in this caper where your partner
               Desmond got knocked off. I just found out who did it. And
               I thought you gents might want to know about it.

PHELPS:        Mr. Spade, that is indeed gratifying news!

STERLING:      Who? Who did it?

SPADE:         You did.

AD LIBS:       CONSTERNATION "Sterling? Ridiculous" etc.

SPADE:         And you, Mr. Pine, and you, Mr. Phelps, and you and you
               and you. The whole bunch of you.

PINE:          What an extraordinary idea! Why on earth did it take ten
               men to commit one murder?

SPADE:         Not one murder. Two! Desmond and his wife. Desmond
               because he was worth more to the corporation dead than
               alive.

PHELPS:        Now, look here, Spade . . .

SPADE:         A few months back you discovered that Desmond had
               been quietly taking his money out of the firm and turning
               it into life insurance. Am I right?

PHELPS:        Yes, but-

SPADE:         (CUTTING IN) Okay. So to avoid an embezzlement rap
               he put those insurance policies against a loan for the cor-
               poration. The loan came due at the same time the market
               took its recent plunge. Am I right?

STERLING:      You haven't said one thing that every broker on Sansome
               Street doesn't already know.

SPADE:       Yeah, Mr. Sterling. But here's something they don't know. About a week ago, you called a Board Meeting in Desmond's absence and told the boys that only Desmond's death could save the corporation. They voted to save the corporation. When Anita Desmond threatened to contest the award of the insurance . . . the corporation decided to kill her too. I don't know which one of you did the actual hiring of the gunsels. Whoever did will probably have to take the rap for all of you.

STERLING:    Very neat, Mr. Spade. But the man who was originally employed to eliminate poor Desmond is now dead. And even if he were not, you would have only the testimony of the self confessed killer. And furthermore, there was never an exchange of money.

SPADE:       A reliable firm like this ought to pay its bills.

STERLING:    You're wasting our time and your own, Mr. Spade. Even if you were to prove all of your charges, there is absolutely nothing in corporation law that could be used against us. In fact, the law specifically provides that no individual may be held responsible for the acts of a corporation.

SPADE:       Can I quote you on that when I give the story to the papers!?

STERLING:    I don't think a paper in town would print it. No editor would believe a story like that.

SPADE:       Maybe not, but you're taking quite a risk. Let's get off the dime, gentlemen. I don't care who takes the rap for killing Desmond and his wife as long as it's not me. I think Mr. Sterling might be a good candidate. Supposing we take a vote on it.

PINE:            (PAUSE) There's certainly something in what he says.

PHELPS:          As I recall, it was Sterling's idea in the first place, wasn't it?

AD LIBS:         (EXCITED) "Why not, I think it's an excellent idea" . . . "We certainly can't risk a scandal of that sort" . . . "We'd be barred from the exchange."

STERLING:        No, wait. I have another suggestion. Spade here is already under indictment for one of the murders, and the police are hunting him for another one. No – don't bother reaching for your gun, Spade. I have one now.

SOUND:           DOOR THROWN OPEN

JACK:            Drop the gun, mister.

SOUND:           GUN DROPPED

STERLING:        Who . . . who are you?

JACK:            Sammy's right, mister . . . A reliable firm like this, reckon should pay off its debts

STERLING:        How much do you want?

JACK:            Five hundred grand. We'll take twenty thousand on account. You ought to be able to lay your hands on that much right away. A bunch of tycoons like you guys.

POBEY:           Watch it, Jack! He's reaching for that gun!

SOUND:           MACHINE GUN BURST . . . STERLING (GROANS) AND FALLS

POBEY:           Now come across with the dough, you guys, or the rest of you'll get it just like he did.

PINE:            My dear man, you don't seem to understand. This is not a bank, it's a brokerage firm. We don't handle cash here!

POBEY:      Don't handle cash. Seven fifty grand for bumping off one guy and he says they don't handle cash.

JACK:       Stop stalling.

PINE:       But I tell you –

SPADE:      Don't look now, boys, but a police car just parked down the street.

POBEY:      We better lam up out of here, Jack.

JACK:       Yeah, but before we go we better clean up the rest of 'em ...

PINE:       No . . . no!

SOUND:      A LONG MACHINE GUN BURST ALL SCREAM

MUSIC:      CLIMATIC BRIDGE AND TO B.G.

SPADE:      And that, Commissioner, is how the firm of Desmond, Sterling, Pine and Phelps was finally liquidated. When the cops walked in, there was nothing left but a very dead Board of Directors. The gunsels got it somewhere between the fourth and fifth floors of the building as they were scamming down the back fire escape. If the boys you sent around hadn't been so anxious to arrest me, you might have got them both alive. It was just luck that one of them lived long enough to talk and clear me. So take this and press it in your memory book, Commissioner. That's the last time I'll ever let a dame talk me into tailing her husband, unless your wife should happen to drop around, in which case it'll give me great pleasure to find out the address of that little blonde you've been seeing over in Milpitas. Period. End of Report.

SOUND:      OPEN DRAWER

EFFIE:      Is that all, Sam?

SPADE:      Yeah, let's see that letter from the commissioner.

EFFIE:      I didn't open it, I though you'd probably want to open this yourself.

SOUND:      OPENING ENVELOPE

SPADE:      Why that pot-bellied walking exhibit of Bright's disease. He's got a nerve.

EFFIE:      How can you tell by shaking the envelope?

SPADE:      My license . . . it ain't here!

EFFIE:      Let me read that letter.

SPADE:      (AFTER A BRIEF PAUSE) Well, what does it say?

EFFIE:      Dear Mr. Spade:   Your license Number 137596, suspended three days ago had been re-approved by the department. However, your license fees appear to be in arrears. Upon payment of the amounts specified below we will be glad to make restoration of same. Very truly yours, Hilda Podge, Secretary to the Commissioner.

SPADE:      Why do I stay in this business, supporting every crackpot on the city payroll?

EFFIE:      Goodnight, Sam.

SPADE:      Goodnight, Sweetheart.

MUSIC:      CURTAIN

# THE ADVENTURES OF SAM SPADE
## "INSIDE THE STORY ON KID SPADE"

PROGRAM #21
FEBRUARY 16, 1947
5:00 – 5:30
9:00 – 9:30

ANNCR: The Adventures of Sam Spade, detective – brought to you by Wildroot Cream-Oil, the non-alcoholic hair tonic that contains Lanolin . . . . Wildroot Cream-Oil "Again and again the choice of men who put good grooming first."

MUSIC: PUNCTUATION . . . . UP INTO TRILL INTO PHONE BELL

SOUND: PHONE BELL

SOUND: TELEPHONE ON FILTER MIKE: LIFT RECEIVER:

EFFIE: (DISTRAUGHT) Hello . . . ..

SPADE: (FILTER) Sam Spade Detective Agency, when you have the time, Miss Perrine.

EFFIE: Oh Sam, for heaven's sake, Sam, get up here quick.

SPADE:      What's happened?

EFFIE:      He's dying, Sam . . . he's dying . . . he's dying . . . .what shall I do?

SPADE:      Who's dying?

EFFIE:      This man. He came in. He's bleeding – (SUDDEN WAIL) Oh, Sam please hurry . . . I can't . . .

SPADE:      Take it easy, angel, I'm on my way.

MUSIC:      THEME AND TO B.G.

ANNCR:      Dashiell Hammett, America's leading detective fiction writer, and creator of Sam Spade, the hard-boiled private eye, and William Spier, radio's outstanding producer-director of mystery and crime drama, join their talents to make your hair stand on end with the Adventures of Sam Spade . . . (MUSIC ACCENT) . . . .Presented by the makers of Wildroot Cream-Oil for the hair.

(COMMERCIAL)

South of the Border, the girls say, "Que quapo"! North of the Border, they say "How handsome!" But everywhere, girls admire the man whose hair is groomed the Wildroot way. For Wildroot Cream-Oil is famous for keeping your hair in trim the way girls like to see it – neat and natural. There's not a drop of alcohol in Wildroot Cream-Oil. What's more, it contains LANOLIN. So get the big economy-size bottle at your drug or toilet goods counter. And ask your barber for Wildroot Cream-Oil – "again and again the choice of men who put good grooming first."

(MUSIC:      SNEAK UNDER) And now, Wildroot brings to the air, the greatest private detective of 'em all . . . in . . . the *Adventures of Sam Spade*!

| | |
|---|---|
| MUSIC: | (UP TO SHOW) |
| MUSIC: | THEME |
| SOUND: | OPEN DOOR STEPS |
| EFFIE: | (FADING ON) Sam, in here quick. |
| | SOUND STEPS LEFTY'S MUMBLE FADES ON |
| LEFTY: | (FADING ON) . . . SURE . . . THINK I'm a dumb? . . . yah, yah, (EXCITED) The left, the left – throw it! (SUBSIDES) . . . Mmmm – ahh – nice, nice . . . sure . . . I'll take him . . . the fifth . . . I'll take him. Ummm. |
| SPADE: | Lefty! . . . |
| LEFTY: | Ahh???? |
| SPADE: | It's me, Lefty, Spade. |
| LEFTY: | Spade? . . . Ahh? . . . (SUDDEN EXCITEMENT) Spade . . . You all right, Sam? You all right? |
| SPADE: | (GENTLY) Sure, Lefty. I'm fine. |
| LEFTY: | (BREATHING HEAVILY) Fine, fine . . . I gotta tell you, Sam . . . yeah . . . |
| SPADE: | (CHOKED) What, Lefty? What's on your mind? |
| LEFTY: | It's in my head, Sam. I can't – I don't know . . . it's in my head . . . keep countin' – slow . . . count slow – it's in my head . . . what? What? What? What? I don't know . . . it's . . . (HE DIES) |
| SPADE: | Lefty!!! |
| MUSIC: | PUNCTUATE |
| SOUND: | DOOR CLOSE GENTLY |

SPADE:      Lefty . . . ah, the poor punchy guy . . . winds up with three police slugs in his belly.

EFFIE:      But . . . how do you know the police shot him?

SPADE:      He was a lammister. He's was doing a bit . . . I heard he crashed out yesterday . . . never figured on his getting this far.

EFFIE:      What was he in for?

SPADE:      Manslaughter. Twenty years to life. He did fifteen of them . . . Guess he went stir-crazy.

EFFIE:      Who is he, Sam?

SPADE:      He used to be my trainer. (SMALL CHUCKLE) Yeah . . . Kid Spade  . . . the bright boy of the ring . . .

EFFIE:      You mean you were once a fighter?

SPADE:      For one season. I got out fast. I didn't want to wind up hearing bells in my head. Like poor Lefty in there.

EFFIE:      Who'd he kill, Sam?

SPADE:      Well . . . (MUSIC: SNEAK IN AND UNDER) I was just a punk kid, a little faster with my mitts than my wits. I was doing a hitch on a banana boat as an oil wiper – we carried a couple of passengers. One of them was the Maestro. The crew named him that the first day out because he wore a wing-collar and a monocle. Well, one day I get into a brawl down in the engine room with a couple of stokers. I was cocky, I guess, and they both went for me. I needed a room to fight them both so I backtracked up the iron steps onto the deck. There I either had to fight or jump over and swim. So I fought. I was the last one left standing, so I guess I won. Somebody grabbed me by the arm. I turned around to let him have it, and saw it was the Maestro.

MAESTRO:    What is your name?

SPADE:      They jumped me . . . I had to . . .

MAESTRO:    Do you know what you have just created . . . in front of my very eyes: A ballet . . . a ballet of destruction! . . . like nothing I have ever seen on the stages of Moscow . . . Paris . . . Brussels . . . the intricate footwork – the quick thinking of your muscles . . . beautiful . . . brilliant.

SPADE:      What're you selling?

MAESTRO:    A great future for you!

SPADE:      I think you're nuts.

MAESTRO:    This we must understand now. I will do the thinking. You will do the fighting.

MUSIC:      BRIDGE AND TO B.G.

SPADE:      And we did. Six weeks later I went in against Pretty Boy Gluskin and took him in four rounds. By the following February I'd had twelve fights. Out of the twelve I had won an even dozen. I was getting to be a valuable boy on the coast. Don't ask me if I liked it, I was still letting the Maestro do the thinking while I did the slugging. He took care of the money for both of us. Yeah, he certainly did.

            (MUSIC:   PUNCTURE)

SOUND:      OUT OF MUSIC: RATTLE OF DICE: EXPEL BREATH: SNAP FINGERS)

STICKMAN:   And the dice read – days in the week! Seven – and the Maestro's down. Pass the dice and make some ice! Lay it on the line, Maestro – we'll pay it on the line.

MAESTRO:     (SHAKY LAUGH) Well – I – I think I have played enough for tonight . . .

SOUND:       (FADING OFF) RATTLE OF DICE:  ETC HOLD IN BG:

STICKMAN:   (FADING UNDER) I lay it or take it. Right or wrong, I go along . . . Maestro –

MAESTRO:     Yes?

STICKMAN:   Mr. Cripp wants to see you. This way . . .

MAESTRO:     Well . . . I – it's getting late and –

STICKMAN:   (HARD) Mr. Cripp wants you now!

MAESTRO:     Ah – yes. Thank you.

SOUND:       STEPS: OPEN, CLOSE DOOR: GAME ROOM OUT:

CRIPP:       Sit down, Maestro.

MAESTRO:     (NERVOUSLY) Well – it's growing late and I –

CRIPP:       This will only take a minute. How's Kid Spade?

MAESTRO:     Sam? He – he's in the mountains. A little rest.

CRIPP:       Great little welter, that Spade. Punch like a heavy, feet like a flyweight . . . (DREAMILY) All my life I dreamed of owning a boy like that. Not for the money, not for what he'd bring – just to own him! Like a fast horse carrying my colors. He leaves 'em all behind . . . You know – I'd be willing to trade you any three of my boys for Kid Spade.

MAESTRO:     Well – that's very generous, Mr. Cripp – but –

CRIPP:       No. I didn't think you would. Cigar?

MAESTRO:     Thank you.

SOUND:      STRIKE MATCH

CRIPP:      There you are. Nothing like a good cigar to promote good feeling in a business talk.

MAESTRO:    (CAUTIOUSLY) Business talk?

CRIPP:      A little matter of 75 hundred bucks; The 35 you dropped tonight – and four G last week.

MAESTRO:    (GIGGLING FOOLISHLY) Yes –I – my luck has been a little –

CRIPP:      That's a very impressive signature you got, Maestro. All those loops and curls: like a perfesser. Looks like a million on these IOUs. I'm sure it's good for the 75 hundred.

MAESTRO:    Oh, of course, of course . . .

CRIPP:      It is? Well, then I figure I've got enough of your paper. I want my money now.

MAESTRO:    (QUICKLY) I can't – I haven't –

CRIPP:      (SOFTLY) Then get it . . .

MAESTRO:    (AGITATED) I must have time!

CRIPP:      I run a cash business!

MAESTRO:    You gave me credit!

CRIPP:      You got assets.

MAESTRO:    What?

CRIPP:      Kid Spade!

MAESTRO:    No!

CRIPP:      Then pay!

MAESTRO:    (HYSTERICALLY) No! I won't let you steal him from me!

He's mine! I found him! I built him and you can't steal him from me!

CRIPP:     I want that boy!

MAESTRO:   I won't give him up!

CRIPP:     Then you'll pay my collectors!

MAESTRO:   It's a gambling debt! You can't –

CRIPP:     My collectors don't carry a summons: a barrel and fifty pounds of cement! (A LONG PAUSE. A SIGH)

MAESTRO:   (SUDDENLY CALM) Very well, Mr. Cripp. You leave me no arguments. And you have added greatly to my education.

SOUND:     OPEN. CLOSE DESK DRAWER: RUSTLE OF PAPER

CRIPP:     I was sure you'd be sensible about this, Maestro. I had the contract drawn up. Just put that impressive signature on the dotted line.

MAESTRO:   May I use your pen?

CRIPP:     Sure . . .

MAESTRO:   Thank you . . .

SOUND:     SCRATCH OF PEN

MAESTRO:   There you are, Mr. Cripp.

CRIPP:     Kid Spade now belongs to me!

MAESTRO:   (SIGHS) Yes . . . your pen writes very easily . . .

CRIPP:     You can keep it. Part of the deal.

MAESTRO:   Thank you. (SIGHS) I shall treasure it as the most expensive pen in the world.

| | |
|---|---|
| MUSIC: | BRIDGE AND TO B.G. |
| SPADE: | What had happened there that night I knew nothing about at the time. I'd been up in the mountains having fun. When I got back I brought something with me that was going to make a lot of difference. We came into the room together. The Maestro was standing by a window staring down into the street as though looking for me. Lefty was sort of crouched down on his haunches alongside the Maestro. He was fifteen years younger than what just died in there, but he was just as punchy. |
| MAESTRO: | Sam . . . where have you . . . Oh? |
| SPADE: | Hello, Maestro . . . Lefty. Maestro, this is Lynn Carter. |
| LYNN: | How do you do? |
| MAESTRO: | (SUSPICIOUSLY) How do you do, Miss Carter. |
| SPADE: | And this is Lefty. He was my trainer. |
| LEFTY: | Hello! |
| LYNN: | Sam has told me so much about you during the past two weeks that I feel I – |
| SPADE: | (CHUCKLING) Probably bored you to death. |
| LYNN: | I found it very colorful. |
| MAESTRO: | Sam – there is something I must tell you. If Miss Carter will excuse us – |
| SPADE: | But there's something I must tell you, Maestro. Lynn and me – we're going to be married! |
| LEFTY: | Married! |
| MAESTRO: | What? |

SPADE:      That's right.

LYNN:       It happened so quickly that I – well, I wouldn't blame you for resenting me. After all, you've been with Sam so long, you'd probably feel that way about anyone who'd take him away.

MAESTRO:    Take him – away? Sam – what does she mean, Sam?

SPADE:      This isn't easy, Maestro. You know how I feel about you. But – well, I'm quitting the ring.

MAESTRO:    (BEWILDERED) Quitting the –

LEFTY:      Sam's quittin'?

SPADE:      (SINCERELY) I'm sorry, Maestro. But I'm going away with Lynn. To New York. Her father owns a – well, he wants us to live there. I'm going to work for him.

MAESTRO:    (QUIETLY INTENSITY) But Sam – Sam, you can't! Not now! I just –

SPADE:      Don't make it tougher for me. We're taking the plane to New York tomorrow night.

MAESTRO:    (GROWING PANIC) No! You can't, Sam! You can't run out on me like this!

SPADE:      (EDGY) Don't needle me, Maestro!

MAESTRO:    But you don't know what's happened, Sam! You can't quit! I sold you!

SPADE:      Sold me! . . . To who!

MAESTRO:    Cripp!

SPADE:      That mobster! Why didn't you ask me first!

MAESTRO:    I couldn't, Sam. I had to –

SPADE:    (HARSHLY) I don't like it! I don't like being bought and sold like so much beef on the hoof! That's why I'm getting out! Lynn was right! Two – three years in the Cripp stable, I'm a punching bag for the new boys: a  gibbering idiot like poor Lefty here!

LEFTY:    Who – who's a –

SPADE:    I'm sorry, Lefty. I just –

LEFTY:    (FURIOUS) Don't call me a – I'll kill – did ya hear –

MAESTRO:    Shut up, Lefty! So Lynn was right! I knew it the minute she walked in here! Smelling of her perfume and –

SPADE:    (WARNINGLY) All right –

MAESTRO:    Yes – it's her fault! Why didn't you leave him alone! He's different from you! But no – you liked the way he looked in the sun in trunks; those smooth muscles – that beautiful body –

SPADE:    That's enough! I'll . . .

MAESTRO:    (OUT OF CONTROL) You had to have him! To show your ritzy friends! A great catch, you scheming, convincing, five-cent –

SOUND:    SLAP HARD ON MIKE:

LYNN:    (SCREAMS) Sam! Don't!!!

SOUND:    PUNCHES:          SCUFFLE:

LYNN:    Lefty! Stop him! He'll kill him! Sam!

LEFTY:    Sam!

| | |
|---|---|
| MAESTRO: | (GASPING) Sam – I can't – (GASPS) |
| LYNN: | Sam! He's choking! Stop! |
| SOUND: | THUD OF BODY TO FLOOR |
| SPADE: | (BREATHING HARD) All right! I'm all right now! |
| LYNN: | (SOBBING) Oh, Sam, Sam. |
| SPADE: | I should have killed him for that! Let's get out of here before I do! |
| LYNN: | Oh, Sam – I – I've never seen you like this before! |
| SPADE: | (HARD) I love you, too – Sweetheart! |
| SOUND: | DOOR CLOSES |
| MUSIC: | BRIDGE AND TO B.G. |
| SPADE: | I slammed out and Lynn didn't catch up with me until I was downstairs. You know something about my temper, Effie. I was worse then. The only way I could meet a problem was with a right cross. But by the time I go out into the street I cooled off and my first instinct was to go back and apologize. I wish I had. If I had I would have heard what was going on in that room when I closed the door. |
| MUSIC: | UP AND OUT |
| MAESTRO: | (WEAKLY) Lefty . . . |
| LEFTY: | Boss . . . you alright, Boss? Your face is a funny color. |
| MAESTRO: | Get – water . . . |
| LEFTY: | Sure, Boss, sure . . . Water . . . |
| SOUND: | POURING WATER IN GLASS |

LEFTY:      There . . . You all right now, Boss?

MAESTRO:    Yes. I'm all right now. You're a good boy, Lefty.

LEFTY:      (LAUGHS DELIGHTEDLY) Sure! Sam's a rat! Lefty's a
            good boy! Lefty's no rat! He called me an idiot! I'll kill
            him, Boss. Lefty's a good boy. He don't like for Sam to do
            the Boss no hurt! I'll kill 'em!

MAESTRO:    Sssssssssh – sssssssshhhhhhhhh . . . You must not get ex-
            cited, Lefty we must think.

LEFTY:      Sure, Boss. Let's think . . . Your lip is all red Boss.

MAESTRO:    (AS THOUGH TO HIMSELF) We have a problem, Lefty
            . . . Mr. Cripp must not hear about Sam quitting.

LEFTY:      Sam's quittin' Boss?

MAESTRO:    If something happened to Sam – an accident – they hap-
            pen every day, Lefty . . .

LEFTY:      Sure! Accidents happen! When I was a little boy I –

MAESTRO:    Then I could go to Cripp and say:   It is a tragic thing,
            Mr. Cripp. A fine boy like that. Your boy, Mr. Cripp. Yes,
            a tragic finale to a promising career."

LEFTY:      Yeah, Boss. That would be some tragic! Some finale.

MAESTRO:    (SUDDENLY) Lefty –

LEFTY:      Yes, Boss?

MAESTRO:    In Stillwell's gym . . . You know where the main steam
            valve for the steam room is?

LEFTY:      What, Boss?

MAESTRO:    The valve, Lefty. The one that lets the live steam into the
            steam room.

LEFTY:      The – Oh, sure, Boss! The gadget that the guy turns off and on the steam with!

MAESTRO:    Yes, Lefty-

LEFTY:      Sure, Boss. It's under the stairs in the basement the other side of the gym. You know, on the side by –

MAESTRO:    Yes, Lefty, yes . . . Do you think you could get under the stairs in the basement?

LEFTY:      Sure! Nobody cares if I go to the basement.

MAESTRO:    Yes, Lefty . . . And do you think you could open the valve as wide as it will go?

LEFTY:      (CONFUSED) Open the – For all the steam to go fast into the steam room?

MAESTRO:    Yes, Lefty . . .

LEFTY:      Boy – that's some hot, all that steam, Boss! You can't stay in all that hot! Did you was up the gym when poor Kelly got all the hot because the valve broke and the door was stuck? Did you was there when they brung him out? Boy – that was some lookin' dead Kelly all right!

MAESTRO:    Yes, Lefty. A very tragic accident.

LEFTY:      Some tragic, all right, Boss.

MAESTRO:    Lefty – take my watch . . . Can you read the time?

LEFTY:      (OFFENDED) Sure! You think I'm dumb?

MAESTRO:    What time is it, Lefty? The little hand is on the five and the big hand is on the twelve –ah.

LEFTY:      Five o'clock!

MAESTRO:    That's right, Lefty.

LEFTY:       (ELATED) See? I'm no dumb! Five o'clock!

MAESTRO:    And at five o'clock tomorrow afternoon, Lefty, you must be in the basement at the gym – by the steam valve – And exactly five o'clock, Lefty, you will open the valve – all the way.

LEFTY:       For all the hot?

MAESTRO:    Yes, Lefty . . . all the hot!

LEFTY:       (AGITATED) But you can't stay in the – Did you was up in the gym when –

MAESTRO:    I won't be in the steam room, Lefty. But Sam will. Alone.

MUSIC:       PUNCTUATE AND TO B.G.

SPADE:       That was the caper. The Maestro was on the spot. He had to get off. There was only one out for him:  Kid   Spade had to die an accidental death – even if the Maestro had to arrange it. He thought he did. But he was wrong. All he arranged was the beginnings of a guy who knew that from here on out he couldn't trust anybody – a guy named Sam Spade.

MUSIC:       FIRST ACT CURTAIN.

ANNCR:       The makers of Wildroot Cream-Oil are presenting the weekly Sunday adventure of Dashiell Hammett's famous private detective . . . SAM SPADE!

MUSIC:       (UP AND RESOLVES OUT)

             (NEW COMMERCIAL)

ANNCR:    Men, here's important news on good grooming: Better than four out of five new users of Wildroot Cream-Oil say they prefer Wildroot Cream-Oil to all other hair tonics. Here is new and even more conclusive evidence that Wildroot Cream-Oil is "again and again the choice of men who put good grooming first." So if you want the well-groomed look that helps you get ahead, socially and on the job, listen: Recently, thousands of people from coast to coast who brought Wildroot Cream-Oil for the first time were asked: How does Wildroot Cream-Oil compare with the hair tonic you previously used. The results were amazing. Better than four out of five said they preferred Wildroot Cream-Oil. And no wonder. Wildroot Cream-Oil gives you the advantages that men consider most important: Wildroot Cream-Oil grooms your hair neatly and naturally. It relieves annoying dryness. And it removes loose ugly dandruff. What's more, non-alcoholic Wildroot Cream-Oil is the only leading hair tonic that contains soothing LANOLIN. So ask for Wildroot Cream-Oil "again and again the choice of men who put good grooming first."

MUSIC:    (ACCENT AND HOLD)

ANNCR:    And now back to "Inside Story on Kid Spade" – tonight's adventure with . . . ..SAM SPADE!

MUSIC:    (UP INTO SECOND OVERTURE AND TO B.G.)

MUSIC:    SECOND OVERTURE AND TO B.G.

SPADE:    The next morning I packed my bag, tried to get out of the hotel to meet Lynn as soon as possible. I had a hunch that he would call me. He did.

MAESTRO:    (FILTER) Sam, I beg you! I will never again be able to rest again if we part this way. Just for a few minutes! Come to see me, Sam . . . come down to Stillwell's Gymnasium. You have all your – your boxing things there. In the locker room. I – I want you to give them to me, a keepsake. I want to keep them, Sam. Please.

SPADE:      I can't – I have to meet Lynn.

MAESTRO:    Call her – you'll meet her later – your plane doesn't leave until six . . .

SPADE:      Well – okay – I'll see Lynn – then'll meet you later at the gym . . .

MAESTRO:    Oh, thank you, thank you, Sam! Believe me, I'll never forget you for this!

MUSIC:      BRIDGE AND TO B.G.

SPADE:      Yeah . . . thank you, Sam, thank you . . . that's what he said. But that wasn't what he was thinking, and he was still thinking for me. Sure, I was being a right guy. I was trying to break clean – but the Maestro was in there waiting to throw the big low punch. And when he hung up the phone, he gave poor Lefty the needle.

LEFTY:      Well, boss?

MAESTRO:    He will come.

LEFTY:      (AGITATED) And – and you'll get him into the steam room?

MAESTRO:    (DREAMILY) Yes, Lefty, yes . . . And I will sit here with him, with the steam thick around us, hiding us from each other . . . and when I begin to feel the live heat, Lefty . . . at five o'clock, I will be talking about old times as I quietly slip out of the room and he will be sitting, sitting there alone, thinking of old times, not knowing I am gone and that he is alone . . . until it is too late. He will hear the sudden rush of steam and feel the scalding heat and he will run to the door – but it will not open and he will pound and scream in agony – but the door will stick and each scream will draw burning steam into his tortured lungs . . . and then they will find him . . . but it will be too late . . . too late . . . too late . . .

MUSIC:      (BRIDGE) AND TO B.G.

SPADE:      That's what I was walking into. And you know I think back now and realize that maybe I knew I was walking into a sack – but maybe I also knew that I had to walk into it – and then either walk out on my own two feet, thinking for myself, or not walk out at all . . . I met the Maestro at the gym. We went down to the locker room and he picked over my gloves and the punching bag like they were the toys of a baby that'd just died. Then he begged to see me in the ring just once more – to go a couple of rounds with one of the boys upstairs. I did. And fifteen minutes later we were in the steam room.

SOUND:      MINOR-PITCHED DEEP-THROATED SOUND OF STEAM ESCAPING LAZILY INTO THE ROOM: ECHO CHAMBER THROUGHOUT SCENE;

MAESTRO:  Ahhh . . . this is fine . . .

SPADE:      Hot!

MAESTRO:  Good for your muscles!

SPADE:      Whew! Steam's so thick, can't see your hand in front of you!

MAESTRO:  Here – feel your way over here, Sam. Sit here. That's

|  |  |
|---|---|
|  | right. Just keep your head down, your eyes closed – and relax. Like me. |
| SPADE: | Yes . . . feels good . . . |
| MAESTRO: | It will begin to feel even better. Later |
| SOUND: | NOTHING BUT THE MEN BREATHING DEEPLY AND THE SLOW, HOLLOW INSIDIOUS SOUND OF THE STEAM:    THEN: |
| MAESTRO: | (SOFTLY) Tell me, Sam. Tell me how you met Lynn. |
| SPADE: | Well . . . she was up at the hotel with her folks. We got to talking. And – I liked her. It felt good just being with her. And her family. I – kind of felt that's what I wanted most was right there. |
| SOUND: | STEAM PRESSURE UP LIGHTLY |
| SPADE: | I – guess I was always a pretty lonely guy. But I didn't know it. Now I do. That makes the difference. I guess I'm tired of hotel rooms and training camps and fight talk and – |
| MAESTRO: | But don't you see, Sam? Maybe you don't love this girl. Maybe it's just your loneliness and what she represents to you: a home, a family . . . |
| SPADE: | I guess that's the crop for any man. |
| SOUND: | SILENCE: MEN BREATHING: STEAM UP A BIT: THEN: |
| SPADE: | (BREATHING HEAVILY) Getting kind of hot, Maestro. Maybe we'd better – |
| MAESTRO: | Remember, Sam? Remember the day we first met? |
| SPADE: | Maestro – I – this heat it – I think we'd – |
| MAESTRO: | (CONTINUING SMOOTHLY) You had muscle power – |

and a burning restlessness, you didn't know what to do with it. I showed you. I found you, found the ring – and in one year you were near the top.

MAESTRO: (START FADE LOWLY) Yes-it was a long year, Sam. A year of hardship. But we went through it together and it brought us closer together. Yes . . . . . . .

SPADE: (MUSIC: SIMULTANEOUS) And that's what I couldn't take. I knew he would go on that way, pulling all the stops, playing every variation on the old theme, as only he could sing it. I didn't know whether I was embarrassed by it or whether I was afraid I'd fall for it. I opened my mouth to say goodbye, Maestro, but somehow nothing came out. The steam was thick enough by now to hide me as I silently groped my way to the door, opened it just enough to slip out, closed it behind me – and left the Maestro talking into the steam, without having to say those last goodbyes. I figured that the Maestro would still be going on, still thinking that the Maestro would still be going on, still thinking that he was thinking for me by the time I was dressed and out of the gym. I wanted to let him have his performance, but I couldn't stay for it. (MUSIC: OUT) But what he'd planned for five o'clock when the little hand was on the five and the big hand on the twelve was going to happen. Poor Lefty didn't know the difference. He had his instructions, and you can imagine, Effie, what those last awful moments must have been like with the Maestro talking to a guy who wasn't there.

MUSIC: EERIE BACKING FOR FOLLOWING SCENE:

MAESTRO: . . . Yes, Sam . . . it was a year of hardship, tank-town fights . . . but then we got your first fight in the big time. Remember that night? How nervous you were? And do you remember the last thing you said to me before you went into the ring?

(HE PAUSES: WAITS A REPLY: DEEP SILENCE BUT FOR HIS OWN BREATHING AND THE MUTED ROAR OF THE STEAM: SILENCE: THE ROAR OF THE STEAM IS NOW MENACING)

Sam – where are you!

(SILENCE: THE DREADFUL KNOWLEDGE THAT HE IS ALONE IN THE CHAMBER HITS HIS BRAIN: HE IS NEAR HYSTERIA)

Sam!

SOUND:      BARE FEET RACING MADLY ACROSS CONCRETE FLOOR:

MAESTRO:    Sam! Sam!

SOUND:      RATTLE OF DOOR HANDLE:      IT HOLDS FAST:

MAESTRO:    (HYSTERICALLY) Sam! Don't leave me here!

SOUND:      FISTS POUNDING ON DOOR FRANTICALLY)

MAESTRO:    Come back! Please come back! Sam! Don't leave me here!

SOUND:      HYSTERICAL POUNDING ON DOOR:

MAESTRO:    (SCREAMING HYSTERICALLY) Lefty! Lefty! Don't – Sam! Sam! Sam!

SOUND:      ROARING RUSH OF INTENSE, LIVE STEAM: AGO-NIZED AND ENDLESS SCREAM:

MUSIC:      WHAMS IN TO TOP IT: BRIDGE OVER:

SPADE:     (QUIETLY) And that's the way he died: knowing it was coming, waiting for it to come . . . That's the way he died.

SPADE:     That Dundy! Where is he? Get on the phone. Get him over here so we can get Lefty out of here!

EFFIE:     He'll be along, Sam. He'll be along. Oh, Sam . . . I'm . . . I'm so grateful.

SPADE:     Grateful? What are you talking about?

EFFIE:     Yes . . . that underneath you're really a softy and couldn't bear to sit there with the Maestro while he talked of old times – because if you had – why, I – I – (IN SUDDEN TEARS) Oh, Sam, it would have been dreadful!

SPADE:     Keep your shoulder down . . . and your chin up . . . that's it. (PATS SHOULDER) (HE KISSES HER)

EFFIE:     (SIGHS) Sam, tell me, Sam. What was she like?

SPADE:     Lynn? . . . I don't know, Effie. She must have been wonderful. I went down to meet her at the airport that same afternoon. It was five-thirty and the sun was setting. It was just the day to be leaving on a plane for New York, I guess.

SOUND:     AIRPORT ACTIVITY:

ANNCR:     (ECHO-FILTER) Attention, please . . . Attention . . . We are holding Flight 17 for passenger Spade. We will hold Flight 17 for only two minutes longer for Mr. Spade. Leaving at Gate Five.

ANNCR:     Flight 17. Flagship to New York. Leading at Gate Five. Flight 17. Board, Please.

SOUND:     GENERAL ACTIVITY INTENSIFIED:

LYNN:       (PROJECTING) Sam – Sam – here . . . ..

SPADE:      (FADING ON) Hello, Lynn. Sorry I'm late.

LYNN:       Hurry! We've only got – what is it, Sam?

SPADE:      Lynn – there's something I – (BREAKS OFF)

LYNN:       Go on, Sam. I think I know.

SPADE:      This afternoon – when you saw me in the Maestro's office – when I blew my top-

LYNN:       Yes, Sam.

SPADE:      There's a lot of violence in me, Lynn.

LYNN:       It frightened me.

SPADE:      We don't know each other, Lynn.

LYNN:       (SINCERELY) Goodbye, Sam. Good luck.

SPADE:      Thanks, Lynn.

ANNCR:      Last call flight 17. Board please.

LYNN:       (OVER ABOVE) And Sam – please – take care of yourself. I – I'll always worry about you . . . (FADING) Keep your chin down and your shoulder up! Goodbye, my dear – goodbye . . .

SPADE:      Goodbye, Sweetheart.

SOUND:      BG PLANES BUILDS TO MIGHTY ROAR

PA VOICE:   (FILTER) (ECHO) Flight 17 – New York – Flight 17 – now taking off – stand back please-

SOUND:      BG PLANE BUILDS TO MIGHTY ROAR:

SPADE:      (A WHISPER) Goodbye . . . Sweetheart.

SOUND:      PLANE TAKES OFF AND DISAPPEARS IN THE DIS-
            TANCE.

MUSIC:      CURTAIN

ANNCR:      Wildroot Cream-Oil has presented The Adventures of
            Sam Spade . . . Dashiell Hammett's famous private detec-
            tive. Produced and directed by William Spier.

(COMMERCIAL)

The man who makes the best impression is the man who
puts good grooming first! And you can do that, fellows,
by using Wildroot Cream-Oil. This grand non-alcoholic
hair tonic is "again and again the choice of men who put
grooming first"! And here's why Wildroot Cream-Oil is
so popular: it gives a man everything he wants in a hair
tonic – grooms his hair neatly and naturally, relieves dryness and removes loose dandruff! What's more, Wildroot Cream-Oil contains soothing LANOLIN, that's so
much like the oil of your skin. And remember, no other
leading hair tonic gives you all of these advantages! So
take Wildroot's Close-Up Test. If a close-up look in the
mirror reveals unruly hair, dryness or loose dandruff, you
need Wildroot Cream-Oil – "again and again the choice
of men who put good grooming first."

MUSIC:      (THEME)

ANNCR:      Sam Spade is played by Howard Duff. Lurene Tuttle is Ef-
            fie. "The Adventures of Sam Spade" is written for radio
            by Bob Tallman and Jason James, with musical direction
            by Lud Gluskin. Next Sunday, author Dashiell Hammett
            and producer William Spier join forces for another ad-
            venture with Sam Spade brought to you by the Wildroot
            Company . . . Makers of Wildroot Cream-Oil for the hair.

MUSIC:        (GOODNIGHT SWEETHEART TO:)

ANNCR:        Smart girls use Wildroot Cream-Oil too – for quick good grooming and to relieve dryness between permanents. Mothers say it's grand or training children's hair. Dick Joy speaking.

              THIS IS CBS . . . THE COLUMBIA BROADCASTING SYSTEM.

# THE ADVENTURES OF SAM SPADE
## "THE SHORT LIFE CAPER"

SUNDAY, JANUARY 11, 1948
5:00 – 5:30 PM PST

9:00 – 9:30 PM PST

ANNCR:    The Adventures of Sam Spade, detective – brought to you by Wildroot Cream-Oil HAIR TONIC, the Non-alcoholic hair tonic that contains Lanolin. Wildroot Cream- Oil "again and again the choice of me who put good grooming first."

MUSIC:    UP INTO TRILL INTO PHONE BELL

SOUND:    (RECEIVER LIFTED: TELEPHONE ON FILTER MIKE

EFFIE:    Sam Spade Detective Agency.

SPADE:    Me. Sweetheart.

EFFIE:    Oh, Sam, I'm so glad you called. That woman was here again.

SPADE:    What woman?

EFFIE:      That Mrs. Short.

SPADE:      What did she want?

EFFIE:      She wanted her money back. What did you do to her, Sam?

SPADE:      Not a thing, Sweetheart. Not my type.

EFFIE:      Well, I must say it's the first time that ever happened. A client wanting a refund. You must have done something, Sam.

SPADE:      Tell you all about it when I get there, Sweetheart. I'm coming right down to dictate my report on the Short Life Caper.

MUSIC:      THEME BACKGROUND

MUSIC:      (OVERTURE)

SOUND:      DOOR CLOSED, STEPS

EFFIE:      (FADE ON) Oh, Sam, you hung up so quickly, I didn't have a chance to tell you –

SPADE:      Bring your book and come on in, Sweetheart.

EFFIE:      Of course, Sam.

SOUND:      STEPS. CHAIR, DESK DRAWER ETC. (EFFIE'S STEPS FADE ON)

EFFIE:      (FADE ON) I must say, I don't see why you even bother sending her a report. The way she talked, wanting her money back.

SPADE:      What did you tell her?

EFFIE:      I told her, Mrs. Short, apparently you do not appreciate that Mr. Spade is one of the most important detectives in the country, and you were very fortunate to secure his services.

SPADE:    Why did you say that?

EFFIE:    Didn't you listen, Sam?

SPADE:    I'm still listening.

EFFIE:    To the radio, Sam!

SPADE:    Oh yeah. Nothing worth bothering about. A few traffic smashes, couple of rumbles to bunco and fugitive, girl jumped off the bay bridge.

EFFIE:    Don't you ever listen to anything but police calls?

SPADE:    Is there something I'm missing?

EFFIE:    There certainly is! This program last night, Sam –

SPADE:    Later, Effie, later. I want to get this Short dame out of my hair first.

EFFIE:    Well, whatever you say, Sam. But I must say –

SPADE:    Down, Effie.

SPADE:    Date: January 11, 1948. To Mrs. Leon Short. From: Samuel Spade, License Number 137596. Subject: The Short Life Caper. (MUSIC SNEAK) (SOUND: RAIN BACK-GROUND: DISTANT SLOSHY TRAFFIC: SKIDDING BUSSES: TROLLEY BELLS: AUTO HORNS: HARBOR SOUNDS: BLEND) It was a wet, dim afternoon in San Francisco. Business was at a standstill everywhere but the emergency hospital. (SIREN IN FAR DISTANCE) But it was dry and comparatively cozy in my office – that is, till you came in. I took your umbrella, shook the water out of

|         | it, helped you off with your rain-cape, and handed you a dry handkerchief (MUSIC:  ACCENT AND OUT) |
|---------|---|
| VERA:   | (WEEPS) I'm sorry, Mr. Spade, I just can't help it. |
| SPADE:  | That's alright; it's a very sad day. |
| VERA:   | It's all so tragic . . . I'm Vera Short, Mr. Spade. |
| SPADE:  | Oh, don't say that. |
| VERA:   | That's my name. And the Continental Detective office in Boston traced him here through the bank. |
| SPADE:  | Traced whom? |
| VERA:   | My husband. (FRESH TEARS) |
| SPADE:  | Wandering husband. His full name, Mrs. Short? |
| VERA:   | Mr. Short |
| SPADE:  | Full name. |
| VERA:   | Leon. Leon N. Short. |
| SPADE:  | N. for what? |
| VERA:   | I-uh-nothing. He felt he needed an initial. Mr. Spade, do we have to spend so much time on little details? |
| SPADE:  | Ninety-nine percent of detective work is collecting little details, Mrs. Short. If you want me to find your husband . . . |
| VERA:   | Oh, but I know where he is. |
| SPADE:  | Maybe you'd better tell me in your own words exactly what your problem is, Mrs. Short. |
| VERA:   | Leon left home, Boston, that is, three weeks ago. He often went on business trips . . . I don't know why I worried |

about this one. But when two weeks went by and I hadn't heard from him, a terrible suspicion came into my mind. I went to the bank. And it's a good thing I did.

SPADE:     You mean he'd drawn out all his money?

VERA:      Oh, no, he couldn't. Practically all of it is in my name. On account of taxes, you know. But he'd sold some securities – more than a hundred fifty thousand dollars. And had the cash transferred out here – to the Golden Gate Bank.

SPADE:     And you think he's selling you short.

VERA:      What would you think – all that cash. (SOBS)

SPADE:     You say you know where he is. Have you talked to him?

VERA:      Just over the phone. He told me to go back to Boston. And I was just being silly about the hundred and fifty thousand dollars because he was going to buy a gold mine with it. And that's what he wanted it for. But I don't believe it.

SPADE:     Why not?

VERA:      What would he do with a old mine here in the sticks? After all, we live in Boston. And it's full of sound investments. (SOBS)

SOUND:     (DRAWER: BOTTLES: GLASS: POURING)

SPADE:     Here. Try this.

VERA:      Oh, you're so thoughtful. (GULPS) Oh, that does help.

SOUND:     (GLASS SET DOWN)

SPADE:     Now I suppose you tell me exactly what you want me to do.

VERA:      He's staying at a terrible hotel. It's not even in the auto club booklet. The Belvedere, it's called. My husband is a Bostonian, Mr. Spade. And he wouldn't be found dead in a hotel like that. I doubt if it's even insurable. You'd think after that terrible earthquake they had here-

SPADE:     Fire, Mrs. Short.

VERA:      Well, whatever it was. But he's there, anyway, Room 213. And the elevator man was fresh and I think they cook coffee in the rooms. The smell. And this man opened the door and he told me my husband didn't want to see me and when I tried to brush past him he was most disrespectful. He kicked me.

SPADE:     I see. Go on, Mrs. Short.

VERA:      Well, isn't that enough? And I think my husband is being held prisoner in that room, maybe even tortured. And something dreadful is sure to happen because he'll never hand over that money.

SPADE:     Is the hundred and fifty thousand still in the bank?

VERA:      Oh, yes. At least it was still there when I called an hour ago.

SPADE:     Mrs. Short, I know you'll take this the way it's intended . . . But . . . maybe your husband really doesn't want to see you. Had you thought of that?

VERA:      Yes, I had. And frankly, if that's the way he feels, it's all right with me, Mr. Spade. But I want to be sure.

SPADE:     (MUSIC UNDER) Your coat, umbrella, and eyes were dry when you left my office, Mrs. Short. I counted over the fifty bucks advance you had left with me, made sure it was not boodle, then did some preliminary spadework by phone. Your story about the big wad of cash at the Golden Gate Bank checked. Leon Short was registered at the Belvedere but had left a do-not-disturb with the operator . . . So I put on my hat, raincoat and galoshes and sloshed out into the downpour (SOUND: WET TRAFFIC AND RAIN) By the time I reached the corner of Geary and O'Farrell, even the fly-specked entrance door of the Hotel Belvedere looked inviting. (SOUND: R E V O L V - ING DOOR: CHANGE FROM TRAFFIC TO HOTEL LOBBY SOUNDS) Across the lobby, behind a dusty potted palm, I found Tiny Stover, the house dick, fast asleep in a dingy, mohair-covered chair. An unlighted cigarette dangled from his mouth. (SOUND: CIGARETTE LIGHTER) I lit it. (SOUND: EXPLODING CIGARETTE

STOVER:      (REACTS) Hey, stay where you are! (SOUND: FUM-BLES: GUN DRAWN: SAFETY CATCH) Reach!

SPADE:       Wake up, Tiny, you're dreaming.

STOVER:      Oh. Oh, it's you, Sam

SPADE:       Since when you smoking trick cigarettes?

STOVER:      Ah, them bellboys, hot-foot, exploding cigarettes, plastic chewing gum. Can't hardly get any sleep around here anymore. (YAWNS) What's on your mind?

SPADE:       Two thirteen. Name of Short.

STOVER:      Short . . . Short . . . yeah. Boston. Checked out couple hours ago. Him and that other old Joe.

SPADE:       Who was the other one?

STOVER:      One of our regulars here. Old time ham actor, name of Savage. Sherwood Savage.

SPADE:      What have you got on him?

STOVER:     Nothing. Not that I haven't tried. He works the bar here. I tagged him for a con merchant but I never caught him at it. All I know, he's a lush, hasn't done any acting or work either since the WPA went out . . . owned three months rent here when he ran into this Leon Short . . . same day pays his room, liquor bill, passes out ten-dollar tips . . .

SPADE:      Hm. A very flush lush.

STOVER:     Right. And if you ask me, there's something funny still going on. Because the day Mr. Short moves down from the St. Mark to bunk with Mr. Savage, Mr. Short suddenly gets very sick. And Savage keeps sending down to the drugstore all the time for different kinds of medicine. The more medicine they send up, the sicker Mr. Short gets.

SPADE:      Know where they moved to?

STOVER:     No forwarding address.

SPADE:      Room been made up yet?

STOVER:     Sam, this is the Belvedere.

SPADE:      Then it's the way they left it. Mind if I give it a quick frisk?

STOVER:     (YAWNS) Go ahead. The lock's broke. Only mind you don't swipe any linen and don't destroy no property.

SPADE:      (MUSIC UNDER) I gave him my word, scout's honor, and trudged up the stairs to room two thirteen. (SOUND TO SUIT ACTION) The door was cracked a couple of inches. I pushed it the rest of the way open and walked in. The room contained a pair of sagging twin beds, a dresser with the knobs broken off, a Venus holding an ashtray (also the knobs broken off), and something that might once have been a chair. But over in the corner was something that didn't belong in the Belvedere. It was new, shiny, and expensive-looking. It was some kind of an electrical heat lamp, and the tag on it said: "Cambria Rentals, for Home & Hospital Use." Pinned to the tag was a voucher made out to one Dr. Maurice G. Milsted, with offices in the Sutter Professional Building. I decided to go to the doctor.

MUSIC:      (UP AND DOWN)

SOUND:      (STEPS DOWN CORRIDOR: DOOR OPENS: MUTED DOCTOR'S OFFICE CHIME)

SPADE:      The neat, modernistic lettering on the door said Maurice Milsted, M.D. A neat little olive-skinned nurse with an old-fashioned Madonna-type hair-do under her starched white cap came out to meet me.

ANN:        Your name, please?

SPADE:      Sam Spade.

ANN:        No appointment?

SPADE:      I'm not a patient.

ANN:        Shall I ask you the rest of the questions?

SPADE:      That could be quite pleasant if we had the time.

ANN:        Your name is Sam and we're in a hurry. We're making some progress.

SPADE:      I sensed that myself.

ANN:        My name is Ann Romero, I'm 24 years old, unattached, and I share an apartment at 565 Geary Street with a girl named Peggy Rea, in case you have a friend.

SPADE:      I don't have, so supposing we meet at the Blue Lamp.

ANN:        Well, it's not the Top of the Mark, but it's cozy.

SPADE:      When do you get through here?

ANN:        Six o'clock. But I've got some x-ray pictures to file. Then I have to sterilize my instruments.

SPADE:      How about seven o'clock. Suture, nurse?

ANN:        You can do better than that, Sam. You know you can.

SPADE:      I'll try, Sweetheart.

ANN:        Door on the left, that's his private office.

SPADE:      I'll thank you on the way out.

SOUND:      (STEPS: DOOR OPENED)

MILSTED:    (OFF: FADING ON) I want that patient to have absolute quiet. I want all the mental patients out of that wing, I won't have them wandering in and out disturbing Mr. Short. No one is to be admitted – especially his wife! And you are not to interfere with any arrangements Mr. Savage has made. Is that clear . . . see you do!

SOUND:      (PHONE HUNG UP: DOOR CLOSES QUIETLY)

SPADE:      (COUGHS)

MILSTED:    Oh. You that costotomy that Dr. Gross promised me?

SPADE:      Should I resent that?

MILSTED:    Oh. Too bad. Sit down. Where does it hurt you?

SPADE:      It doesn't.

MILSTED:    All well, eh? Miss Romero will give you your bill on the way out. If it starts bothering you again take one of these every hour.

SPADE:      Dr. Milsted, I am not a clie- I mean, patient of yours.

MILSTED:    Of course you aren't.  You're that costotomy of Dr. Gross's. I don't want to frighten you, I don't want to be unethical, but Gross is the last man on earth I'd go to for a costotomy. I could show you-

SPADE:      Shut up!

MILSTED:    Hmm. Torsional spasm. Should never attempt- I've told him- costotomy's worthless in a case like yours anyway.

SPADE:      Look, will you please be quiet and let me talk?

MILSTED:    Go on, son. Get it off your chest. What did you say your name was?

SPADE:      Humboldt. I'm with the Cambria Rental Service. About that electrical heater you ordered for a patient of yours in the Belvedere Hotel.

MILSTED:    Oh. The Desert Air Lamp. What's the matter with it? Isn't it helping you?

SPADE:      I'm not your costotomy, Doctor. Remember? Your patient checked out without informing us as to the change of address. Now if you'll just-

MILSTED:    Oh, you mean the hyperplastica.

SPADE:      Hyperplastica, yes.

MILSTED:    Well, he won't be needing your lamp much longer.

SPADE:      Why not?

MILSTED:    Got a minute? (SOUND: DESK DRAWER) Look at this. Read x-rays?

SPADE:      Well, I'm a little rusty. What's that shadow in the middle of it?

MILSTED:     Don't wonder you didn't recognize it. That is the liver of Leon N. Short. Notice the shading along here- brimstone, or Feuerstein's syndrome, bevertail condition of the left lobe, note the degradation of the Tenal impression. (SPADE ADLIBS SAGELY UNDER) The most beautiful stasis cirrhosis I have ever been privileged to see- complete hopeless hyperplastic perihepititis. Any questions?

SPADE:       Yeah. What's the matter with him?

MILSTED:     Well, the medical term for it is gin drinkers' liver, otherwise known as hobnail liver. Advanced stage. The man's as good as dead. I've moved him to Sunnyrest Sanitarium down the peninsula. It's expensive, but I think you'll like it there. Alcohol is forbidden. Costotomy is a serious matter. And don't you ever forget it.

SPADE:       Thank you and goodbye, Dr. Milsted.

SOUND:       (STEPS DOOR CLOSED)

SPADE:       Wheeoooo.

ANN:         What's the matter, Sam? Did he hurt you?

SPADE:       I'm not hurt, just terribly, terribly angry.

ANN:         You said you were going to thank me on the way out.

SPADE:       So I was.

ANN:         (IN CLINCH) Mmm. I bet you like your steaks rare.

SPADE:       Yeah. Can we have dinner at a quarter of seven?

MUSIC:       (BRIDGE & TO BACKGROUND)

SPADE:       After my consultation with Dr. Milsted, I decided that the job of finding your husband wasn't going to be as easy as I'd thought. The only picture I'd seen was an x-ray of a diseased liver, and I wasn't sure I'd be able to recognize him from that. There was a picture in the newspaper morgue but for identification purposes it was worse than the x-ray. But there were plenty of pictures of Sherwood Savage, the man he had disappeared with. It seemed he'd been quite an actor in his day. I took one with me to see if I could get it autographed. (MUSIC CHANGES MOOD)

SPADE:    The Sunnyrest Sanitarium was just what you'd expect it to be. It was smack in the middle of the fog belt- (SOUND: AUTO CRASH: SCREAMS) around the corner from the airport- (PLANES TAXI, TAKE OFF: AIRPORT PA QUACKS IN B.G.) across the bay from a Naval Artillery range. (SOUND: HEAVY CANNON FIRE AND REVERBERATION) Sunnyrest- a Haven for the Weary. I held my hands over my ears and pushed the doorbell with my nose. (SOUND: NERVE WRACKING DOORBELL)

SOUND:    (DOOR FORCES OPEN: VIBRATES AND GLASS RATTLES)

VOICE:    (GASPS)

SPADE:    This is the Sunnyrest Sanitarium?

VOICE:    (WHEEZES)

SPADE:    A patient. Mr. Short.

VOICE:    (WHEEZES)

SPADE:    Thanks, I will.

SOUND:    DOOR CLOSES)

VOICE:    (GASPS)

SPADE:      No, no, don't bother! You just stay there in your hammock. I'll find my way all right.

SOUND:      (CLIMBING STAIRS UNDER LINE)

VOICE:      (OFFSTAGE) Wait a minute. Whatcha want?

SOUND:      (STEPS CONTINUE UPSTAIRS AND DOWN HALL)

VOICES:     (OVER SOUND OFFSTAGE) (ADLIB) (POKER GAME IN ONE ROOM:      OTHER SCREWY SOUNDS)

SOUND:      (STEPS OUT:      KNOCK ON DOOR)

SHORT:      (OFF) Come in!

SOUND:      (DOOR OPENED)

SPADE:      This IS Mr. Short's room?

SHORT:      Yes. I'm Shor- I mean Savage. Sherman Savage I meant to say- that is Sherwood. That's Mr. Sav- I mean Mr. Short over there on the bed.

SAVAGE:     Savage-the lights-it's growing dark.

SHORT:      There, there, Sherw- I mean, Leon. Try to rest. Try to forget.

SAVAGE:     Forget . . . aye . . . forgetfulness . . . Death is the physician of him whom medicine cannot cure. Nietzsche. Come closer. It's so dark . . . so dark . . . who stands beside my bier?

SPADE:      My name is Spade. I can see you're pretty sick. I won't take much of your time.

SAVAGE:     Spade! A Spade to dig my grave. (STAGY GRUESOME LAUGHTER) (FADE UNDER) The end is come of pleasant places- the end of tender words and faces. The end of all, the poppied sleep. Groans and convulsions, and dis-colored faces, friends weeping round us, blacks and ob-sequies, make death a dreadful thing. The pomp of death is far more terrible than death itself. (USE ABOVE AS NEEDED FOR BACKING)

SPADE: (MUSIC UNDER) If it hadn't been so pathetic, it would have been funny. And even if I hadn't recognized the man in the bed from his picture, I would have tagged him as a ham actor playing a very corny death scene. His lines were very bad, but I had an uncomfortable feeling that he was really dying.

SAVAGE: (OUT IF NARRATION) Ah, yes, the poppied sleep. Swinburne. And you, young man, have you brought the money?

SPADE: What money?

SAVAGE: From the bank-the hundred and fifty thousand dollars. You're not from the bank?

SPADE: Well, no, not exactly, I-

SAVAGE: Gadzooks! It's the undertaker.

SHORT: Have you made all the arrangements for my-I mean, Mr. Short's burial?

SAVAGE: You keep out of this. I'm the one who's dying. I'll discuss my own funeral arrangements. Sit down, stop adlibbing, and don't upstage me.

SHORT: Very well, Mr. Sav- I- Mr. Short.

SAVAGE: Zounds, man, don't you even know your own name?

SHORT: (MURMURS) Sorry, I- Sorry.

SPADE:      Look, I don't want to interfere, but Mrs. Short is very upset.

SHORT:      Vera! Vera sent you?

SAVAGE:     Quiet. I'll deal with this interloper. Mr. Spade, you have spoken with my doctor?

SPADE:      Yeah.

SAVAGE:     Then you know. He has given me the very most a week to live. I know not what Vera has told you. But it is greed and greed alone that has made her seek me out. She has brought me nothing but unhappiness. I desire only one benison from the gods- to spend my last few days in this peaceful haven. I beg of you, do not bring her here.

SHORT:      Yes, indeed, Mr. Spade, that would spoil everything.

SAVAGE:     You would not deny the last request of a dying man?

SPADE:      In this case . . . no . . . I don't think I would.

MUSIC:      (BRIDGE AND TO BACKGROUND)

SPADE:      And I didn't. When a man goes to that much trouble to shake a woman, I think he deserves a break. There was only one way the caper could possibly add up. Your husband had to run into poor old Sherwood Savage in the Belvedere Bar, probably just after Savage had learned he had only a few days to live. Between them they hatched their plot; Savage was going to be buried under the name of Leon Short, and your husband would be free of you forever. It was as simple as that. Which all goes to show that if you keep your eyes open, work diligently, and apply your knowledge of human nature to the problem at hand, you can be as wrong as the next guy. I was- dead wrong. Sam Spade, Detective.

MUSIC:     (UP TO FIRST ACT CURTAIN)

ANNCR:     The makers of Wildroot Cream-Oil are presenting the weekly Sunday Adventure of Dashiell Hammett's famous private detective . . . SAM SPADE!

MUSIC:     UP AND RESOLVES OUT

ANNCR:     Now, here's important news on good grooming. Better than four out of five users of Wildroot Cream-Oil say they prefer Wildroot Cream-Oil to all other hair tonics. Here is a new and even more conclusive evidence that Wildroot Cream-Oil is . . . "again and again the choice of men who put good grooming first." So I you want the well-groomed look that helps you get ahead, socially and on the job, listen. Recently, thousands of people from coast to coast who brought Wildroot Cream-Oil for the first time were asked. "How does Wildroot Cream-Oil compare with the hair tonic you previously used?" The results were amazing. Better than four out of five who replied said they preferred Wildroot Cream-Oil. And no wonder. It gives you the advantages that men consider most important. Wildroot Cream-Oil grooms your hair neatly and naturally . . . relieves annoying dryness . . . and removes loose dandruff. What's more, non-alcoholic Wildroot Cream-Oil is the only leading hair tonic that contains soothing Lanolin that's like the oil of your skin. So ask for Wildroot Cream-Oil hair tonic . . . "again and again the choice of men who put good grooming first."

MUSIC:     ACCENT AND HOLD

ANNCR:     And now back to "The Short Life Caper" tonight's adventure with Sam Spade.

MUSIC:     UP INTO SECOND OVERTURE

MUSIC:    OVERTURE AND TO BACKGROUND

MUSIC:    (SECOND OVERTURE)

SOUND:    (PHONE RINGS)

SPADE:    Yes?

VERA:     (ON FILTER) Mr. Spade, this is Vera Short.

SPADE:    Oh, yes, Mrs. Short, I've been trying to reach you. I talked to your husband, and-

VERA:     Did he say anything about that hundred and fifty thousand dollars?

SPADE:    It was mentioned.

VERA:     What did he do with it? The bank says they sent it to him out at Sunnyrest. In an armored truck. And he signed for it.

SPADE:    Well, it's his money, Mrs. Short.

VERA:     Nothing of the sort. It's mine, now that he's dead.

SPADE:    Well, I'm sure he left it to some worthy cause.

VERA:     That's no concern of mine. I think it was most inconsiderate of him. Mr. Spade I want you to come down here at once.

SPADE:    Where are you?

VERA:     I'm at an establishment called the Sunset Mortuary. They're preparing Leon's remains for shipment back to Boston.

SPADE:    Uh- you've actually seen your husband's body?

VERA:     Of course I have. I had to be sure it was him- I mean he! Now you hurry right down here.

SPADE:    Okay, Mrs. Short. I'm practically there.

MUSIC:    (BRIDGE)

SOUND:    (MUTED STEPS ON COMPOSITION FLOOR)

VERA:    (FADES ON) Well, I must say, it took you long enough to get here. So much to do before that train leaves. I came West without a stitch of black, and prices they're getting for caskets out here . . .

SPADE:    Most everything's like that, Mrs. Short. Slightly higher west of the Rockies.

VERA:    Mr. Spade, I want that money. The whole hundred and fifty thousand. Unless you locate it before I leave town, I shall sue for the fee I paid you plus mental anguish. Unless you'd care to return it now?

SPADE:    Listen, Shorty, you'll be lucky if I let you catch that train.

VERA:    (GASPS)

SPADE:    That ham actor's makeup may fool them in Boston, if you keep him in the coffin with the lid screwed down, but every cop on O'Farrell Street knows Sherwood Savage. He's a local landmark. You and your husband picked the wrong pigeon.

VERA:    What are you talking about?

SPADE:    I figured it wrong, Short. I figured your husband was pulling a simple disappearing act. How much insurance do you and Mr. Short stand to collect if you bury Mr. Savage under your husband's name?

VERA:    Insurance? My husband never carried any insurance. Why should he? Mr. Spade, I think you're confused. I think you'd better come with me. He's right in the next room.

SOUND:    (STEPS: VERA'S, SPADE FOLLOWS

VERA:    (OVER SHOULDER) Here I've been thinking you did such a grand job- except for losing track of that money. And all the time, I think you've been looking for the wrong man. I want you to take a good look now.

SOUND:    (DOOR OPENED)

MUSIC:    (PUNCTUATE AND TO BACKGROUND)

SPADE:    I looked, and then I didn't know where to look. The man in the coffin was the man I had tagged as Leon Short as the Sunnyrest joint- and not Sherwood Savage who worked so hard playing Leon's death scene. My mind was reeling. Everything went black. When I regained my senses I was surprised to find myself in the Stutter Professional Building outside the door of Dr. Maurice Milsted's office.

(SOUND:    DOOR OPENED: CHIME AS BEFORE)

ANN:    (GASPS) Oh, Oh, it's you. You startled me.

SPADE:    I may startle you some more before I leave here, Sweetheart.

ANN:    Now, please don't be angry with me. I was really going to meet you at the Blue Lamp. Honestly I was. Only I happened to think of something and it worried me so I had to come back and make sure.

SPADE:    It wasn't a picture of somebody's liver.

ANN:    How did you know?

SPADE:    Never mind that. I want some answers from you.

ANN:    They can't arrest me, can they? It was just a mistake. I got the labels mixed up and put Mr. Savage's name on that acute hyperplasty. And the hyperplasty died last week, and here's his name on Mr. Savage's x-ray you see. And doctor has had poor Mr. Savage thinking he's at death's door. So I stopped in at the Belvedere Hotel to make a phone call and I happened to see Mr. Savage and he looked so healthy, carrying a big heavy suitcase, he was smiling. I couldn't get it out of my mind, how a man could look so happy if he really believed he was dying. But I've got to find that other plate and I can't imagine where it's gone to.

SPADE:     Have you looked in the upper left hand drawer of the doctor's desk?

ANN:     Oh, no, I never go into his private office.

SPADE:     He in there now?

ANN:     No, it's much too late.

SOUND:     (STEPS: DOOR YANKED OPEN)

ANN:     (SCREAMS)

MUSIC:     (PUNCTUATE AND UNDER)

SPADE:     She was right. It was much too late. The drawer the x-ray film had been in was open and the contents dumped on the floor. There was a rank smell in the air. It smelled like burned cellulose. What was left of the most beautiful stasis cirrhosis Dr. Milsted had ever been privileged to see was in an ashtray. The doctor's right hand, holding a charred matchstick between a rigid thumb and forefinger rested beside it. What was left of the doctor was slumped across the red-stained green desk-blotter. He's been shot through the head.

MUSIC:      (UP TO CLIMAX: CHANGES MOOD: DROP TO B.G.)

SOUND:      (BARROOM BACKGROUND)

SAVAGE:     Break out another Jera boam, bartender, I'm treating the house.

BARTENDER:   Sure you can pay for all this, Mr. Savage?

SAVAGE:     Drat your insolence, sir! You are looking upon a man of wealth. I honor this bistro with my presence. High descent and meritorious deeds, unless united to wealth, are as useless as seaweed. Horace wrote that, sir, in the 25th century B.C., and it's still true. Ah, I see an acquaintance down the bar who has not yet tasted of my hospitality. Step up here, sir, and you shall be my honored guest. You see before you a man risen from the dead.

SPADE:      Yeah. High as a kite.

SAVAGE:     Gad, your rapier-like wit!

SPADE:      Making a little free with champagne, aren't you?

SAVAGE:     Ah, a man's gift maketh room for him, and bringeth him before great men. Proverbs eighteenth chapter, sixth verse.

SPADE:      Why did you do it?

SAVAGE:     Our deeds determine us as much as we determine our deeds. If you mean Milsted he was a quack and a malpracitioner. I have done humanity a great service.

SPADE:      Did you think you'd get away with it?

SAVAGE:     Come, let us sit upon the ground and tell sad stories of the death of kings. Will you join in a booth, sir? Keep your fat lunch-hooks off that bottle, barman, I'll carry it myself.

Over here, Mr. Spade, far from the maddening crowd, (SITS) Ah, this is better. (DEFIANT) Well, it's quieter than Sunnyrest. Um. Where shall we begin.

SPADE:     How about your first meeting with Leon Short?

SAVAGE:   Right here, sir, in this very booth. I had just come from that quack, Milsted, who had informed me that me liver had at last given out. That Boston bumpkin- ah, I've played them many atime- cold as codfish. He plied me with liquor, a dying man, hoping to accelerate my demise, no doubt, and then he made his foul proposition.

SPADE:     And you agreed to let yourself be buried under his name. I guessed that much when I saw you play that lousy death scene.

SAVAGE:   I couldn't get into it, somehow. Never could play against amateurs. That feller Short- kept forgetting his name.

SPADE:     What were you going to get out of it?

SAVAGE:   Not a farthing, sir. A mean, miserable man. But misers are very good people; they amass wealth for those who wish their death. In short, no pun intended, this worm, in ex-change for my hapless body, agreed only to keep it in liquor and out of the rain until death did us part. I was on the point of eviction from this foul hostelry, me credit at the bar had been rescinded, and so I agreed. Am I boring you?

SPADE:     No, you're taking off this part real good.

SAVAGE:   I have not trod the boards these forty years for nothing, sir! Well, when that sawbones Milsted telephoned me to say that it was all a hideous mistake and that I was not going to die after all, it occurred to me that, as the scene had been set for Mr. Short's death anyway, he might as well play the part himself. As soon as the money arrived from the bank, I fetched him a blow across the head with my walking stick and took a taxi back to town, first having packed the money in a valise. Milsted agreed to write the death certificate, but the scoundrel afterwards demanded the whole hundred and fifty thousand, which I deemed exorbitant. So I shot him.

SPADE:      Why are you telling me all this?

SAVAGE:     A generous and free-minded confession doth disable a reproach and disarm an injury. Montagne.

SPADE:      It won't work, Savage. Not in the State of California.

SAVAGE:     I am aware of that. Remember, sir, I have faced Death and looked him squarely in the eye. He hold no terrors for me now.

SPADE:      But the hundred and fifty grand.

SAVAGE:     Ah, you were going to say I can't take it with me. Yet that money was my sole and only motive. There is a pretty puzzle, oh? What?

SPADE:      So pretty I don't get it.

SAVAGE:     It was ever my ambition in life, since first, a beardless boy, I played to the groundlings, to build a great theatre that would bear my name. At last this ambition lay within my grasp. The Sherwood Savage Shakespeare Memorial. The valisco is enroute at this very moment to a trusted friend of mine (who shall remain nameless) and him I have appointed treasurer of the Sherwood Savage Shakespeare Memorial Fund. When finally that great theatre rears its lofty towers, I daresay Vera will be content to write it off her income taxes. Indeed, what else can she do? Will you have another drink?

SPADE:      I guess you've got time for another round.

SAVAGE:     Barkeep! Drinks all around! A farewell toast from an actor to the greatest audience of his career! (CROWD REACTION) Tell me, Mr. Spade, do they have adequate lighting in that- er- gas chamber?

SPADE:      Yeah. Real bright spotlight.

SAVAGE:     How many seats in the house?

SPADE:      Only a few. But the press will be there.

SAVAGE:     (SIGHS) Well, I never played to the critics. Perhaps I should have. Well, I shan't be disappointed in my notices, shall I? Won't be here to read them. Eh? (MUSIC: SNEAK) Drink up, Mr. Spade. Drink washes off the daub and discovers the men. Old Proverb.

MUSIC:      (UP TO CLIMAX AND OUT)

SPADE:      Period. End of report.

EFFIE:      Imagine. After doing all that for her, she had the gall to demand her money back.

SPADE:      Well, she had a point there. A hundred and fifty grand ain't hay.

EFFIE:      But as Mr. Savage pointed out, she can just write it of her income taxes.

SPADE:      I'm not sure she can, but I sincerely hope not.

EFFIE:      So do I. Oh, Sam, about that radio program I listened to last night . . .

SPADE:      Type that up, Sweetheart, then I want to hear all about it.

EFFIE:      Here it is, Sam. I hope I spelled hyperplastica right.

SPADE:      If you did we'll add ten bucks to the bill.

EFFIE:      Oh, Sam, you're so great, it's such a privilege to work for you.

SPADE:      Well, thanks a lot, Angel. Shall we dance?

EFFIE:      Sam, I don't understand why you don't take more interest in things.

SPADE:      What things?

EFFIE:      Well, the radio, for instance. Do you realize that you were on the air for a whole hour last night?

SPADE:      That's a lie. I was at Sunnyrest Sanitarium.

EFFIE:      Well, not you, Sam, but that Howard Duff, you know, that handsome actor that plays you on Sunday nights and we saw him in that picture about a prison or something?

SPADE:      Yeah, and that reminds me. Take a letter to his agent. Tell him I'm tired of getting that guy's fan mail, and further more I have never made a single penny out of that show, and furthermore they never even asked permission to use my name. And furthermore . . .

EFFIE:      That's not true, Sam, you signed a paper. And you said at the time I quote you this might be good for business.

SPADE:      Yeah, this Duff gets my mail and I get his- that's great for business.

EFFIE:      Well, all right, if you're not interested in all the nice things Robert Montgomery said about you.

SPADE:      Montgomery, eh? The movie star? What show was that?

EFFIE:      Suspense.

SPADE:    Oh yeah, I listened to that a couple of times. They had a thing there on ballistics, where the bullet-

EFFIE:    Oh, that was ages ago, Sam. They've got a whole new thing now. And it's on for a whole hour. There's never been anything like it. It said in the paper.

SPADE:    Hmm. What'd they say about me?

EFFIE:    They said you were the- the dean of private eyes or something like that.

SPADE:    Pardon my long grey beard.

EFFIE:    They didn't mean it like that, Sam. Maybe that's not the word they used. I'm not sure, Sam, but it gave a very nice impression. You know a whole hour and Suspense and Robert Montgomery sounds so dignified and- Sam, aren't you interested in anything but money?

SPADE:    Yeah, I am. And when you're a little older, Effie-

EFFIE:    Oh, you! (MUSIC SNEAK) Goodnight, Sam!

SPADE:    Goodnight, Sweetheart!

MUSIC:    FINAL CURTAIN

# THE ADVENTURES OF SAM SPADE
## #138-X3 "THE JANE DOE CAPER"

TO BE TRANSCRIBED SATURDAY, APRIL 30, 1949

ANNCR:     The Adventures of Sam Spade, Detective- brought to you
           by Wildroot Cream-Oil Hair Tonic, the non-alcoholic hair
           tonic that contains Lanolin. Wildroot Cream-Oil, "again
           and again the choice of men and women and children,
           too."

MUSIC:     (UP INTO TRILL INTO PHONE BELL)

SOUND:     (PHONE RINGS:   RECEIVER LIFTED: TELEPHONE ON
           FILTER MIKE)

EFFIE:     Sam Spade Detective Agency.

SPADE:     Me, Sweetheart.

EFFIE:     Oh, Sam, was it an interesting case?

SPADE:     Fascinating, in a depressing sort of way.

EFFIE:     Oh, that's good.

SPADE:     Good?

EFFIE:      Yes, because I know those who depress you the most pay off the best. And we do need the money.

SPADE:     Well, don't send out for champagne. My client is on the way to Minneapolis. And besides, she's dead.

EFFIE:      You should have collected in advance, Sam.

SPADE:     Well, I couldn't very well do that. She was dead when I met her. And her name wouldn't have been any good on a check anyway. Stay where you are, Sweetheart. I'll be right down to dictate my report on the Jane Doe Caper.

MUSIC:     (THEME AND TO BACKGROUND)

MUSIC:     (OVERTURE)

SOUND:    (DOOR CLOSED: STEPS)

EFFIE:      (FADE ON) Sam, you say the most abstracting things on the telephone.

SPADE:     You don't need a phone.

SOUND:    (STEPS)

EFFIE:      And what do you mean, her signature wasn't good.

SPADE:     Her name was Jane Doe, which means anybody, or no-body.

EFFIE:      There you go again. And what do you mean she was dead when you met her.

SPADE:     Just that. Come on, let's get this over.

EFFIE:      Sam, you're all unwrought.

SPADE:     Date: Fill it in. To: Detective Lieutenant Dundy, Homicide Detail, San Francisco Police. Subject: The Jane Doe Caper. Dear Dundy: (MUSIC SNEAK) You were there at the start of it, but just for the record, I had dropped in at the City Morgue for a routine checkup on a missing person job. I didn't think I'd find my client's husband there. In fact everything about her told me that her husband, unless he was out of his head, was at least out of the country. Think he turned out to be. But that's another story. What I did find, not on a morgue slab, but leaning over one, was you.

SOUND:    (DRIPPING WATER ON ECHO: STEPS ON ECHO: AND OUT)

DUNDY:    Hello, Sam. What brings you here?

SPADE:    Morbid curiosity. And you, Lieutenant?

DUNDY:    This girl. Harbor Patrol brought her in.

SPADE:    Golden Gate Bridge?

DUNDY:    Could have been. Looks like suicide . . . What's the matter with the world, Sam? A girl with a young appealing face like that . . . everything to live for.

SPADE:    Who was she?

DUNDY:    Don't know, yet. Tagged her Jane Doe.

SPADE:    (MUSIC UNDER) And that's when I took my first real look at her. She couldn't have been in the water more than a few hours. Her shoes were missing- they would be- but the rest of her clothes were intact, and even with the soaking they'd got in the bay, you could still see that they had style, and had cost someone a lot of money. But something about her didn't seem to belong to those clothes. Her features were good, but she looked too young, and her skin looked as if it had never worn makeup. Her hands were smooth- almost too smooth- and neatly manicured, but her nails were too short. And around her throat, where you would have expected to see a necklace or a string of pearls, there was a cheap silver medallion. She looked lonely and out of place, even in death, and I could sense that your thoughts were running in the same direction.

DUNDY:    Funny how some of them get to you, isn't it, Sam?

SPADE:    Yeah.

DUNDY:    It's things like this that make me think sometimes I should have gone into some other line of work. A cop is not supposed to have any personal feelings. But I can't help it. A young girl like that . . . everything to live for . . .

SPADE:    Why do you keep saying that?

DUNDY:    Well . . . had money, anyway. Must have. Look at the way she's dressed. She could have sold that fur coat for enough to go away somewhere and start over.

SPADE:    You're sure of that, Dundy.

DUNDY:    You're darn right. That's mutation mink. My wife wants one.

SPADE:    She'll never get one at the rate you're going.

DUNDY:    Now, Sam . . .

SPADE:    Dundy, of all the bay suicides, can you remember a single one that didn't take off his coat before jumping?

DUNDY:    Well, now, Sam, I don't- Say! Come to think of it-

SPADE:    That's using the old noodle. Keep it up, Dundy, I'll see you around. Hey, Maxie?

SOUND:      (STEPS SLIGHTLY)

DUNDY:      (SLIGHTLY OFF) Wait a minute, Sam.

SPADE:      (STEPS OUT) Yeah, Dundy?

DUNDY:      You got a hunch about this one?

SPADE:      You want to hire me?

DUNDY:      Now, Sam . . . .

SPADE:      Let me know how it comes out.

MAXIE:      Sammy! What can I do for you?

SPADE:      That stiff tagged Jane Doe.

MAXIE:      Autopsy report just came down. Drowning. Multiple frac-
            tures and shock. She took the jump alright.

SPADE:      Let's see that report. And don't tell Dundy, I asked for-

MAXIE:      Sure, Sammy. Make yourself at home.

MUSIC:      (IN AND CONTINUE BACKGROUND)

SPADE:      There are a lot of Jane Does in morgues all over the coun-
            try. A lot of them get buried under that name. I don't
            know what there was about this one. You felt it too- in
            your subtle way. I couldn't shake the feeling that Jane
            Doe needed a friend- even if it was too late. (MUSIC
            CHANGES MOOD) None of the obvious means of iden-
            tification were there. No labels in the clothes, no clean-
            er's marks, no dental work (and that was another thing
            that didn't fit the body of a well-dressed woman, because
            she needed some). The only thing that seemed to belong
            to her was that little cheap medallion. When I left the
            Morgue, I was carrying it in my pocket. My next stop was

a little supply house on Columbus Avenue with a sign in the window, "Imported Medals Our Specialty." Don't ask me why I picked that one. Maybe because she looked kind of Italian . . .

| | |
|---|---|
| SOUND: | SHOP DOOR CLOSES: LIGHT TRAFFIC OFF |
| CLERK: | (FADES ON) Yes, sir? May I help you? |
| SPADE: | This medal. Do you sell them here? |
| CLERK: | Why, ah . . . ah . . . no. We haven't carried this design in over ten years. |
| SPADE: | But you used to sell them? |
| CLERK: | Yes. Before the war. It was an Italian import. I believe we had only one sale on them. A job lot for a graduating class. |
| SPADE: | Do you remember what school? |
| CLERK: | It would probably have been one of the poorer neighborhoods. Probably Benedict. Over on Lombard. |
| MUSIC: | BRIDGE |
| SOUND: | CHURCH CLOCK TOLLING THREE PM KIDS PLAYING OFFSTAGE TWIST DOORBELL: STEPS APPROACH WITHIN: DOOR OPENED |
| FITZ: | Good afternoon. Won't you come in? |
| SPADE: | Thank you. |
| SOUND: | STEPS: DOOR CLOSED: BACKGROUND DOWN |
| FITZ: | What can I do for you? |
| SPADE: | My name is Spade. I'm a private detective. I'm trying to trace down the identity of a girl who might have gone to school here. |

FITZ:      Is she in trouble?

SPADE:     She's dead, Father-

FITZ:      Poor child . . .

SPADE:     The only clue to her identity was this medallion. She was wearing it when the body was recovered.

FITZ:      Oh, yes, I remember these. Have you a picture of this girl?

SPADE:     Yes . . . It's not very pleasant . . .

FITZ:      I have seen death before, many times . . . (SIGHS) Oh, yes. Poor child.

SPADE:     Do you recognize her?

FITZ:      Something about her . . . yes, perhaps. There have been so many. You see- there on the wall- the framed photographs. (SOUND: STEPS UNDER) each one a group of a dozen or more children dating back for more than twenty years. Here it is- the class of 1940. (MUSIC UNDER)

SPADE:     I looked at it. A group of eight boys and ten girls. The girls were wearing identical white dresses and white veils, identical self-conscious expressions, and wearing identical medals. I couldn't tell one from the other. And best the kindly old dean could do for me was the names and addresses of the ten girls. (MUSIC UP AND DOWN) (SOUND: TRAFFIC B.G.: STEPS ON SIDEWALK) The first four addresses were dead leads. The fifth didn't look any more or less promising than the others had. It was just another frame house with lace curtains in the windows, a downhill sag, and a sign- "Doorbell out of order."

(SOUND:    STEPS TO WOOD PORCH: KNOCK ON DOOR: STEPS FROM WITHIN: DOOR OPENS)

SPADE:      You're Mrs. Armanda?

LOUISA:     How you know me?

SPADE:      I got your address from the Father at Benedict School.

LOUISA:     Oh. Come in.

SOUND:      STEPS: DOOR CLOSES: TRAFFIC DOWN: STEPS UN-
            DER:

LOUISA:     I sorry for my poor house. When my husband die, they
            take his boat for debts. My son, he's a-gamble everything.

SOUND:      (STEPS OUT)

SPADE:      Does your daughter live at home, Mrs. Armanda?

LOUISA:     (A BEAT) Julia? Why you talk about her? She is in trouble?

SPADE:      I don't know. You didn't answer my question.

LOUISA:     No. She don't live home no more. She is leave her own
            people. She is make shame on us all.

SPADE:      Mrs. Armanda, I don't want to alarm you unnecessarily,
            but if the girl I have in mind is your daughter you'd better
            know about it. Here's a picture of the girl. Is it Julia?

LOUISA:     (LONG PAUSE) She is dead. What happen to this girl?

SPADE:      The police think she committed suicide. I'm not so sure.
            She isn't your daughter?

LOUISA:     No, She is no daughter of mine. Why you come here?

SPADE:      I told you. At the school.

LOUISA:     He's make a mistake. He is a good man. But he is old, he
            make too many mistake. What he say about this girl in the
            picture?

SPADE:      He thinks it would be tragic if she were buried as a suicide if she wasn't.

LOUISA:     (LONG PAUSE) No. She is no daughter of mine.

SPADE:      Have you ever seen her? Maybe in church?

LOUISA:     I don't think this girl go to my church. We are all poor here. She wear too fancy clothes. You go, now. I got to start supper for my son.

SOUND:      STEPS

SPADE:      All right, Mrs. Armanda. (SOUND: ESTABLISH STEPS: DOOR OPENS: TRAFFIC UP) Are you sure there isn't anything more you want to tell me?

LOUISA:     Goodbye.

SOUND:      DOOR CLOSED

SPADE:      (MUSIC IN) It was a funny kind of a bum's rush. Her voice said "goodbye," but her eyes seem to be pleading with me to stick around. I watched through the dingy glass pane in the door until she disappeared. Through the portiers into the living room. Then I opened the door and slipped back into the hallway.

SOUND:      (DOOR CLICKS SHUT: TRAFFIC DOWN)

LOUISA:     (WELL OFF, SLOWLY FADE ON) (WEEPING)

BULL:       (WELL OFF, FADING ON) Now, come on, now, Mother. I know how you feel, but this is not going to bring her back. Am I right? You've got yourself to think of and the rest of your family. She wasn't thinking of you when she took that way out. Am I correct?

LOUISA:     I don't believe it. I don't believe she killed herself. And even if she did, I got to claim my own.

BULL:       I'll take care of everything. I'll give her the biggest funeral you ever saw. And I'll see that you don't ever want for anything. Take care of you for life. That's the way Julia would have wanted it. Am I right?

LOUISA:     I don't know what is right. I know you want to be kind, but I know what I feel here. I go to her.

BULL:       It's too late.

LOUISA:     Why you say that?

BULL:       I told you I was taking care of her. Her body's been claimed. She's on the way to Minneapolis.

LOUISA:     Now I know what you are. I go to police. I tell them everything. I'm gone go to police-

BULL:       No, you're not-

SOUND:      (VOLLEY OF SHOTS)

LOUISA:     (SCREAMS AND DIES)

MUSIC:      (PUNCTUATE AND TO B.G.)

SOUND:      (RUNNING FOOTSTEPS: DOOR SLAMS OFFSTAGE)

SPADE:      All I saw was a pair of broad shoulders draped in a checked sports-jacket, before the back door closed behind him. (SOUND: STEPS OUT: DOOR YANKED OPEN) By the time I got to it, he was half way down the stairway on the face of the hill, leading to the street at the rear of the house. (SOUND: TWO MIKE SHOTS) I threw a couple of shots at him. Between the fog and night closing in, I didn't expect them to connect, and they didn't. Two seconds after he made it to the street, I saw a car pull away from the curb. I guessed that he was in it, but that didn't help, because all I could see was the roof of it. I went back into the room where Mrs. Armanda had fallen. I didn't need a mirror test to know that she was dead. But I needed something better than that to find out why.

MUSIC:    (UP TO FIRST ACT CURTAIN)

ANNCR:    The makers of Wildroot Cream-Oil are presenting the weekly Sunday adventures of Dashiell Hammett's famous private detective . . . SAM SPADE!

MUSIC:    UP AND RESOLVE OUT

Now! Here's important news on good grooming! If you want the well-groomed look that helps you get ahead socially and on the job, listen: Recently thousands of people from coast to coast who bought Wildroot Cream-Oil for the first time, were asked: "How does Wildroot Cream-Oil compare with the hair tonic you previously used?" The results were amazing. Better than 4 out of 5 who replied said they preferred Wildroot Cream-Oil. Remember, non-alcoholic Wildroot Cream-Oil contains LANOLIN. It grooms the hair naturally; relieves dryness and removes loose, ugly dandruff. So, if you want your hair to be more attractive than ever before, get the generous new 25 size of Wildroot Cream-Oil- America's leading hair tonic- on sale at all drug and toilet goods counters. It's also available in larger economy bottles and the handy new tube. By the way, smart gals use Wildroot Cream-Oil too . . . and mothers say it's grand for training children's hair. Get Wildroot Cream-Oil – "again and again the choice of men and women and children, too!"

MUSIC:

ANNCR:     And now back to "The Jane Doe Caper" tonight's Adventures with Sam Spade.

MUSIC:     SECOND OVERTURE

MUSIC:     (OVERTURE AND TO BACKGROUND)

SPADE:     I put the call in to Homicide. The house that Jane Doe had lived in was as bare and lacking in character as that tag they had put on her body in the morgue. I felt embarrassed and maybe a little disappointed when I started reconstructing her life from the things I found. She'd slept on an iron cot that sagged in the middle. The only other items of furniture in the room were a broken chair that had been mended with wire, and a dresser that looked as if it had been salvaged from a junkyard. Stuck in the frame of the dingy mirror was a blurred snapshot of a man in dungarees and a seaman's watch-cap. On the dresser top were a bottle of cheap perfume, a shoot-gallery-type doll, and a pair of rubber gloves. In the top drawer was a beaten-up patent leather purse containing an empty lipstick container, a ditto change purse, a filled-in application for hospital insurance, and a card of membership in the Fish Cannery Workers Union of the Pacific. I decided that union Card might be worth following up. But I didn't need it.

SOUND:     (RAPPING ON DOOR OFFSTAGE) (SPADE'S STEPS REGISTER AND OUT WITH: DOOR OPEN)

TONIA:     Oh, pardon me, I didn't know Julie had company. Just tell her Tonia came by to see how she is.

SPADE:     Maybe you'd better come in.

TONIA:     Oh, I wouldn't think of butting in on-. (STOPS) Is something wrong?

SPADE:      Come on in.

SOUND:      (HER STEPS IN:    DOOR CLOSED)

TONIA:      Who are you? Is Julie in trouble?

SPADE:      Everybody seems to think Julie should be in trouble. Why?

TONIA:      Are you a cop?

SPADE:      No.

TONIA:      Well, then, I'm going.

SPADE:      Wait a minute. I'm not quite a cop. But if you're a friend of Julie's the police will be looking you up. So maybe I can help you on your answers.

TONIA:      Where is Julie?

SPADE:      She's dead.

TONIA:      Poor Julie. I shouldn't say it, but I told her she was taking a terrible risk.

SPADE:      Tell me about it. You and Julie worked together?

TONIA:      Yes, out at the Apex Cannery. We were on the tuna-belt together, till she got moved up to Inspector. Maybe I should explain. The difference between an inspector is that we girls put the fish in the can and the inspector gets more money because all she does is look at them after they're in the can. Only you don't get there after only a month. So I said to Julie, I don't know what you've got on Mr. Driscoll, but be careful of it.

SPADE:      Who's Mr. Driscoll?

TONIA:      Why, he owns the cannery.

SPADE:     And he was friendly with Julie?

TONIA:     Was he friendly? You should have seen the fur coat he sent her. Mutation mink, no less. Just the other day.

SPADE:     I saw it.

TONIA:     Oh. Was she wearing it when they found her?

SPADE:     Why do you say that?

TONIA:     I know what happens when a girl pushes her luck too far. She winds up in the bay. Isn't that where they found Julie?

SPADE:     Look, Tonia, I don't know how much of this is shrewd guesswork on your part, or how much you really know. I don't know how much Julie's mother knew either. Well, she'll never tell us now.

TONIA:     You mean- Mrs. Armanda, too?

SPADE:     Yeah. She clammed up when she should have talked to me. Otherwise I could have saved her.

TONIA:     (FRANTICALLY) I don't- I don't even know who you are?

SPADE:     My name is Sam. I'm a friend of Julie's.

TONIA:     She never mentioned-. (A BEAT) But, yeah, I think so. Listen, Sam, I don't know what it was. All I know is, Julie was tired of being poor. She always had big ideas. One day she just got up right in the middle of work with a raw fish still in her hand and went straight into Mr. Driscoll's office. I yelled after her, "Where are you going with that fish?" And she said, "I'm going to hit Bull Driscoll for a raise with it." And that's how it started.

SPADE:     I take it she got the raise.

TONIA:     And that's not all. Always before she was panning the boss, like we girls. But after that, stars in her eyes. And then she started receiving the presents. She thought he was that way about her. But some of the looks he gave her behind her back were as cold as those when they dig them out of the freezers in the Mexican boats.

SOUND:     (SIRENS START FADING ON FROM A DISTANCE)

SPADE:     Listen, Tonia, hear that siren? That's the cops. If they find us here they'll have us both down at the Hall half the night answering questions. So what do you say we finish this conversation somewhere else?

TONIA:     Where the cops are concerned, you don't have to ask me twice. Come On.

MUSIC:     (BRIDGE AND TO B.G.)

SPADE:     I only got one more lead out of Tonia. The identity of the man in the snapshot stuck in Julie's mirror. His name was Chris Gorelli, and his address was aboard his boat at Fisherman's Wharf.

SOUND:     (STEPS ON CONCRETE: THEN JUMP TO HOLLOW WOODEN FLOAT: WATER SLOSH ACCOMPANIES STEPS ALONG THIS: THEN OUT)

SPADE:     Hello! Anyone aboard?

CHRIS:     (WELL OFF) Whaddya want?

SOUND:     STEPS JUMP TO BOAT: A FEW ON DECK: THEN OUT

CHRIS:     (CLOSER BUT STILL SLIGHTLY OFFSTAGE) Come on in the cabin if you want.

SPADE:     Thanks, I will. (MUSIC IN) He looked up at me as I came in. His bloodshot eyes were dull, as if with drink or grief or maybe both. He waved me a perch on the opposite bunk, then pressed his forehead into his hands, as if trying to squeeze the pain out of it.

CHRIS:      Phew! (COUGHS) Who are you?

SPADE:      The name is Spade. Here's my I.D.

CHRIS:      Private—. Who hired you?

SPADE:      Nobody.

CHRIS:      Meaning Bull Driscoll?

SPADE:      I don't know Driscoll. How well do you know him?

CHRIS:      Never met him. But maybe my luck will change.

SPADE:      You mean you've been trying to get to him?

CHRIS:      Yeah. I been hanging around that cannery all day. He never showed.

SPADE:      Did he have a reason to kill Julie?

CHRIS:      (AFTER A BEAT) What was your interest in Julie?

SPADE:      I only saw her once. On a morgue slab. They'd tagged her Jane Doe. I didn't think the name suited her.

CHRIS:      Huh! I thought you guys only worked for money. Or you get some smart ideas from those glad rags she was wearing?

SPADE:      Okay, have it your way. Maybe it'll turn out to be smart after all. If a simple little girl like Julie could shake that much out of Driscoll, a smart boy like me should be able to really bleed him.

CHRIS:      (COUGHS) I don't get it.

SPADE:     What do you know about Driscoll?

CHRIS:     Smart operator. Took the pile he made running liquor during Prohibition and invested it in quick freezers. That way he don't wait for the tuna to run up here, he gets them in Mexican waters and brings them in frozen- the year around.

SPADE:     (MUSING) Yeah . . . I'm going to hit Bull Driscoll with it for a raise . . . "

CHRIS:     Huh?

SPADE:     Does Customs ever get a look at those fish before they're unloaded?

CHRIS:     Fat lot of good it'd do. It'd take dynamite.

SPADE:     You mean they unload 'em and thaw 'em out before they're inspected.

CHRIS:     Hey! You think he was running something in those fish and Julie was-

SPADE:     I don't know. All I know is Julie was dressed fit to kill. And I mean just that.

MUSIC:     BRIDGE AND TO BACKGROUND

SPADE:     I didn't tell him what else I thought. I left him to ponder that one while I headed for the nearest phone booth to dig out Bull Driscoll's home address. When I came out, I headed uptown walking just slow enough for a drunk man to tail me without too much trouble. He was still behind me when I leaned on the doorbell at 1133 Taylor, where the trail ended.

SOUND:     TRAFFIC B.G.: DOOR BUZZER OFF: STEPS WITHIN:

DOOR OPENED

BULL:    Good evening.

SPADE:    Mr. Driscoll?

BULL:    Right the first time.

SPADE:    You were Julie Armanda's employer?

BULL:    Right the second time. Come in.

SOUND:    STEPS: DOOR CLOSED: MORE STEPS UNDER

BULL:    We can talk in here. (STEPS OUT) Sit down. You're from the police, am I right?

SPADE:    You're only half-wrong.

BULL:    About the tragic shooting of Julie's mother. Correct?

SPADE:    You're still only half-wrong.

BULL:    I never met the family. But as far as Julie is concerned, I know her to be a fine girl. Never thought much of that fellow she's engaged to. Drunk. Given to violence. Made a scene at the cannery one time. Has he been questioned?

SPADE:    I talked to him.

BULL:    Bad apple, am I right?

SPADE:    You may be less than half-wrong on that one. But let's get off the dime. You know perfectly well that Julie is dead, am I right?

BULL:    Why do you say that?

SPADE:    You admit you know about the shooting of Julie's mother. Ergo, you read the papers. Ergo, you read the little item about the Jane Doe in the mutation mink and other glad rags. Ergo, you must have guessed who she was, since you brought her those clothes. Am I correct?

BULL:     Well . . . I admit I had my selfish reasons for not wanting to become embroiled. She's been despondent ever since I told her that . . . well . . . she'd mistaken my intentions . . . understand what I mean?

SPADE:    Yes . . . But not in the way you think I do. I think she committed suicide when she went into your office with that fish in her hand, and come out with a promotion.

BULL:     Uh huh! You're a shamus, am I right? With ideas, am I correct?

SPADE:    Just a couple of hunches.

BULL:     Your hunch is that Julie was blackmailing me. Well, you're wrong. She merely discovered a little irregularity that was going on one of my boats was a smuggler. You follow?

SPADE:    So far, I'm ahead of you.

BULL:     Then you'd better talk till I catch up.

SPADE:    Okay, I will. You've got a nice apartment here. Good taste. You don't strike me as the kind of a guy who would give a twenty thousand dollar wardrobe to a girl who obviously didn't know how to wear it. You're also smart enough to know that you could have got results a lot cheaper, if all you wanted was to keep her quiet for awhile.

BULL:     Then why did I do it. Tell me that.

SPADE:    I know how it worked. The cops never identified her because it never occurred to them that a girl dressed like that might just be a poor little girl in a fish cannery. They're probably still looking for a missing heiress, unless you really did have that body claimed and shipped to Minneapolis.

BULL:      (A BEAT) Say that again.

SPADE:     Biggest funeral you ever saw. Take care of you for life. Brother, you sure did.

BULL:      (BURSTS OUT LAUGHING)

SPADE:     (SHOUTS HIM DOWN) I'm glad you think it's funny. That makes it a lot easier. I don't think it's funny when a poor dumb old woman gets filled with lead because she wants to claim her daughter's body. I don't think it's funny, dressing a poor confused little dame up in the only fur coat she'd ever touched, so she could keep a date with her murderer.

BULL:      Quite a humanitarian, aren't you?

SOUND:     (A FEW STEPS)

SPADE:     I don't talk it very well. But I'll try and show you what I mean. (SOUND:   GRABS HIM AND PULLS HIM TO HIS FEET)

BULL:      (REACTS)

BULL & SPADE: (ADLIB FIGHT)

SOUND:     (SCUFFLE AND FIGHT: BODY FALL AND CRASHING FURNITURE ON CUE)

SPADE:     (HEAVY BREATHING UNTIL:)

SOUND:     (DOOR BUZZER: STEPS TO DOOR: DOOR OPENED)

SPADE:     You're a little late, Chris.

CHRIS:     Get out of my way.

SPADE:      Don't be an idiot.

CHRIS:      (PULLING AWAY) I know what I'm doing. (QUICK FADE) Leave me alone!

SPADE:      (STUMBLES) Don't do it, Chris! You don't-

SOUND:      (GUN EMPTIED: GUN THROWN)

CHRIS:      Okay, you can call the cops. I'm finished.

SPADE:      You stupid fool! I had him nailed.

CHRIS:      For what? He didn't kill Julie. I did. (A little pause) Yeah.

SPADE:      Why?

CHRIS:      You saw her; you said she was dressed to kill. Yeah, I got the wrong idea. (STARTS BREAKING) I thought I was losing her to a guy that could afford to dress her up like- When I saw her leave the house in those clothes . . . on her way to meet him . . . (SOBS INTO):

MUSIC:      (UP TO CLIMAX AND OUT)

SPADE:      Period. End of sob story.

EFFIE:      (SOBS)

SPADE:      Ef . . . I said end of sob story.

EFFIE:      It's not the story, Sam. It's you.

SPADE:      What did I do wrong?

EFFIE:      Nothing. That's it. You're just perfect, that's all. To give up all that time and money and sacrifice yourself so self-sacrificingly, all for a poor nameless girl, who wasn't even in a position to thank you.

SPADE:      True, Effie. All too bitterly true. But I'm just a tiny bit less wonderful than you think.

EFFIE:      (STOPS CRYING) You are?

SPADE:      That's better. Now dry off your notebook and go type that up. When you return, I will tell all.

EFFIE:      All right, Sam. (FADE) But if you think you're going to shatter my delusions . . .

EFFIE:      (FADE ON) Here it is, Sam. And if you dare say one word against you . . .

SPADE:      Perish forbid!

EFFIE:      But what is it that you so mistakenly think reflects to your dishonor?

SPADE:      What?!

EFFIE:      The all you were going to unburden to me because you're too modest to take credit (SOBS) for your good deeds.

SPADE:      I've decided you're right, Ef. I mustn't shatter your delusions.

EFFIE:      Please, Sam. So I can talk you out of it.

SPADE:      Well, I played it stupid, that was all.

EFFIE:      (STOPS CRYING) I know, Sam, but only to throw them off the scent.

SPADE:      Don't make excuses for me. I should have known all along that Driscoll didn't kill Julie. He was smart. He wouldn't have left that cheap little medallion on her.

EFFIE:      (FRESH SOBS)

SPADE:      Now, now . . . I wasn't that bad.

EFFIE:      No, Sam. It just proves all over again how wonderful you
            are. You cracked the case in spite of all the mistakes you
            made.

SPADE:      Okay, you win. Dry up and go home.

EFFIE:      (BLOWS NOSE) Goodnight, you sweet wonderful man.

SPADE:      (CLEARS THROAT) Goodnight, Sweetheart.

MUSIC:      UP TO FINAL CURTAIN

# THE ADVENTURES OF SAM SPADE
## "DEATH & COMPANY"

PROGRAM # 5
FRIDAY AUG 9, '46
4:00 – 4:30 PM

# KECA

| | |
|---|---|
| ANNCR: | The hair-raising adventures of Sam Spade, detective, brought to you by the makers of Wildroot Cream-Oil for the hair. |
| MUSIC: | PUNCTUATION . . . UP INTO TRILL . . . INTO PHONE BELL |
| SOUND: | PHONE BELL |
| EFFIE: | Sam Spade Detective Agency. |
| SPADE: | (FILTER) Hello, Sweetheart. |
| EFFIE: | Sam! . . . Is it over? |
| SPADE: | Yeah, baby, all over, the firm of Death and Company is out of business for good. |

EFFIE:        Oh, Sam . . . How about Eddie Malley?

SPADE:        Just killed two people. Stay there, Sweetheart, I'll be down to dictate my report.

MUSIC:        THEME AND TO B.G.

ANNCR:        Dashiell Hammett, America's leading detective fiction writer and creator of Sam Spade, the hard-boiled private eye, and William Spier, radio's outstanding producer director of mystery and crime drama, join their talents to make your hair stand on end with the Adventures of Sam Spade . . . (MUSIC ACCENT) . . . presented each week by Wildroot Cream-Oil, the non-alcoholic hair tonic that will put your hair back in place again . . . grooming it neatly, naturally the way you want it. Men, no matter how capable you are, it often takes people a long time to find out how much you know and what good work you can do. But if you're always sure about your appearance, you make a successful impression right away! So spruce up with Wildroot Cream-Oil hair tonic- and get the handsome, successful look that helps you get ahead on the job. Wildroot Cream-Oil not only grooms your hair, but relieves dryness and removes loose dandruff. There's not a drop of alcohol in Wildroot Cream-Oil. It contains lanolin. So ask for Wildroot Cream-Oil. (MUSIC:  SNEAK UNDER) And now, Wildroot brings to the air the greatest private detective of em' all . . . in the . . . Adventures of Sam Spade!

MUSIC:        UP TO OVERTURE

SPADE:        Ready, Effie?

EFFIE:        Ready, Sam.

SPADE:    Ummm. Date: August 9, 1946 To: San Francisco Police Department – attention: Detective Lieutenant Dundy. Subject: Death and Company. From: Samuel Spade- License Number 137596 . . . . On the morning of August 7 . . .

EFFIE:    That reminds me:   Your license fee is due Monday.

SPADE:    What? We just paid it!

EFFIE:    (PATENTLY) That was a year ago, Sam.

SPADE:    (GRUMBLING) Why do I stay in this business! Supporting every crack-pot on the city payroll! Okay- take it out of petty cash.

EFFIE:    (SIGHING) That'll be another twenty-five you owe me.

SPADE:    We'll discuss that later. Where were we?

EFFIE:    . . . On the morning of August 7 . . .

SPADE:    (MUSIC UNDER) Yeah . . . a man who introduced himself as Martin Chappel came to my office. He was about 45, solidly built, but shaky and washed out. His eyes were red-rimmed and the lower lids sagged as he told me his wife had been snatched.

(MUSIC:    THIN PUNCTUATION)

CHAPPEL:  She went to a matinee yesterday afternoon, Mr. Spade. She never returned home. This letter came in the mail this morning.

SPADE:    Let me see it.

SOUND:    CRACKLE OF LETTER

CHAPPEL:  Yes, sir . . .

| | |
|---|---|
| MUSIC: | SIMULTANEOUS |
| SPADE: | It was a run-of-the-mill ransom demand, crudely printed in all capital letters on cheap note paper. It was addressed to Chappel:  Dear Sir:        If you want to see your wife alive again go to the lot on the corner of Turk and Larkin Street at twelve tonight and put $5000 in $100 bills under the pile of bricks behind the bill board. If you call in the police we'll let you know where to find the corpse. We mean business . . . It was signed Death and Company. |
| CHAPPEL: | (HYSTERICAL) Death and Company! How could this happen to us! Why . . . why! |
| SPADE: | Throwing a whing-ding won't get us anywhere. Here . . . have a drink. |
| SOUND: | DESK DRAWER:  BOTTLES EFFECT |
| CHAPPEL: | I'm sorry. But this . . . Thank you, sir. |
| SPADE: | That's better. Your wife go to this matinee alone? |
| CHAPPEL: | I don't know. She told me she was going when I left for the office in the morning. But she didn't say which show or who she was going with. |
| SPADE: | You check with her friends? |
| CHAPPEL: | Yes. Late last night- when she didn't come home I telephoned all of them. No one had seen her. |
| SPADE: | (ABRUPTLY) What business you in? |
| CHAPPEL: | Why . . . I . . . I have a small advertising agency. |
| SPADE: | Do much traveling? |
| CHAPPEL: | Yes. Maybe six months of the year I'm- (SUDDEN REALIZATION) What are you trying to say, Mr. Spade? |

SPADE:      I think you know. It's brutal but necessary. Has Mrs. Chappel ever stayed away overnight before?

CHAPPEL:    No! It's nothing like that! If you knew her you wouldn't ask that!

SPADE:      (SOFTLY) Just for the record.

CHAPPEL:    What shall I do, Mr. Spade?

SPADE:      Can you manage the five thousand?

CHAPPEL:    Yes.

SPADE:      Get it.

CHAPPEL:    (SOME RELIEF) I'm glad you feel that way. I want my wife back safe. I don't care about the money.

SPADE:      It's the only way to play it. Now about the police-

CHAPPEL:    No! Not the police! I'm afraid they'll-

SPADE:      I can't handle a snatch without letting the police in.

CHAPPEL:    But that's why I came to you! I don't want-

SPADE:      Listen. I'll handle the police. They'll keep their hands off until Mrs. Chappel is safe home. But in a snatch I must keep them informed. If something goes wrong, I'm not going to be the fall guy!

CHAPPEL:    (AFTER A PAUSE) All right, Mr. Spade. If you think it's best . . .

MUSIC:      BRIDGE ON TO B.G.

SPADE:      I thought it best. I called Lieutenant Dundy, gave him a run-down, and at eleven o'clock that night, he and Sergeant Polhaus joined me at Chappel's bungalow. At first, Dundy was all for making the Turk and Larkin Street brick pile a midnight target for half the San Francisco Police force.

But I waved the history of kidnapping from Ross to Parker in front of his nose, showed him that statistics were on our side: less grief if you pay first and hunt the gunsels after- and he finally listened to reason. Chappel thanked me, and at eleven-thirty he left his house alone with the five grand wrapped in a sheet of brown paper. He was back in less than an hour. He was wet with perspiration and his face was yellow. Dundy barked at him before he even closed the door behind him.

SOUND:    CLOSE DOOR

DUNDY:    (SHARPLY) Did you leave the money?

CHAPPEL:  (WEAKLY) Yes, sir.

DUNDY:    Did you see anybody?

CHAPPEL:  No. Nobody. I found the pile of bricks like it said in the note and I left the money and I didn't see anybody.

DUNDY:    (GROWLING) Well- nothing to do now but wait!

MUSIC:    SIMULTANEOUS

SPADE:    So we waited. Chappel sat in a big chair, staring into space. He chewed his thumb slowly. He did that all night. Polhaus dozed on the sofa. Every once in a while he'd make funny noises with his mouth, look up, blink at Chappel, grin foolishly, doze off again. Dundy and I played gin-rummy. I won $27.42. The night hours seemed to crawl. Dawn was beginning to poke its fingers through the windows when the phone broke the tense silence (SHRILL PHONE BELL). Dundy lunged for it. (CLATTER OF PHONE)

DUNDY:      Yeah? . . . Yeah? It's gone and you didn't . . . ? (VIO-
            LENTLY) Were you asleep! Shut up! Go back to head-
            quarters! I'll see you later!

SOUND:      HANG UP PHONE VIOLENTLY

CHAPPEL:    What- did they?-

DUNDY:      The money's gone.

SPADE:      You were having the spot cased?

DUNDY:      Callahan and Moore. They saw nothing!

CHAPPEL:    (AGHAST) You- you had the place watched?

DUNDY:      It was all right. A couple of men in an apartment down the
            block with field glasses. Nobody could tumble to that,

CHAPPEL:    (HYSTERICALLY) You promised! Mr. Spade- they promised!

SPADE:      Moore says the money was gone?

DUNDY:      Yeah, says they watched all night. Didn't see anybody but
            the money is gone. They must be blind.

CHAPPEL:    How could you do this! You promised you wouldn't- You
            gave me your-

SOUND:      PHONE BELL: CLATTER OF PHONE

DUNDY:      Yeah?

VOICE:      (FILTER) Mr. Chappel? This is Death and Company.

DUNDY:      (AS BEFORE) Spade! Take those ear-phones!

VOICE:      (CONTINUING) We got the dough alright! But we
            warned you not to tell the police. You like to play games
            with Death and Company? Okay. You got the whole city
            to look in to try to find the body . . . the body . . .

SOUND:     (CLICK)

DUNDY:     Hello! Hello . . . Hello!

SOUND:     (CLATTER PHONE)

CHAPPEL:   Good Lord- what happened, what happened?

DUNDY:     Well, Sam . . . that tears it. That voice sounded familiar. You know who? Sounded like Eddie Malloy.

CHAPPEL:   She's dead! I knew it! I knew it! She's dead!

SPADE:     (VIOLENTLY) Don't look at me, Dundy! I warned you to keep your boys away! From here on out, it's strictly a police job-and brother, you're welcome to it!

MUSIC:     BRIDGE, AND TO B.G.

SPADE:     All the rest of that day and late into the night, the police chased around like mice in a cheese factory. They didn't find the body. I just sat tight. I had a hunch that Death and Company had me penciled in for another scene . . . Early the next morning, a babe named Mona LaRue Malloy came to my office. She was a worn twenty-five, good looking in a determined sort of way.

MONA:      . . . and it is an utmost difficulty, Mr. Spade. I simply cannot make ends meet since that rat, if you'll excuse the expression, deserted me. (SHE SNIFFLES)

SPADE:     What do you do for a living now?

MONA:      I am a receptionist, Mr. Spade.

SPADE:     Where?

MONA:      At the Blue Bottle Bar and Grill.

SPADE:     I see what you mean.

MONA:      It is a very nice atmosphere but the tips are very skimpy of late.

SPADE:     How did a nice, refined girl like you ever marry an ex-con like Eddie Malloy?

MONA:      (SNIFFLES) He turned my head with flattery.

SPADE:     And now . . .

MONA:      All I desire, Mr. Spade, is to locate Eddie Malloy's whereabouts so I can get a divorce in a legal manner so I can hold my head up when it comes to a question of honor, so to speak.

SPADE:     Well, I don't usually handle business like this. For one thing, there isn't much money in it-

MONA:      Mr. Spade, You will be amply reimbursed. Eddie has a record as long as my arm, he's wanted now on six counts, and when you find him, we can bleed the rat for all he's worth.

SPADE:     You have no idea where he might be?

MONA:      None.

SPADE:     Not much to go on.

MONA:      That's why I come to you, Mr. Spade. I have been informed that you have even better connections than the police to find a character such as Eddie. Please, Mr. Spade. (SHE SNIFFLES)

SPADE:     All right, Mrs. Malloy. I'll buzz around.

MONA:      Oh thank you, Mr. Spade! You're a real gentleman.

MUSIC:     BRIDGE AND TO B.G.

SPADE:          That night, I buzzed a few of the hep-boys, and in two hours I had the address where Malloy was holed-in. The El Royale, a flea-bag over on Drumm Street. I got over there about ten o'clock (SOUND TO AC-TION) found Apartment Number 12 on the second floor, (KNOCK) rapped on the door. No answer. (KNOCK) I tried again. Still no answer. I went down-stairs to the superintendents' apartment, was about to knock (DOOR OPEN) when the door creaked open and an old bat left over from the silent version of "Dracula" stuck her nose out.

OLD WOMAN:      (CROAKING) What'cha want?

SPADE:          I want to talk to Malloy.

OLD WOMAN:      Who's Malloy?

SPADE:          It's okay. Pobey sent me.

OLD WOMAN:      (CACKLING) Pobey sent me, Pobey sent me! Who's Pobey?

SPADE:          (HARD) Don't get cagey with me! I'll beat your ears off! You know Pobey?

OLD WOMAN:      (LAUGHING) Tough guy. Raise a hand to me, I'll cut your heart out!

SPADE:          Put that knife down before I ram it down your throat!

OLD WOMAN:      Malloy ain't here! Ain't seen him since yesterday!

SPADE:          Where'd he go?

OLD WOMAN:      Out of town. On business.

SPADE:          Where'd he go?

OLD WOMAN:      Break a leg!

SOUND:      DOOR SLAM HARD

MUSIC:      PUNCTUATE ON TO B.G.

SPADE:      The old witch almost chopped my fingers off with the door. I went back upstairs to Malloy's apartment. (KEY . . . BOLT) The third key I tried threw the bolt. (STEPS) I walked into the living room. The windows were locked tight. I looked around . . . (STEPS) walked into the bedroom, (DOOR KICKED OPEN) kicked the door open—and saw it . . . It was lying on the floor midway between the bed and a window looking into the court. It was the body of a tall slender woman with curly red "hair." She had been beaten and strangled to death. Mrs. Chappel had been dead for several days, the place was full of dust, and obviously nobody had been here since it happened. I left it the way I found it and went into the hall to phone Dundy. Just as I reached for the phone (SOUND: PHONE RINGS) . . . (SOUND: PHONE PICKED UP) Hello?

VOICE:      (ON FILTER) This is Death and Company . . . Have you found her?

SPADE:      Yeah.

VOICE:      You can call the police now. You have my permission.

SPADE:      Why the cape and whiskers act, Malloy? Don't you know this call can be traced?

VOICE:      (STARTS TALKING UNDER SPADE'S LINE) Too bad you were so clumsy. It would have been so simple if you'd just taken my advice. Maybe next time you have better sense . . . goodbye . . . .goodbye . . .

SPADE:      Goodbye.

VOICE:    Goodbye . . . Good . . . (SOUND: PHONE SLAMMED DOWN)

MUSIC:    PUNCTUATES

SPADE:    I stood there looking at the phone for a couple of minutes. And decided not to make that call to Dundy. I had a hunch about Death and Company, and I was going to give it a whirl.

MUSIC:    UP FOR FIRST ACT CURTAIN AND TO B.G.

ANNCR:    The makers of Wildroot Cream-Oil are presenting the fifth in a new series of programs bringing to the air for the first time, the adventures of Dashiell Hammett's famous private detective . . . SAM SPADE!

MUSIC:    UP AND RESOLVES OUT MIDDLE

ANNCR:    (COLD) There are some things that you and I know for sure . . . We know that a man who is mighty careful about his appearance will have a head start in climbing the ladder of success. And we know that a smart man like that will be mighty careful about what he uses to keep his hair in trim. Recently an important consumer jury of hundreds of men in Metropolitan New York voted on the five advantages in a hair tonic which they considered most important. And Wildroot Cream-Oil has all five of those advantages . . . One- Wildroot Cream-Oil grooms your hair neatly and naturally- never leaves it sticky or greasy. Two; Wildroot Cream-Oil relieves annoying dryness. Three- it removes loose dandruff.

Four- it's non-alcoholic And Five-it contains soothing LANOLIN. Remember-no other leading hair tonic gives you all five of these important advantages. No wonder four out of five in a nation-wide test preferred Wild-root Cream-Oil to all other hair tonics they'd tried. So next time you visit your barber, ask for Wildroot Cream-Oil. And get the big economy size bottle of Wildroot Cream-Oil at your drug or toilet goods counter.

| | |
|---|---|
| MUSIC: | ACCENT AND HOLD |
| ANNCR: | And now back to "Death and Company" . . . to-night's adventure with . . . SAM SPADE! |
| MUSIC: | SECOND OVERTURE |
| SPADE: | The Blue Bottle Bar and Grill was one of those dark joints with a lot of neon behind the bar, a dance floor in the back room with booths around it, and a juke box big enough for a family of midgets to keep house it. It was early and nobody was there except the bar-tender. |
| BARTENDER: | What'll it be, mister? |
| SPADE: | Gimme a shot. |
| SOUND: | DRINK POURED |
| SPADE: | Where's Mona? |
| BARTENDER: | She don't work here no more. |
| SPADE: | Know where I can find her? |
| BARTENDER: | If you've got a nickel you can talk to her. |
| SPADE: | What's the number? |
| BARTENDER: | Don't need a number, just put it in the juke box. |
| SPADE: | She hiding in there? |

| | |
|---|---|
| BARTENDER: | Guy that rents those things came around and offered her a job. Said he needed a nice refined voice like that. She sits in a room somewhere and plays the records that come over the wire. |
| SPADE: | Know where the room is? |
| BARTENDER: | Spend a nickel and ask her. |
| SPADE: | Okay. |
| SOUND: | STEPS NICKEL IN JUKE BOX |
| MONA: | (ON FILTER) This is Mona. What selection do you wish to hear, please? |
| SPADE: | Sam Spade, Sweetheart. |
| MONA: | We do not have any selections by that singer. |
| SPADE: | I didn't think you had. Listen, baby, I found the joint where Malloy's been staying. |
| MONA: | Whom am I addressing? |
| SPADE: | Sam Spade, Sweetheart. |
| MONA: | Oh, Mr. Spade . . . Did you talk to that rat? |
| SPADE: | He wasn't home. The place was empty. |
| MONA: | You mean there wasn't anything there? Did you look in the closets? |
| SPADE: | What did you think I'd find there? |
| MONA: | Some luggage perhaps. Or some clue as to the whereabouts of the place he has scrammed to? |
| SPADE: | The trail's cold, Sweetheart. I think Mr. Malloy has left San Francisco. |

| | |
|---|---|
| MONA: | But, Mr. Spade . . . I employed you to find that cheap gunsel. You can't just throw me to the winds! |
| SPADE: | Stick to your music, Sweetheart. There's more future in it. |
| MONA: | Excuse me, Mr. Spade. The Silver Slipper has a request, but don't go away. (SOUND: STEPS BACK TO THE BAR) |
| BARTENDER: | (FADING ON) She still trying to locate Malloy? |
| SPADE: | Yeah, you know him? |
| BARTENDER: | Used to hang around here. |
| SPADE: | How long ago did Mona take this new job? |
| BARTENDER: | 'Bout a week ago. She'll be back here. |
| SPADE: | How come? |
| BARTENDER: | Ah, she's too stupid to hold down a job like that. Gets the records all mixed up. Always dropping the needle so they stick in the groove. |
| SPADE: | Gimme a couple nickels. |
| BARTENDER: | Whyn'cha go and see her? It'll save you money in the end. |
| SPADE: | This one's for the telephone. |
| BARTENDER: | ADLIBS IN B.G. UNTIL EFFIE ANSWERS: THEN DOOR CLOSE BOOTH |
| SOUND: | STEPS . . . NICKEL IN PHONE DIALING |
| EFFIE: | (ON FILTER) Sam Spade Detective Agency. |
| SPADE: | Mr. Spade in? |

EFFIE:      No, he's just been arrested for counterfeiting three-dollar bills. What do you want, Sam?

SPADE:      I want you to go to 120 Drumm Street, Apartment 12. In the little hall there's a phone. Call me.

EFFIE:      Where can I reach you?

SPADE:      At the Blue Bottle Bar and Grill. Third bottle from the end of the bar.

MUSIC:      BRIDGE

SOUND:      PHONE RINGS. STEPS . . . RECEIVER LIFTED . . . PHONE BOOTH DOOR CLOSED

SPADE:      Yeah?

EFFIE:      Sam, I'm here in this place now. What do you want me to do?

SPADE:      Where're you standing now?

EFFIE:      In the little hallway where the phone is.

SPADE:      Facing the hall door?

EFFIE:      Yes.

SPADE:      Turn slowly around and look through the door into the bedroom that opens on the court.

EFFIE:      (MURMURS) Turn slowly around . . . Sam, this is silly, why don't you tell me what you want me to do? I- (SCREAMS)

SPADE:      That's what I wanted you to do, Sweetheart. Now get out of there fast.

MUSIC:      BRIDGE

EFFIE:      And then people started running in there from all over the house. A man grabbed me on the stairs and tried to hold me, but I kicked him in the shins and got away. And furthermore, if you ever play a trick on me like that on me again, Sam Spade, I'll-

SPADE:      Look, Sweetheart-I wanted the body to be found- but I didn't want to be the guy that found it. I-

SOUND:      PHONE RINGS . . . OFF HOOK

SPADE:      Hello!

DUNDY:      (FILTER) Sam? Dundy.

SPADE:      What brilliant pinch have you engineered this time, Captain Midnight?

DUNDY:      Girl named Mona LaRue-Malloy's ex-wife. She walked into Malloy's flat, found Mrs. Chappel's body and started screaming her head off. We picked her up about a half an hour ago.

SPADE:      What'd she tell you?

DUNDY:      She said she hadn't seen Malloy for over a week. Denies she was at the flat or screaming or anything else.

SPADE:      My, my, that's confusing.

DUNDY:      Mona also told us she hired you to find Malloy for her. She said you went up to his apartment this morning and told her you didn't find anything there. The landlady's story checks with hers. What about it, Sam?

SPADE:      You seem to have found out everything all by yourself, Dundy.

DUNDY:      I think you better tell me what else you're holding back on this caper, and don't give me any double-talk.

SPADE:      Don't pressure me, Dundy. I get amnesia.

DUNDY:      Okay, Sam. If that's the way you want to play it, but I'm warning you-

SPADE:      Yeah, I know, I'll never get to be president this way. But if you'll leave me alone, I'll find Malloy for you.

SOUND:      HANG UP PHONE

MUSIC:      BRIDGE AND TO B.G.

SPADE:      My next stop was an office building over on California Street. Chappel and Chapman, the advertising Agency that Martin Chappel was president of, was on the tenth floor. His office was about the size of the one Mussolini was forced to vacate. The walls were paneled and in one end there was a lot of radio equipment, old scripts, a recording machine, and stuff . . . He was alone and still looking pretty miserable.

CHAPPEL:    Who-? Oh, hello, Mr. Spade.

SPADE:      I guess you know they found your wife.

CHAPPEL:    Yes. Dreadful as it is, it's better to know definitely than to be kept in that horrible suspense.

SPADE:      The cops picked up Malloy's ex-wife.

CHAPPEL:    Did she talk? Did she tell them anything?

SPADE:      Not yet. And I don't think she will.

CHAPPEL:    I want that man brought to justice, Mr. Spade! I don't care how much it costs me.

SPADE:      You've paid your fee, Chappel. I didn't find your wife. But I think I know a way to find her killer.

CHAPPEL:    How? I'll try anything.

SPADE:      You'll have to trust me and do just what I tell you to. First of all, I want you to get some money out of the bank go over to headquarters and bail Mona LaRue Malloy out of jail.

CHAPPEL:    Very well, but that's mad. She may even be an accomplice!

SPADE:      That'll make it even better. If she thinks Eddie's taken a powder and left her to face the rap, she'll find him. All we have to do is to put a tail on her and she'll lead us to him.

CHAPPEL:    It's wild, but it's worth trying.

SPADE:      Okay, get going before the bank closes.

MUSIC:      BRIDGE AND B.G.

SPADE:      The story broke in the mid-afternoon edition of the Chronicle and by evening the other papers had picked it up. Playing it up big with banner heads, pictures of Chappel bailing Mona LaRue out of jail, of Mrs. Chappel before and after, the whole caper. They intimated that Eddie Malloy was now off the hook, and that suspect number one, because of his peculiar action, was Chappel, himself. I'd planted the story that way. I figured that now the heat was off, Eddie Malloy would show. Around six, I'd rifted over to the Blue Bottle Bar and Grill.

SOUND:      OUT OF MUSIC BAR ROOM SOUNDS . . . NICKEL IN JUKE BOX

MONA:       (ON FILTER) This is Mona. What number do you wish to request, sir?

SPADE:      Anything you've got handy, Mona dear.

MONA:      This is a very popular number at the present time, sir.

SOUND:     NEEDLE DROPS AND SCRATCHES AROUND RE-
           CORD

MONA:      Oops! Sorry.

MUSIC:     LOMBARD TYPE OF "AMOR" . . . THEN STICKS IN
           THE GROOVE NEEDLE LIFTED

MONA:      I am sorry, that record is apparently defective, so to
           speak. I will try another.

SOUND:     GREAT PILE OF RECORDS FALL AND CRASHES

MONA:      There has been a slight accident. One moment please. I
           will play this one while we are waiting.

VOICE:     (ON FILTER) Are you run down, overworked? Tired?
           Nervous? Try Sil-Flax in the large economy size . . . size
           . . . size . . .

MONA:      I am sorry. That is apparently a transcription, so to speak.
           Here is a new number that has just come in. Lud Gluskin
           and his Versatile Juniors . . . Would you like that, sir?

SPADE:     Never mind, forget it.

MALLOY:    Wait a minute; I want to talk to her, Mona?

MONA:      (FILTER) This is Mona. What number did you wish to re-
           quest, please?

MALLOY:    Mona, this is Eddie.

MONA:      I do not wish to have any further trouble with you, Eddie
           Malloy.

MALLOY:    Where are you? I've got to see you.

MONA:    I am sorry. We do not have that selection in stock.

SOUND:    CLICK

MALLOY:    Hey, wait a minute, Mona!

BARTENDER:    You're wasting your time, Malloy.

MALLOY:    (COMING BACK) Gimme a shot.

SOUND:    (GLASS SET DOWN: DRINK POURED)

SPADE:    What happened, Malloy. She get tired of you?

MALLOY:    I don't know. She picked him up in here. He had a lot of dough, or his wife did. I told him if he didn't keep away from Mona, I'd hurt him.

SPADE:    What's his name?

MALLOY:    Oley, what is this guy, a gum-shoe?

BARTENDER:    You can trust him, Eddie. Eddie Malloy, Sam Spade.

SPADE:    I've been waiting some time to meet you, Malloy- tell me, how would you like to get something on a character named Martin Chappel?

MALLOY:    You got something?

SPADE:    Maybe. I was just going to pay him a visit up at his office . . . like to go along?

MALLOY:    Brother, lead the way!

MUSIC:    (BRIDGE)

SOUND:    DOOR UNLOCKED OPENED . . . LIGHTS SWITCHED ON

SPADE:    Come on in, Malloy.

MALLOY:     (SUSPICIOUS) What's this place? This ain't no office.

SPADE:      That's what they call it in the advertising business. Put the gun away, Malloy. There ain't any secret panels.

SOUND:      SWITCH RADIO WARMS UP

MALLOY:     Phonograph records everywhere. Looks like the place had been hit by a wave of bobby-soxers.

SPADE:      Sit down. I'll play you a record.

SOUND:      RECORD ON TURN TABLE:    NEEDLE    TESTED ON FINGER:    REACTION ON LOUDSPEAKER: RECORD NOISE INTO:

VOICE:      (FILTER) Are you run down, overworked? Tired? Nervous? Try Sil-Flax in the large economy size . . . size . . . size . . .

SOUND:      NEEDLE PICKED UP

MALLOY:     Hey, what's the pitch?

SPADE:      You've heard these things over the radio, haven't you, Malloy? Well, this is one of the places where they make them.

MALLOY:     You mean that's Chappel's racket?

SPADE:      I thought you knew about it.

MALLOY:     I don't know from nothing. I'm getting out of here.

SPADE:      (TOUGH) Sit down, Malloy. I haven't finished.

MALLOY:     You going to make me sit here and listen to that stuff all night?

SPADE:      Maybe the other side of the record is better.

| | |
|---|---|
| SOUND: | RECORD TURNED OVER: RECORD NOISE INTO: |
| VOICE: | This is Death and Company. We got the dough all right . . . dough all right . . . dough all right . . . |
| MALLOY: | Hey, that sounds like– |
| SOUND: | NEEDLE SQUAWKS ACROSS RECORD |
| CHAPPEL: | All right, Spade, stand over against that wall. You, too, Malloy. |
| MALLOY: | You dirty double-crossing–! |
| CHAPPEL: | Shut up! |
| SPADE: | What a vile temper you have, grandmother. |
| MONA: | Don't let's bandy words with these jerks, Martin. |
| CHAPPEL: | You keep out of this, Mona. |
| SPADE: | I had a hunch you two would show up together. |
| CHAPPEL: | You had everything all figured out, didn't you, Spade? |
| SPADE: | Why, you cheap amateur, I nailed your wife's kidnapping for a phony the night you went to that lot to deliver the money. When the money wasn't there the next morning without the police seeing anybody come to get it, I was pretty sure you hadn't even left any money there. |
| CHAPPEL: | Strange you didn't take the police into your confidence, or were you planning to shake me down for part of the insurance money? |
| SPADE: | So it was your wife's insurance you were after. I kind of thought that was it. You and Mona had it all tied up in a nice little package. Bump off your wife, play it for a kidnapping, plant the stiff on Malloy here, and count on his past record to convict him. |

MALLOY:     That Death and Company . . . where did they get my voice?

SPADE:      Eddie-they had an actor make it who sounded as much like you as possible . . . Mona had the ideal set-up working for an outfit that fed recorded music over a telephone line to a string of juke boxes around town. So Chappel put the Death and Company spiel on a phonograph record and Mona played it over the phone. When Mona got her juke box records mixed up this evening, and put on an advertising record by mistake I had the line between her and Chappel, had them both cold.

MONA:       Why stand around gassing with him, Martin? Let him have it.

SPADE:      Two more corpses won't help you explain things to the police.

CHAPPEL:    Not two more, Spade. Only one. The police know you were looking for Malloy. If you are found shot in my office, all I have to do is turn him in, and he'll take the rap for both killings. With a record like Eddie's they don't even bother to question anyone else.

SPADE:      So you made it work after all.

CHAPPEL:    Yes. I'm sorry to have to do this, Spade, but-

MONA:       Martin. Watch out! (SCREAMS)

SOUND:      TWO SHOTS

MUSIC:      PUNCTUATE

SPADE:      So you see, Lieutenant, the deaths of Martin Chappel and Mona La Rue were not murder, but self-defense on the part of Eddie Malloy, whose quick action with his .45,

|        | thus saved his life and  . . . .incidentally mine . . . which I suppose you will hold against him. Try to be big about it. Period. End of Report. |
| EFFIE: | Hmmph. |
| SPADE: | What are you hummphing about? |
| EFFIE: | I won't even discuss it, Mr. Spade. |
| SPADE: | Still mad at me for sending you on that little screaming errand? |
| EFFIE: | When I went to work for you, Mr. Spade, I understood that I was being engaged as a receptionist and secretary. Being sent into strange apartments with corpses in them is not my idea of a receptionist's duties. |
| SPADE: | Okay, Sweetheart. I didn't know you felt that way about it. |
| EFFIE: | I'm serious, Sam. I've been reading the help wanted ads. Look at this. "Receptionist wanted. Seventy-five dollars a week. No typing . . . " |
| SPADE: | Huh? Who's paying dough like that? |
| EFFIE: | It says right here. (IT DAWNS ON HER AS SHE READS IT) The Blue Bottle . . . Bar . . . and Grill. That's very strange, Sam. I didn't know they had receptionists in places like that. |
| SPADE: | Hummph. |
| EFFIE: | But it's very strange. |
| SPADE: | Very strange, indeed. |
| EFFIE: | Sam, I don't think you care whether I go to work as a receptionist at the Blue Bottle Bar and Grill or not! |

SPADE:      Well, I don't like to stand in your way, Effie. I'd like to see you get ahead.

EFFIE:      Sam, it won't work! You can't force me to resign like this. I'm going to stay here till you pay me every penny of back pay you owe me.

SPADE:      That's the way I like to hear you talk.

EFFIE:      Goodnight, Sam.

SPADE:      Goodnight, Sweetheart.

MUSIC:      CURTAIN

ANNCR:      Wildroot Cream-Oil . . . presents "The Adventures of Sam Spade" . . . Dashiell Hammett's famous private detective, produced and directed by William Spier.

(NEW COMMERCIAL)

Men-you'll learn a lot about the way girls think from this recent survey. Asked how they felt about a man's appearance, 97 out of 100 girls said they definitely dislike a man whose hair is dry and unkempt looking. So don't look that way. Spruce up with Wildroot Cream-Oil. It grooms your hair neatly and naturally. And as our survey shows, that's exactly what girls like to see. Wildroot Cream-Oil keeps your hair handsomely in trim . . . protects it from summer sun, wind and water! So Wildroot's famous F.N.Test. Check your scalp. Signs of dryness or loose dandruff tell you . . . you need Wildroot Cream-Oil right away.

MUSIC:      THEME TO B.G.

PROGRAM NUMBER SIX
DECEMBER 22, 1950

# The Adventures of Sam Spade
## "THE CAPER CONCERNING THE THING"

CAST:

SPADE . . . . . . . . . . . . . STEPHEN DUNNE
NBC WESTERN DIVISION PROGRAM

EFFIE . . . . . . . . . . . . . . .LURENE TUTTLE

MGR . . . . . . . . . . . . . . HOMER CANFIELD

KINGSLEY . . . . . . . . . . . . WALLY MAHER

PRODUCTION MGR . . . . . . .HARRY BUBECK

CLERK . . . . . . . . . . . . . .LURENE TUTTLE

ARTIST AGENCY . . . . . . REGIS RADIO CORP.

TONY . . . . . . . . . . . . . . . SIDNEY MILLER

PRODUCER-DIRECTOR. . . . . . . . .WM. SPIER

DOCTOR . . . . . . . . . .WHITFIELD CONNER

ASSISTANT . . . . . . . . . . . . . MAGGIE FOSS

NURSE. . . . . . . . . . . . . VIRGINIA GREGG

WRITERS . . . . . . . . . . . E. JACK NEUMANN
AND BASSLER, WHITFIELD CONNER,
JOHN MICHAEL HAYES

ANDREA . . . . . . . . . . . VIRGINIA GREGG

MUSICAL SUPERVISOR . . . ROBERT COURTNEY
WILL WRIGHT
ARMBRUSTER POBEY
WALLY MAHER

NBC DIRECTOR. . . . . . . . BILL YAEGERMAN

KLAUS . . . . . . . . . . . . . SIDNEY MILLER

ENGINEER. . . . . . . . . . . RAOUL MURPHY

SOUND . . . . . . . . . WAYNE KENWORTHY

ANNOUNCER . . . . . . . . . . DON RICKLES

ANNCR:    The National Broadcasting Company presents- The Adventures of Sam Spade, Detective!

MUSIC:    THEME INTO TRILL INTO PHONE BELL:

SOUND:    (PHONE RINGS . . . RECEIVER UP)

EFFIE:    Sam Spade Detective Agency.

SPADE:    Me, Angel.

EFFIE:    Sam . . . .what's going on? What's happening to you lately? I'm completely in the dark.

SPADE:    Well, you should be. For all you know, I've been out fighting sharp-elbowed crowds, wearing shoeleather, last year's argyles, and my patience down to a frazzle . . . just to buy you a Christmas present.

EFFIE:     Were you, Sam?

SPADE:     No . . . but it sounded good, didn't it? Maybe I'll take the coward's way out and give you a television for Christmas. I wonder if they have a screen you can buy an inch at a time.

EFFIE:     Oh, Sam . . . you're in a good mood. I can tell.

SPADE:     Really? Well, my acting must have improved. I know I'm in a mood, Effie . . . but I wouldn't exactly describe it as good.

EFFIE:     Sam, you can't fool me. At Christmas time you're the happiest person in the world.

SPADE:     All right, If you want proof positive, I am about to enter with some kind of a story . . . which is precisely what this one is, only what kind I'm not sure. You can sprinkle holly and snow where you will throughout it. Maybe it'll help.

EFFIE:     What's it going to be about, Sam?

SPADE:     About twenty-nine minutes and thirty seconds . . . get out Phil Harris's distinguished recording of it. I think there only be a clue in this verse– and we're going to need it because it's the "Caper Concerning The Thing."

MUSIC:     UP AND OUT

SOUND:     DOOR OPENS . . . STEPS

SPADE:     Ef- Effie-

SOUND:     STEPS RUNNING ON

EFFIE:      Sam! What's that green branch you're holding- oh, mistletoe!

SPADE:      Ready? Eyes closed dreamily? Lips puckered? (THEY KISS) Merry Christmas, Sweetheart.

EFFIE:      Mmmm-m-m-m thank you, Sam, But . . . aren't you rushing the season a little? Today is only Friday, and . . .

SPADE:      Every day is Christmas when I'm with you, Eff.

SOUND:      DESK DRAWER . . . BOTTLE

EFFIE:      Sam . . . I've just been dying of curiosity ever since you called.

SPADE:      Curiosity about what?

EFFIE:      The Thing. You said this was going to be a caper about The Thing. Is . . . is that "The Thing?"

SPADE:      Well, as far as I know, Effie . . . it might even be "The Thing."

EFFIE:      Tell me what it is, Sam . . . tell me what it is.

SPADE:      (DRINKS) Well . . . Effie. I don't know. You'd blab it all over town.

EFFIE:      Sam . . . Sam . . . I promise I won't say a word to anybody. Just tell me, please!

SPADE:      All right, I'll tell you what I know.

EFFIE:      (DELIGHTED) Oh, Sam . . . come on. I'm ready to take it down. Who should I address this to . . . Phil Harris?

SPADE:      No . . . just put . . . TO: To Whom It May Concern.

EFFIE:      To Whom It . . . ? Sam, you can't send a report to just anybody.

SPADE:     Look, Effie, if you can think of anybody to address it to when we're finished . . . well, that's up to you. DATE: Fill it in. TO: (PAUSE) FROM: Samuel Spade, San Francisco, The Earth, license number 137596. SUBJECT: "Caper Concerning- The Thing" (MUSIC: SNEAK) I hate the type of call that came last Wednesday . . . the whispered tones, the hushed urgency . . . as if someone had a hair-triggered bazooka stuck in his ear, and loaded because nine times out of ten it's someone with a detective story complex just trying to locate a fraternity brother in town. (SOUND: PHONE RINGS UNDER) I'm afraid, this time, what with worrying about Effie's Christmas gift, and all, I was a little bored and unimpressed.

SOUND:     PHONE UP

KINGSLEY:  (FILTER) (HUSHED FURTIVE TONES) Sam Spade, the detective?

SPADE:     The same. You can speak up.

KINGSLEY:  Listen carefully. Spade, I'm five-eleven, one hundred seventy-five pounds. I'm wearing a brown tweed suit, no hat, no overcoat. My hair's blond, eyes blue-

SPADE:     Can you cook?

KINGSLEY:  Please, this is serious. I'm phoning you from the telephone booth in the lobby of the Crescent Hotel on Turk Street.

SPADE:     That figures. A place like that is uniform mystery atmosphere.

KINGSLEY:  Come right over, please. I'll be waiting for you. It's urgent, and there's money in it.

SPADE:     Well! All right . . . for money I'll play. But first tell me who you-

SOUND:      CLICK IN FILTER . . . DEAD LINE BUZZ

SPADE:      Hello . . . hello . . .

SOUND:      HE PUTS DOWN RECEIVER

MUSIC:      IN AND UNDER

SPADE:      This was a variation on Standard Script Plot 38- he hung up before I could find out his name, or turn him down . . . but, since he was expecting me, I thought I'd saunter over to the Crescent Hotel and watch his act in full. And it was good. (SOUND:    HOTEL LOBBY SOUNDS B.G.) He was lurking behind a potted palm looking more conspicuous than he would have if he'd been lying drunk in front of the preservation desk. And he had exactly the right amount of red in his eyes . . . as if he'd just seen Joseph Stalin in the men's room. His feeling for detail was superb . . . down to the three-day beard, wrinkled shirt, mud-caked shoes . . . and darting blood-shot eyes. He even jumped when I got near him.

KINGSLEY:   Oh . . .

SPADE:      Hello . . . My name's Spade. You phoned me.

KINGSLEY:   Oh, thank goodness you came over. Here . . . this is for you.

SPADE:      A hundred dollar bill. That's a good start. Why am I taking it?

KINGSLEY:   For the moment . . . to keep an eye on this key . . . here.

SPADE:      What's the key for?

KINGSLEY:   I . . . look, I don't think it's safe for us to just stand here in the lobby.

SPADE: Oh sure, of course. I should have known. It isn't safe to talk here. Somebody's after you.

KINGSLEY: (STARTING TO GET CONFUSED) I . . . Spade.

SPADE: Suppose you start by telling me your name.

KINGSLEY: I'm . . . I . . . I . . . I . . . I'm going to tell you a lot . . . of things. I . . .

SPADE: What is it? What's the matter with you?

KINGSLEY: (GROANS) Spade, I'm . . . I'm . . . (DESPAIR) . . . I'm not gonna make it . . . they're going to win . . . after all.

MUSIC: IN AND UNDER

SPADE: It looked a little too genuine. His eyes rolled back in his head, seemed to take a sudden fixed stare at nothing in particular . . . and then he pitched forward into my arms. I lowered him gently to the carpet. I tried cold water, hand-rubbing, a double slug of bourbon from the bar . . . but nothing worked. And they had a lady manager!

CLERK: (FLUTTERING) We can't just let him lie there in the lobby. We simply can't!

SPADE: Ever see him before?

CLERK: No. Never. People are staring . . . simply staring. It's bad for the hotel.

SPADE: Instead of standing there, editorializing, why don't you do something?

CLERK: What could I do? I'm not a surgeon, or a little-bearer, you know.

SPADE: You might try calling police emergency. After all, it's your hotel.

MUSIC:     IN AND UNDER

SPADE:     And she did. I rode over to the police emergency hospital
           with my unconscious and unknown client. A frisk of his
           clothing revealed no billfold, papers, or cards that would
           identify him. At the hospital I hung around the desk, ex-
           amining the hundred dollar bill, which passed all the stan-
           dard tests . . . until a doctor named Miller came out with
           some news. The man was doped to the ears, and they
           wouldn't find out who he was until he came to. I had his
           money in hand, so I tried to find out who he was. I re-
           traced my steps to the hotel. Nobody there had ever seen
           him before. Questioning around the neighborhood made
           me think my client had been out of his bailiwick, because
           no one seemed to recognize his description. The sight of
           a locksmith shop recalled to me that I had one clue.

TONY:      You want what?

SPADE:     Do you have any idea what this key might fit?

TONY:      Ah let me see . . . mmm . . . oh . . . ah . . . uh-huh.

SPADE:     Well . . .

TONY:      Is easy. Come to me anytime, I tell you anything you want
           to know about any key.

SPADE:     About this one.

TONY:      Mmm . . . oh . . . ah . . . uh-huh. Is for locker. In bus depot,
           train station. Airport, maybe. Easy.

MUSIC:     IN AND UNDER

SPADE:     For him, maybe, but not for me. I tramped around to
           transit storage lockers in three bus stations, two railroad
           terminals, and one airport. About four in the afternoon,

the key finally fit locker one thirty-nine, Berkeley bus sta-tion. (SOUND: FADE IN BUS STATION NOISES IN B.G.) I was just in the act of opening it when an ache in my bad knee cautioned me to look around. I spotted two men in dark suits, needing shaves (the men, that is) who were putting the double whammy on me. I didn't open the locker, but withdrew the key, strolled briskly over to the crowd at the main desk, brought a stamped envelope, and mailed the key to my office . . . an ingenious ruse. The two hoods followed close on my heels as I was leaving the depot . . . but I led them a fast five minutes chase through the place and they fell far behind, and out of sight. I went back to the emergency hospital. Doctor Miller was just going off duty.

MUSIC:        OUT

DOCTOR:    I've been trying to phone you, Sam.

SPADE:       What's up?

DOCTOR:    Your client's name is Kingsley Benedict, the Second!

SPADE:       Did he finally come around?

DOCTOR:    Not when I last saw him. His family sent a doctor and a private ambulance down for him early this afternoon. Took him to a private sanitarium . . . the Bide-A-Wee over in Berkeley.

SPADE:       Berkeley, huh? (PAUSE) How'd his family know he was here?

DOCTOR:    Not more than an hour after you left, Missing Persons sent out a routine call for a man answering his description. I notified them I had this guy, so they came around and took a look at him. It checked.

| | |
|---|---|
| MUSIC: | IN AND UNDER |
| SPADE: | I talked to him a little longer and got the details. My client was apparently a member of the rich and powerful Benedict dynasty of our city. (MUSIC:    SHIFT    MOODY) I found the Bide-A-Wee home out in Berkeley, perched between two gloomy mountains that glowered down on the California campus. A damp cold fog was blowing in from the bay as I was admitted by a nurse. |
| SOUND: | CLOSE DOOR |
| NURSE: | Yes . . . ? |
| SPADE: | My name is Spade. I'd like to see Kingsley Benedict, please. |
| NURSE: | Oh . . . |
| SPADE: | He's here, isn't he? |
| NURSE: | Yes, certainly. But Dr. Hoffman's gone for the day. |
| SPADE: | Dr. Hoffman. |
| NURSE: | Yes . . . he says who can see people and who can't. |
| SPADE: | Are you in charge now? |
| NURSE: | Only when he's not here. |
| SPADE: | Then why don't you say who can see people, and who can't just this once. |
| NURSE: | Kingsley Benedict is in no condition to see anyone . . . and besides, I just couldn't let you in. I just couldn't! |
| MUSIC: | IN AND UNDER: |
| SPADE: | I was going to rassle her for it . . . but I thought I'd try something unethical first. And it worked. She just hap- |

pened to have fifty dollars change for the hundred dollar bill I got from Kingsley. She forthwith led me down a
straight narrow hall to a private room on the corner, and
told me I had to hurry. (SOUND:   OPEN DOOR) My
client was lying peacefully on an unrumpled bed. He was
quiet- remarkably quiet. His eyes were wide open . . . but
he said nothing.

NURSE:      There he is. Dr. Hoffman would fire me if he-

SPADE:      How long's he been like this?

NURSE:      Ever since I came on duty . . . two hours ago.

SPADE:      Would you mind telling me what's the matter with him?
            What this is all about?

NURSE:      Your money only bought you a look.

SPADE:      I have another fifty.

NURSE:      I wouldn't dare tell you for ten times that. Now get out of
            here . . . please . . . before I get in trouble.

SPADE:      I took another look- The fresh blue welt, high on my cli-
            ent's right arm, told me that he'd been re-doped, right to
            the hilt . . . and that he wouldn't talk to anyone for some
            time . . . possibly not until the next day. A glace at his bed
            chart did not record a narcotic. I was wondering about
            that all the way back to my office where I found a visitor
            waiting. He was large, smooth-jowled, dressed in impec-
            cable clothes. He first gave me an unctuous smile- and
            then a surprising piece of paper.

BASSLER:    Mr. Spade, a check made out to you for one thousand
            dollars. There you are.

SPADE:      Pretty . . . what's it for? –and who are you?

BASSLER:    John Bassler, Attorney-at-law. This is just a retainer for allowing me to talk with you.

SPADE:    I don't usually charge that much, but it's Christmas.

BASSLER:    And I hope you have a happy one. Now another check for three thousand dollars . . . there.

SPADE:    And this one is for . . . ?

BASSLER:    Repeating the conversation that ensued between you and a man named Kingsley Benedict today.

SPADE:    I see.

BASSLER:    And another check for five thousand dollars . . . made out to you . . . and all in order.

SPADE:    And I'll never guess what this one is for.

BASSLER:    For turning over to me, certain items that the aforementioned Benedict left in your care.

SPADE:    Who's playing Santa Claus with all this money?

BASSLER:    The checks bear my signature. What do you say, Mr. Spade?

SPADE:    Very little. Here is your five thousand dollar check. Thank you. And here is your three thousand dollar check. Thanks again. I'll keep the thousand dollar one . . . on which you'll probably stop payment tomorrow . . . but it'll be fun to pretend, and maybe I can beat you to the bank.

BASSLER:    Do I understand you correctly, Mr. Spade?

SPADE:    I hope so, Mr. Bassler.

SOUND:    SNAP OF BRIEF CASE

BASSLER:    Money, Mr. Spade, is the only thing that counts in this world. I'm sorry you haven't learned that obvious lesson.

SPADE:      Mr. Bassler- even at a time of the year when I'm supposed to like everyone, I don't like you. Get out!

SOUND:      QUICK STEPS OFF:

BASSLER:    (SL. OFF) Alright, Mr. Spade . . . but I hope you won't live to regret this rudeness. (UP) Eddie! Jack!

MUSIC:      IN AND UNDER

SPADE:      He just yeah hoped plain I wouldn't live, because answering his call, my two Neanderthal shadows from the bus stationed moved truculently into the office. I prepared to defend myself, American style . . . but fisticuffs were not their intention. (SOUND:  SCUFFLING)  Instead, they just jumped on me with the finesse of overscale television wrestlers, and slapped a damp cloth over my face. In the one good whiff I had, the odor of chloroform screamed through my nostrils. And a few seconds later I went out for good! –like a bug in a killing bottle!

MUSIC:      UP TO FIRST ACT CURTAIN:

MUSIC:      SECOND ACT OVERTURE AND TO BACKGROUND

SPADE:      When I came out of the chloroform, I was lying in a cushiony chaise-lounge, in a very elegant room looking at a very earthly red-head. And she was staring at me. I let this go on for a few minutes, until she got to smiling. It was nothing less than cozy.

ANDREA:     Feel better, darling?

SPADE:      Not at all, why don't you comfort me?

ANDREA:     They shouldn't have done this to you . . . they really shouldn't! You're rather pretty.

SPADE:      That chloroform facial must have done something for me. I must tell Max Factor. But tell me- where do you fit in this gang?

ANDREA:     Why, darling, I'm Andrea. Andrea Benedict, Kingsley's sister.

SPADE:      Who's side of the fence are you on?

ANDREA:     Yours, of course. Look at you- poor baby- Mr. Bassler's gruesome sometimes . . . do you feel like talking?

SPADE:      No . . . but coax me.

ANDREA:     Sam . . . I want it too.

SPADE:      I'm afraid to ask this, but – want what?

ANDREA:     The thing. And dear, Sam, I know you're going to make a bargain.

SPADE:      I am?

ANDREA:     Of course. It's no good to you . . . at all. No good whatso-ever.

SPADE:      If you say so.

ANDREA:     It's just a matter of when and how . . . so somebody's got to make money from it, why not us?

SPADE:      What're we talking about?

ANDREA:     Him, Sam.

SPADE:      Him?

ANDREA:      I haven't much time . . . look, darling, you want to get out of this and make some money on it. Double his offer and you'll be all right. Accept it, and you'll regret it. Then I'll buy it from you. See you later, darling.

MUSIC:       UNDER

SPADE:       With that she willowed her way through two French doors at the far end of the room. I tried to get up and follow her but a spell of dizziness came over me, and I settled back on the chaise-lounge feeling like an aging-actor who couldn't catch the ingénue. But I didn't get much rest . . .

COURTNEY:    (OFF . . . YELPING) Don't jostle me . . . I'm not made of pig-iron!

SOUND:       SQUEAK OF WHEELCHAIR FADES ON:-

SPADE:       First came his voice . . . then the squeak of rubber wheels on the floor . . . then two familiar beefy faces pushing what looked to be the most expensive wheelchair in the world. All it needed was fog light and a mink tail. In it sat a white-haired old man, with hard black eyes.

COURTNEY:    Hah! How does it feel to be dealing with a man who knows how to deal with people? Tell me!

SPADE:       Sorry, no interviews today.

COURTNEY:    I am Courtney Benedict.

SPADE:       Oh . . . father of Kingsley?

COURTNEY:    Grandfather. I'll not mince words with you, Spade. One minute of experience is worth a thousand words.

SPADE:          True, but I'd like a few thousand words on why I was drugged and shanghaied.

COURTNEY:       You could never prove what happened to you.

SPADE:          Perhaps not . . . well let's get down to it. Why am I here?

COURTNEY:       You're entitled to know. My grandson delivered to you a certain object, which you have been reluctant to turn over to my representative . . . even under the inducement of more money than you make in a year.

SPADE:          Don't remind me.

COURTNEY:       Now would you consider turning this object to me . . . or would you rather consider losing your license, having your credit cut-off, and your reputation forever ruined?

SPADE:          You could do all those things?

COURTNEY:       I most certainly could.

SPADE:          You are a really nasty, terrible old man, aren't you? A veritable Scrooge.

COURTNEY:       Come, come, Spade, none of this Christmas sentimentality, make a decision.

SPADE:          You leave a rather awkward choice.

COURTNEY:       How I built the family fortune, young man. Leaving people awkward choices. Now quickly . . . are you in or are you out?

SPADE:          Well . . . there's a little matter of reparations for professional embarrassment, general inconvenience, and some bodily injury.

COURTNEY:       Which come to say five thousand dollars?

SPADE:      Let's say ten . . . I have a lot of shopping to do before Monday.

COURTNEY:   Ten. Now, where is the object for which we bargain?

SADE:       In a locker . . . in a bus terminal.

COURTNEY:   The key?

SPADE:      In the mail. It should be at my office tomorrow morning in the eleven o'clock mail, along with the Christmas cards.

COURTNEY:   Shrewd. All right, Mr. Spade, may we consummate the deal at that time?

SPADE:      All right. Sure.

MUSIC:      IN AND UNDER:

SPADE:      We shook hands and parted in mutual distrust. I grabbed a taxi back to my apartment and was followed very closely all the way. Inside my place I was not surprised to find that the phone was out of order and that I had been well ransacked. A glance out the window disclosed I was going to be with company all night long. So I turned to my library shelf and settled down to my copy of "Thurston the Magician" (which I only use when a case calls for Thurston type rusing.) I found my solution on page twenty-three, under disappearing coins, practiced for four hours, then I looked inside my treasure chest of old keys, till I found one that would do and fell happily fell asleep, chuckling at my own cleverness. The next morning I was followed to the doorway of my office building. And upstairs I had an expected guest, John Bassler, who waited with me until the mailman came. (MUSIC:    ON)

POBEY:      (SL. OFF) Oh . . . 'morning, Mr. Spade . . . (SNIFFS) This
            one's perfumed.

SPADE:      (COUGHS) Please . . .

POBEY:      . . . and this one's from New York . . . .from Gypsy Rose
            . . . and oh yeah, one more . . . mmm . . . feels like it's got
            a key in it or something.

SPADE:      Really. That's pretty good feeling, Mr. Pobey.

POBEY:      (FADES ON) Yes, Mr. Spade, it . . . oh, excuse me, I didn't
            know you had anybody with you.

BASSLER:    Quite all right, sir, bring it in here.

POBEY:      Here's your letter Mr. Spade . . .

SPADE:      Thank you.

POBEY:      (FADES) See you tomorrow . . .

SOUND:      DOOR CLOSES OFF

BASSLER:    The letter, please?

SPADE:      Oh . . . here you are.

SOUND:      LETTER RIPPED OPEN . . . KEY FALLS OUT ON DESK:

BASSLER:    Thank you, Mr. Spade. Your check will be delivered this
            afternoon.

MUSIC:      IN AND UNDER:

SPADE:      The minute he stepped out of the door I went into action.
            I took the real envelope with the real key (which I had
            palmed according to Thurston) out of my sleeve . . . put it
            in my inside pocket and cased the street outside. Making
            sure Bassler had taken his hired help with him, I locked

up the office, went downstairs, rented a car and headed for the Bridge. On the way I stopped in a pawnshop and located a black bag, a pair of smoked glasses, and a used stethoscope. Twenty-five minutes later, with an album of Spellbound under one arm, I was again standing in the foyer of the Bide-A-Wee Sanitarium.

KLAUS:     Doctor who . . . ?

SPADE:     Doctor Martin Carver.

KLAUS:     Oh, yes, Dr. Carver. Your business is what?

SPADE:     One of your patients. Courtney Benedict sent me to look at his son, Kingsley.

KLAUS:     Oh, yes, Kingsley, a most unfortunate case.

SPADE:     May I see him now? I'm rather in a hurry.

KLAUS:     Of course . . . of course . . . If Mr. Benedict says so, you may do anything. Come this way.

SOUND:     STEPS UNDER DOOR OPENS:

KLAUS:     In here. The waiting room.

SPADE:     Look here, Hoffman . . . Mr. Benedict is paying for my services at the rate of five hundred dollars a day. I don't think he'd appreciate you keep me waiting.

KLAUS:     On the contrary, Doctor, he might appreciate that gesture most uncommonly. I must prepare the patient. Besides, what is money to a Benedict? (EFFORT) Wait here.

SPADE:     Hey!

SOUND:     DOOR SLAMS SHUT . . . LOCK CLICKS

MUSIC:     IN AND UNDER:

SPADE:    The push he gave me into the waiting room was not as friendly as it might have been . . . and when the door closed I heard the unmistakable click of a lock. There was only one window in the room . . . and it was covered by a heavy, wire net. I had walked right into it. Five minutes later the door opened, and Dr. Hoffman come back in. This time his face was decidedly unfriendly.

KLAUS:    I have just talked with Courtney Benedict by phone. He says he knows nothing about you . . . that I am not to let you see Kingsley.

SPADE:    I am not accustomed to this sort of unprofessional treatment, Dr. Hoffman. Courtney Benedict obviously has a forgetful mind.

KLAUS:    He was intensely angry . . . over some business with a man named Spade . . .

SPADE:    I know nothing about that. But I have this personal note calling me here to examine his son. Would you care to see it?

KLAUS:    I most certainly would.

MUSIC:    IN AND UNDER:

SPADE:    I bent over my little black bag, fumbled around a while, and finally found just the right prescription. My fist, I pulled it out and swung it at Dr. Hoffman. (SOUND: BLOW) It caught him on the side of the face, and he fell in his tracks. I left the waiting room, locking the door behind me . . . and went unmolested to Kingsley's room. (DOOR OPEN) He wasn't there. So I began searching . . . and I looked through many a horrible and nightmarish cell before I found him . . . on the top floor . . . this time he was in a straitjacket . . . and he was awake. I untied the jacket.

KINGSLEY:        Oh- oh-

SPADE:      Can you walk?

KINGSLEY:   I'll crawl if I have to.

SPADE:      Here . . . lean on me.

KINGSLEY:   I'll make it. I know the way out . . . I'll show you.

SOUND:      STEPS:

KINGSLEY:   Did they . . . did they get the thing?

SPADE:      Not yet.

KINGSLEY:   Good, Spade, good.

MUSIC:      IN AND UNDER

SPADE:      Nobody stopped us . . . the frightened nurse was the only obstacle, waiting at the door. I was going to give her my other fifty, but thought better of it and tied her up instead. More ethical. The dialogue came later in the car. He thanked me for getting him out of there and I said:

SOUND:      CAR MOTOR

MUSIC:      OUT:

SPADE:      You can repay my efforts by satisfying my curiosity. What do you have that everybody in your family wants?

KINGSLEY:   Don't you know . . . haven't you looked yet?

SPADE:      I haven't had a chance to open that box.

KINGSLEY:   I never liked my grandfather, Sam. I didn't go for the way he pushed people around . . . the way he made his money . . . built his empire . . . just the kind of man he is.

SPADE:      Oh- so you got something on him. He found out about it . . . doped you up to keep you from talking to anybody . . . but you got away long enough to get to me.

KINGSLEY:     Yeah. One day last week I happened to run across something . . . well something that'd make him change his mind about a lot of things. If it were shown around town it'd topple him off his throne overnight. He'd be smashed .. . he'd have to crawl into a hole. That's what's in the box.

SPADE:     Mm-huh. And what do you intend doing with it now?

KINGSLEY:     Let's go out and get it.

MUSIC:     IN AND UNDER:

SPADE:     At the bus terminal I took a plant at the doorway, while Kingsley walked firmly over to locker one thirty nine and extracted a small cardboard box, unmolested. When he came to me, there was a look of triumph on his face . . .

KINGSLEY:     This'll make the old buzzard knuckle down and pay attention I . . .

BASSLER:     (FADE ON) Just a minute there . . . I thought I'd find you two here . . .

KINGSLEY:     Bassler...what do you want?

BASSLER:     I phoned the sanitarium and learned you had escaped with Mr. Spade, Kingsley. Mr. Spade, I owe you many apologies but that can come later . . . Kingsley, your grandfather's had a stroke.

KINGLSEY:     If you think I'm going to fall for that . . .

BASSLER:     Please- come with me. This is no trick . . . for safety's sake, bring Mr. Spade . . . if you don't believe me.

MUSIC:     IN:

SPADE:     Fifteen minutes later we were all standing in the library of the Benedict home, warming our hands in front of the fireplace.

Kingsley was still clutching the cardboard box. (SOUND: DOOR OPENS OFF) Finally, a servant beckoned us all into the bedroom. Old Courtney Benedict was lying on the bed, eyes open, motionless. Andrea walked over to us. She took her brother's hand and looked up at him.

ANDREA:     Kingsley . . . he's going to be paralyzed for the rest of his life . . . a stroke . . . He can't talk . . . he can only move his eyes. (SOBS)

KINGSLEY:  Oh no . . . Andrea . . .

ANDREA:     Kingsley . . . it doesn't matter now, does it . . . he can't hurt you or me now . . . he can't hurt anyone, anymore . . .

MUSIC:       UNDER

SPADE:       Kingsley stood there transfixed. A muscle in his cheek moved spasmodically. Then, without a word, he turned and walked out. All of us followed him. He moved over to the fireplace, then with a decisive movement he did it: He threw the box on top of the flames. A moment later it was all gone and we were standing there looking at the ashes.

MUSIC:       CLIMAX AND B.G.

SPADE:       I quietly picked up my hat, and left. Period. End of report.

EFFIE:        Sam! What was in that box!?! What?

SPADE:       You go type that up, angel.

EFFIE:        But-

SPADE:       Go on . . . scoot . . . Question period later.

MUSIC:       PHRASE OF THEME

SOUND:      STEPS ON

EFFIE:      (FADE ON) Here it is, Sam, all typed up. Now tell me.

SPADE:      Hmmm? Tell you what?

EFFIE:      Sam Spade, you either tell me what was in that box or I'll walk out of here right now and never come back.

SPADE:      Really?

EFFIE:      If you don't believe me, you just keep on not telling me.

SPADE:      Well- I'm going to miss you, Ef.

EFFIE:      You'd- you'd let me go, just like that?

SPADE:      I can't meet your ultimatum.

EFFIE:      Oh?

SPADE:      Because I don't know what was the secret of the Benedicts. I don't know what else was in that box. And I'm glad I don't.

EFFIE:      But, Sam . . . if anybody else was listening to your story, wouldn't they be disappointed not to find out?

SPADE:      We'll have to risk that. I trust Kingsley's judgment. He must have thought the old man had been brought to justice or he wouldn't have destroyed the evidence. It was a family matter- let's leave it like that.

EFFIE:      I suppose you're right.

SPADE:      Suppose I'm right! You know I'm always right! After all, who's the employer here? The boss? Who pays you?

EFFIE:      That's a good question. As long as you've brought it up, Sam- I was wondering . . . regarding my back salary..

RECORD GOES ON

EFFIE:      Sam- (OFF) - Sam – off – off – off – Sam!

SOUND:      PHIL HARRIS RECORD

SPADE:      Please don't talk while the music is playing.

EFFIE:      All right – turn it off.

SPADE:      What, what, what is it, Effie?

EFFIE:      It's about Phil Harris. We have a letter from him – about the Thing- The Thing For Kids For Christmas. And it says: You know, "The Thing" can be anything you think an underprivileged child would like for Christmas. In your town there are civic groups who are cooperating with this "Thing for Kids" campaign. Send your new or used toys to the collection centers in your town, and help make some child's Christmas brighter. It'll make you happier, too. That's what it says, Sam.

SPADE:      And that's a nice note to end on.

EFFIE:      I think so. (MUSIC: SNEAK) Goodnight, then, Sam. And Merry Christmas.

SPADE:      Merry Christmas, Sweetheart.

MUSIC:      UP TO CURTAIN

# THE ADVENTURES OF SAM SPADE
## "THE JUDAS CAPER"

SUNDAY, APRIL 11, 1948
6:00-6:30 PM DST
10:00-10:30 PM DST  #81

SPADE:      Date: April 11, 1948. To: Mrs. Teresa Delafield. From: Samuel Spade, License Number 137596

EFFIE:      How many copies, Sam?

SPADE:      No copies.

EFFIE:      Just the one for our files?

SPADE:      No copies!

EFFIE:      All right, Sam . . . Subject?

SPADE:      Leave that blank . . . ah . . . Dear . . . Dear Terry: This won't be easy reading and it's not . . . oh, cross that out, Effie.

EFFIE:      Yes, Sam . . .

SPADE:      Ah . . . I wish . . . No. I hope. No. Start a new page.

| | |
|---|---|
| SOUND: | (PAGE TORN FROM NOTEBOOK) |
| EFFIE: | Sam, maybe if you- |
| SPADE: | It's okay. I've got it now. Dear Terry:    ( M U S I C SNEAK) It started out as a straight bodyguard job. The body was yours, and my so-called client was your mother-in-law. I liked the tone of her letter, the size of the check, I liked the house, a big rambling English type mansion in St. Francis Wood, and I liked her. |
| MUSIC: | (ACCENT & OUT) |
| SOUND: | (BIRDS: OUTDOORSY BACKGROUND) (STEPS ON GRAVEL) |
| SPADE: | (SINGS: OUT WITH) |
| IRENE: | (OFF) Mr. Spade! Mr. Spade! Over here! |
| SPADE: | Hm? Oh. |
| SOUND: | (STEPS FROM GRAVEL TO FLAGSTONES) |
| IRENE: | (ON CUE) (FADES ON) Do you mind? It's such a lovely day. I thought we might just as well have our little talk in the garden. |
| SPADE: | Sure. It's nice. You're Mrs. Delafield? |
| IRENE: | Mrs. David Delafield. Won't you sit down? |
| SPADE: | Thank you. |
| IRENE: | I don't suppose you detectives ever drink lemonade. |
| SPADE: | Why not? Is there something wrong with it? |
| IRENE: | Well, it's pink. I like it that way because it reminds me of the circus. Say when! |

SOUND:      (POURING: ICE CLINKS IN PITCHER)

SPADE:      Uh . . . when.

IRENE:      Well! Isn't this pleasant. They all turn up their noses at my lemonade. Except my daughter-in-law, Theresa. I'm very fond of her, Mr. Spade. In so many ways she reminds me of my own daughter, whom I lost when she was a child.

SPADE:      Oh, I'm sorry.

IRENE:      If anything were to happen to Terry, I should have no one left.

SPADE:      You're a widow?

IRENE:      Oh, no. There's my husband. He's living, but . . . yes, he's alive. And my son, but you know how it is when boys grow up. He's so much like his father.

SPADE:      I see. Well, aside from that, what's worrying you, Mrs. Delafield?

IRENE:      I'm not sure. I want to make sure without involving the police, and without arousing anyone's suspicions. I understand your investigations are confidential?

SPADE:      Unless there's a crime that can't be overlooked.

IRENE:      Well, there's none as yet, thank heaven. But I have the strangest feeling, Mr. Spade. I can't quite put my finger on it . . . but I have this feeling . . . that my son, Russell, is trying to hurt Terry in some way.

SPADE:      What brought this feeling on, Mrs. Delafield?

IRENE:      Well, it may be only my imagination, but the man at Spaulding's told me it's practically impossible to clean a gun when it's loaded. And the doctor said it was definitely sleeping medicine in the bottom of the glass after her bed burned up. And she never drinks brandy.

SPADE:      It was brandy in the glass?

IRENE:      Oh, no, lemonade. The brandy was poured all over the bedclothes, to make it burn better, I think. But of course it may be only my imagination . . .

SPADE:      Now let's get this straight. Your son said he was cleaning his gun when it went off and then what?

IRENE:      Oh, it missed her. But it scorched her hair a little . . .

SPADE:      And then somebody dosed her with sedative and set fire to her . . .

IRENE:      Oh, I managed to get her out in time . . . But it could have been quite dangerous.

SPADE:      Yeah. I agree. Now, tell me, Mrs. Delafield, how'd you happen to write me instead of some other detective?

IRENE:      Oh, because your name is Spade.

SPADE:      That figures.

IRENE:      Because of my Aunt Minnie Spade on my mother's side. I'm afraid I've told a little white lie about you. You don't mind?

SPADE:      No, not as long as it stays white.

IRENE:      Well, I wrote a little note to myself. Here...you'd better read it.

SPADE:      (MUSIC: UNDER) "Dear Aunt Irene:    I shall be passing through San Francisco very shortly and unless you notify me to the contrary I shall avail myself on your gracious hospitality. I look forward to meeting Uncle David, Cousin Russell, and Cousin Terry, of whom you have written me such glowing reports. Signed, Samson Lovett Spade. P.S. Remember the ice-box cookies? Also pink lemonade. Boy, oh boy!"

MUSIC:      (ACCENT AND OUT)

TERRY:      (OFFSTAGE) Boody! Where are you?

IRENE:      Over here, dear! By the bird-bath! (ASIDE) That's she, now, Mr. Spade.

SPADE:      Who?

IRENE:      Your cousin Terry.

SPADE:      My-? Now wait a minute, Mrs. Delafield.

IRENE:      Shh! Confidential. Remember?

TERRY:      (FADING ON) Boody, he's at it again, I've been looking all over the-. Oh. Sorry. I didn't know you had a guest.

IRENE:      Not a guest, darling. One of the family.

TERRY:      This family is improving by the minute.

SPADE:      I was thinking the same thing myself.

IRENE:      Delafield or- Lovett?

SPADE:      Lovett.

IRENE:      Minnie Lovett's boy, who married that Mr. Spade in Seattle, your cousin Samson, dear.

SPADE:      By a previous marriage, of course. Just call me Sam.

IRENE:      Well, if you'll excuse me, I have a foul headache. (SOUND: BIRD BICKERING MAKING RACKET) Shoo . . . .you naughty, naughty, birdies. Shoo! Shoo!

TERRY:      Hmmmmmm . . . ..by whose previous marriage, cousin Samson?

SPADE:      Aunt Minnie's.

TERRY:      Lovett?

SPADE:      Mmmmmm . . . Lovett. How about cousin Russell?

TERRY:      Delafield . . . pure Delafield. He and his old man are in the bar drinking each other under it.

SPADE:      Why?

TERRY:      It's all Boody's fault. She keeps telling Russell he's trying to kill me. It's bound to depress him. What have you got on for this afternoon?

SPADE:      Just what I'm wearing.

TERRY:      Mmmm . . . I like it. My car's parked down by the potting shed. Shall we go for a ride? I mean, I'll show you around the grounds.

SPADE:      Oh sure, sure. Love it.

MUSIC:      (BRIDGE AND TO B.G.)

SPADE:      And I did, every minute of it. It was a beautiful spring day; the birds were chasing each other all over the place, squirrels; chipmunks; girl-scouts selling cookies, boy-scouts buying them . . . .something was in the air. It was a sky-writer advertising a movie. We stopped looking for four-leaf-clovers and turned around to watch him. The plane spelled out "April Showers." I wondered if it meant anything.

(SOUND:     THUNDER CLAP: WIND AND RAIN) It did. (SOUND: THUNDER: HEAVY RAIN)

| MUSIC: | (TO CLIMAX AND OUT UNDER) |
|---|---|
| SOUND: | (DOOR CLOSE ON HEAVY RAIN: CONTINUE STORM B.G. THROUGHOUT) (HURRYING FOOTSTEPS START CLIMBING STAIRS AND OUT AS:) |
| BIZ: | (ALL INTERIOR SOUND AND DIALOGUE ON SLIGHT ECHO) |
| IRENE: | (FADES ON) . . . Terry. Terry. Is that you? |
| TERRY: | (WEARILY) Yes, Boody. |
| IRENE: | (SLIGHTLY OFF STAGE) Who's that with you? Oh, Cousin Sampson. You naughty, naughty children. Where have you been? |
| SPADE: | Uh . . . Cousin Terry was just showing me the potting shed. |
| IRENE: | Oh, did you see my glorious marigolds? Oh, but of course, you saw everything. Well, but never mind that now. Russell's terribly drunk. I'm afraid he's been drinking again. And, the man from Spauding's said that the new bullets he brought out today don't fit any gun in the house. He said they're for elephants. What does it all mean Mr. Spade . . . I mean, Cousin Sampson? |
| SPADE: | Where is Cousin Russell now? |
| IRENE: | He's in Terry's room, but we took the matches away from him I don't know what to do about the gasoline smell in the library, but we can have tea in the morning-room, if Cousin Sampson doesn't mind our informality. |
| SPADE: | Love it. That's what I like about this family. |
| IRENE: | Thank you. Now you go right along with your cousin |

|  |  |
|---|---|
| | Terry. Send Russell down to me, I want to talk to him, tell him I'll give him his matches back if he'll come. And then I want you both to light a fire in the hearth and then I want both of you to dry off all those wet things. |
| TERRY: | All right, Boody. All right! 'Come on, Sam! |
| SOUND: | (CLIMBING STAIRS) |
| IRENE: | (FADE) Tea's in the morning room. Daylight saving, you know! |
| TERRY: | (MUTTERS) Ooh. That woman. Some day she's gonna drive me stark staring mad! |
| SOUND: | (STEPS IN CORRIDOR) (OUT) |
| TERRY: | My room. Come on in. (SOUND:   DOOR OPENED: STEPS: CLOSED) |
| BIZ: | (ECHO OUT) |
| RUSSELL: | (OFF: MOANS) |
| TERRY: | Oh lord. Help me scrape him off the carpet. |
| SPADE: | (SOUND: MOVEMENT: SCUFFLE) Come on you lush. Straighten up. |
| RUSSELL: | I'm innocent, I never touched her. Take me home. |
| SPADE: | Sure. Sure. Up on your feet. |
| RUSSELL: | I live in St. Francis Wood. Hey, Terry, who is this guy? |
| TERRY: | None of your business, what are you doing in my room? |
| RUSSELL: | A husband's got a right. A hus . . . .. .. |
| TERRY: | Get out! |

RUSSELL:    All right, if that's the way you want it. My old man's got influence, he'll close this joint. Sleep on it (FADE) I'll let you know in the morning.

SOUND:    (UNCERTAIN FOOTSTEPS TO DOOR: DOOR OPEN AND SLAM)

TERRY:    Phew (EXHALES) Well, Sam, that's your cousin Russell.

SPADE:    How'd you happen to marry him?

TERRY:    Light the fire, Sam. Pull up that love seat, and I'll tell you all about it. Just a minute, I'll slip on a robe.

SPADE:    Okay. (SOUND: STEPS: MATCH STRUCK: CRACKLE OF FIRE) I'm looking over a four-leaf clover, etc, etc.

TERRY:    (FADES ON) Well, that's cozier. Sit here beside me and your cousin Terry will tell all.

SPADE:    Okay, but first I think I ought to tell you I'm not your-

SOUND:    (OFFSTAGE: MAN FALLING DOWN STAIRS: CRASH OF LAMPS VASES, ETC.)

RUSSELL:    (YELLS THROUGHOUT SOUND) Who pushed me?

TERRY:    Well, he made it down the stairs.

SPADE:    I hope there's a doctor in the house.

TERRY:    He never hurts himself.

SPADE:    Why'd you marry him?

TERRY:    Well, we were brought up together, and everybody seemed to expect it. So I guess we did too.

SPADE:    What do you mean, "brought up together"?

TERRY:    My parents were killed in a plane accident when I was a

baby. Old Mr. Delafield, your Uncle David, by that previous marriage, was appointed my guardian.

SPADE:      I see. Now, about that previous marriage . . .

TERRY:      Russell and me? It never meant a thing. I could get an annulment tomorrow if I had a good excuse.

SPADE:      What has he been giving you . . . but excuses? Or are you waiting for him to make it down those stairs head-first, one of these days?

TERRY:      Sam, don't. Sam, please don't. It's not what you think.

SPADE:      Then, what have you been waiting for all this time?

TERRY:      Haven't you figured it out yet?

SPADE:      Yeah, and it doesn't add up.

TERRY:      Try again, Sam.

SPADE:      Uh, uh.

TERRY:      Why? I know you aren't my Cousin Sampson.

SPADE:      Oh, well. Well, in that case come here.

SOUND:      (ON CUE: BARRAGE    OF    HEAVY    GUNSHOTS) (SOUND OF RICOCHET SLUGS)

TERRY:      (SCREAMS) Russell!

MUSIC:      (PUNCTUATE AND TO B.G.)

SPADE:      I couldn't make out were the gunman was. The slugs were spattering in every direction. I dumped you on the floor, rolled the love seat over on top of you, and reached for my own gun. But I never got to use it. About then the lead stopped flying, and I smelled some smoke that wasn't powder smoke. It came from the rug in front of the fireplace, where a bunch of live coals had showered out on it. I ground them out with my heel. (SOUND:     T O SUIT ACTION) Then I took the poker and started digging into the fireplace. What I raked out were ten empty steel-jacketed cartridges of point-five hundred caliber. (MUSIC ACCENT) I was beginning to believe it was true what they said about Russell.

MUSIC:    (ACCENT AND OUT:) (SOUND: DOOR BURSTS OPEN)

DELAFIELD: (FADES ON) Stay out there, Irene, till I find out if it's safe.

IRENE:    (FADES ON) Terry, Terry, my poor little girl. What happened? Did he miss you again?

DELAFIELD: I'm not sure I blame Russell, Irene. I'm not sure it's at all proper for this a . . . a . . . what did you say his name was?

IRENE:    This is Cousin Sampson, David dear. This is your Uncle David.

SPADE:    Let's drop all that shall we, Mrs. Delafield? My name is Samuel Spade, I'm a private detective.

DELAFIELD: Well, my apologies, that makes it all right, of course. And you can give me a straight answer. What did happen?

SPADE:    Somebody, maybe your son, I'm not sure, loaded the fireplace with live ammunition.

IRENE:    It was Russell! I wondered why he ordered those ridiculous big bullets.

DELAFIELD: Why didn't you tell me of this?

IRENE:    Well, they didn't fit any of the guns, and when he tried to set fire to the library rug and worrying about the gasoline smell and everything, I completely forgot.

DELAFIELD: This settles it. I don't care if he is my own son. He's going out of here in a straitjacket tonight.

TERRY: No, no, you mustn't. You know what he said he'd do if you ever tried to send him away.

DELAFIELD: It can't be any worse than it is. You stay here, Terry. You always upset him. Come on, Spade. (SLIGHT FADE OFF) Irene, he always listens to you, come along.

SOUND: (MOVEMENT: STEPS ON ECHO: STEPS DOWNSTAIRS)

SPADE: (MUSIC IN) The ground floor was big, but there weren't many rooms and no hiding places that I could see. We didn't find Russell anywhere. By this time your mother-in-law was in tears, but I couldn't tell what old man Delafield was thinking.

IRENE: (SOBBING QUIETLY)

DELAFIELD: Irene, stop that. You know it has to be done. You go upstairs and look in his room. I'll search the west wing. Spade, you cover the grounds. Try the potting shed. He often hides down there.

SPADE: Huh?

DELAFIELD: The potting shed. (FADES) Come along, Irene.

SPADE: (MUSIC IN) I didn't have any intentions of searching the potting shed. I went outside to look for another way in so I could follow them. That's when I saw you, Terry, slip out of the side door; remove your shoes, and take out across the lawn. I took out after you, using gum-shoes. They didn't go fast enough in the wet grass to beat you to the potting shed.

(SOUND:    OFFSTAGE:         TWO SHOTS ON ECHO)

TERRY:     (SCREAMS) (TWICE ON ECHO) (ALSO OFFSTAGE)

MUSIC:     (KNIFE CHORD AND UNDER)

SOUND:     (RUNNING STEPS AND OUT) (HEAVY RAIN ON ROOF: DISTANT THUNDER)

SPADE:     The first thing I saw was you. You looked as if you had fainted and I think you really had. The second thing I saw was your husband, Russell Delafield. He looked dead, and he was, and I was pretty sure that the slugs in his head would match the dainty little automatic that lay under your dainty white hand.

SOUND:     (RAIN UP & INTO:)

MUSIC:     (UP TO FIRST ACT CURTAIN)

MUSIC:     (SECOND OVERTURE)

SOUND:     (DOOR CRACKED: CLOSED SOFTLY)

EFFIE:     Sam.

SPADE:     Yes, Effie?

EFFIE:     Lt. Dundy of homicide is in the outer office.

SPADE:     Tell him to go away.

EFFIE:     All right, Sam.

SOUND:     (DOOR OPENED AND CLOSED: PAUSE OPEN AND CLOSE AGAIN)

EFFIE:     Sam.

SPADE:     What now?

| | |
|---|---|
| EFFIE: | He won't. |
| SPADE: | All right. Show him in. |
| SOUND: | (DOOR OPENED) |
| EFFIE: | (FADES) Oh, Lt. Dundy, he just this moment came in through his private entrance. |
| DUNDY: | (OFFSTAGE) Humph. |
| SOUND: | (FADE ON HEAVY FOOTSTEPS:    DOOR CLOSED: STEPS REGISTER AND OUT) |
| DUNDY: | Hello, Sam. |
| SPADE: | Sit down, Dundy. |
| SOUND: | (OF DRAWER BOTTLES:  GLASS AND BOTTLES SET DOWN ON DESK) |
| SPADE: | Drink? |
| DUNDY: | No thanks. |
| SPADE: | So that's the way it is. What's eating you? |
| DUNDY: | The Delafield case, or the potting shed mystery, I think the papers are calling it. |
| SPADE: | I made my statement at the inquest. Anything wrong with it? |
| DUNDY: | Why no, Sam. You're in the clear. We just want you to stay there. |
| SPADE: | Thanks a lot. Now if you'll pardon me, Dundy, I've a million things to do . . . |
| DUNDY: | Wait a minute, Sam. |
| SPADE: | Look, Dundy, the coroner's jury handed in an open verdict. "Death due to misadventure, suicide, and, or ho- |

micide by person or persons unknown." Maybe I should repeat that, "person or persons unknown," Dundy. The guy was a lush. He was off his nut. And his own mother says he threatened suicide every time he opened a fresh bottle which was just about every hour on the hour.

DUNDY:     Those shots, Sam. One was fired eighteen inches from his head, the other twenty inches from his head.

SPADE:     Twenty and eighteen. That makes thirty-eight. Is that how you figured out the caliber of the gun?

DUNDY:     Sam, the absolute maximum distance of the weapon from the wound in suicide . . .

SPADE:     Is twenty inches. I looked it up too. So what are you worried about?

DUNDY:     Two shots, Sam. A man with a hole clean through his head is supposed to have time to pump another one before he fell down?

SPADE:     Nuts. I've seen 'em with as many as five and they were suicides. Reason? Reflex and self loathing.

DUNDY:     But, Sam. The medic says the first slug caused instant death.

SPADE:     (SERIOUSLY) Really, Dundy?

DUNDY:     That's right Sam.

SPADE:     Which one of those slugs was fired first, Dundy? The first one or the second?

DUNDY:     Well . . . a . . . a . . . Now look here, Sam. That's not my department. That's up to ballistics. You know that.

SPADE:     Then stop waving it in my face. Now, you've got one more minute. If it isn't any better than that, it'll cost you for an interview.

DUNDY:     Now climb down, Sam. I just wanted to ask you for a little help. We went out to see this girl, this Teresa Delafield. She wasn't available for further questioning. And, what do you know, she wasn't there.

SPADE:     What do you know?

DUNDY:     Her mother-in-law says she left with you.

SPADE:     What do you know?

DUNDY:     Did she or didn't she?

SPADE:     Yeah, she rode in on the same bus with me. She had some shopping to do. Anything else?

DUNDY:     Yeah. Sgt. Polehaus just happened to run into your landlady . . .

SPADE:     Where did he catch her?

DUNDY:     (CONSULTING NOTES) Ah . . . In the furnace room, your building. Says here:    statement of landlady. My tenant, Samuel Spade, informed me yesterday two p.m. his sister from Tacoma was arriving to keep house for him.

SPADE:     Ah . . . But which one of my sisters?

DUNDY:     Says here. Statement of landlady continued. I would say she is the Hedy Lamarr type. Black hair and I would say violet colored eyes. I did not hear no names mentioned. He referred to her only as Pussy Cat.

SPADE:     (CHOKES) That's a lie. And, furthermore I sleep on the sofa.

DUNDY:     Sam, Sam. Let's get off the dime.

SPADE:     That's my line.

DUNDY:      We know you're hiding her out and it's not doing her or
            you any good.

SPADE:      Do you want to book her for murder, Dundy?

DUNDY:      Course not, Sam. We just want to talk to her.

SPADE:      What's stopping you?

DUNDY:      Well we don't want to go busting in anywhere without a
            warrant.

SPADE:      You mean, you can't get a warrant. So you come suckin'
            around me. You're wasting your time. When you get that
            warrant come and show it to me and I'll show you the
            writ I just had my lawyer draw up for her.

DUNDY:      Okay, Sam. But you're making a terrible mistake. Seems
            to me I remember a girl named Bridget O'Shaughnessy.

SPADE:      Yeah, Dundy. But you've got to admit- when I made a
            mistake it's a beaut.

MUSIC:      (BRIDGE)

SOUND:      (SPADE CLIMBING STAIRS)

SPADE:      I'm looking over a four-leaf clover . . .

SOUND:      (STEPS IN CORRIDOR OUT: DOOR UNLOCKED:
            OPENED)

SPADE:      Yoo hoo. Hey, Pussy-Cat, where are you?

SOUND:      (DOOR CLOSES:  STEPS)

TERRY:      (OFFSTAGE In here, Sam. In the kitchenette. (SOUND:
            GLASS CRASH) Help!

SPADE:      What's the matter? What happened!

(SOUND: STEPS ACCELERATE AND OUT ABRUPTLY)

Good grief! What happened?

TERRY:      Help me up.

SPADE:      Here. (BIZ:          HELPS HER UP)

TERRY:      (WAILS) Three hours.

SPADE:      You mean it only took you three hours to do all this dam-
            age. (SOUND: PICKING UP BROKEN BITS OF CROCK-
            ERY ETC. AND DUMPING IN WASTEBASKET: UNDER
            DIALOGUE).

TERRY:      I wanted to surprise you.

SPADE:      Well stop wailing. I couldn't be more surprised.

TERRY:      Oh, Sam. You are a darling. (CLINCH) Darling, why are
            you fidgeting?

SPADE:      My foot . . . it's stuck . . . in something.

TERRY:      What, Sam?

SPADE:      There's something on my shoe.

TERRY       (WAILS)

SPADE:      Well, it's not your fault. It could happen to anybody.
            What is it!?

TERRY:      My date-nut torte.

SPADE:      Your what?

TERRY:      My date-nut torte.

SPADE:      Is that legal?

TERRY:      I guess I'm just not the domestic type, Sam.

SPADE:    Good. Come in the living room. We'll have a drink.

SOUND:    (STEPS:    MOVEMENT)

TERRY:    You sit down there, and stretch out. This is one thing I do know how to do. (SOUND: MIX DRINKS)

SPADE:    Anything happen today, besides the date-nut torte?

TERRY:    I saw a darling little straw sailor just around the corner.

SPADE:    Stay away from those guys. They're fickle.

TERRY:    A hat, darling. Here's your drink.

SPADE:    I told you not to leave the apartment. Why did you?

TERRY:    Well, I had to get the dates and walnuts, and I bought a paper. Have you seen it?

SPADE:    Yeah.

TERRY:    The potting shed mystery:  Isn't that silly? And that awful old picture of me. Boody must have given it to them. (SERIOUS) Oh, Sam. They're after me, aren't they?

SPADE:    Come here. Sit down.

TERRY:    (CLOSE) Yes, Sam.

SPADE:    Are you scared?

TERRY:    Should I be?

SPADE:    I'm not sure. Should you be?

TERRY:    Sam, I thought you believed in me. I was sure you believed in me, Sam.

SPADE:    I'm trying, Pussy-Cat. I'm trying mighty hard.

TERRY:    Maybe I should give myself up. I will if you say so.

SPADE:      I'm not saying one way or the other.

TERRY:      Why not, Sam.

SPADE:      I guess you never saw anybody sweating under the lights down at headquarters. They do things to you.

TERRY:      What kind of things?

SPADE:      Nothing. Eyestrain. I'd hate to see lines under those pretty eyes of yours.

TERRY:      Oh, Sam. Why couldn't I have met you before . . . before . . .

SPADE:      Forget it. Forget about before. It's all over. You're in the clear, and I'm going to keep you there . . . if, I can keep myself there.

TERRY:      You're taking a terrible chance for me. Aren't you?

SPADE:      Forget it.

TERRY:      We could.

SPADE:      Could what?

TERRY:      Forget everything. But, not here.

SPADE:      Any suggestions?

TERRY:      Darling, I know this doesn't sound very nice. Especially to you, but it's the only way I know to say it. I have money, I even have a passport. I'll tell you something else I bought while I was out this afternoon. An airline ticket.

SPADE:      To romantic places?

TERRY:      I suppose so . . .

SPADE:      Why didn't you use it?

TERRY:      I don't know. I just bought the paper and came back here.

SPADE:      Why!

TERRY:      Sam. Stop torturing me. You know why . . . you know, you know, you know.

SPADE:      Stop it!

TERRY:      You know darling . . . you know. Don't you?

SPADE:      Yeah, yeah, I know.

MUSIC:      (BRIDGE)

SOUND:      (BIRDS, ETC. AS IN FIRST SCENE) (SPADE STEPS)

IRENE:      (FADES ON SINGING "WHAT DO THEY DO ON A RAINY NIGHT IN RIO")

SPADE:      Good morning, Mrs. Delafield.

IRENE:      (BREAKS OFF ON TRILL) Ooops. Mr. Spade, you startled me.

SPADE:      That's a very nice singing voice you have.

IRENE:      Was, Mr. Spade. But, thank you anyway. I was in the theater, you know.

SPADE:      I sensed that, somehow.

IRENE:      You did? Why nobody has spotted me for show people in years. You're a remarkably sensitive young man. Would you like to see my scrapbook?

SPADE:      Yeah . . . someday. Don't want to take up your time right now.

IRENE:      Of course. You're so busy with the arrangements.

SPADE:      Oh yes, the arrangements.

IRENE:      Terry has phoned me and told me everything. Of course it's awfully short notice, after . . . well I suppose abroad it would be all right. Never look back. That's what I said when I left the theatre. What's done is done. Eleven years in the Chocolate Soldier, then oblivion; just a rich man's petted darling.

SPADE:      Do you ever think of making a comeback?

IRENE:      An old lady's idle fancies, Mr. Spade. I've slipped out in the late afternoon and taken a secret path I know, down past the potting shed. Pausing there, sometimes, I've pretended it was a theatre and all the pots were people, row upon serried row, an audience you know. And, I've spoken a few little lines, plucked from memories garden (AS LADY MACBETH) "Go get some water, and wash this filthy witness from your hands. (SPADE:    " H U H ") Why did you bring these daggers from the place? They must lie there:    go carry them, and smear the sleepy grooms with blood."

SPADE:      That's pretty potent stuff. I don't remember that from the Chocolate Soldier.

IRENE:      Macbeth, my dear boy, Macbeth. "Here's the smell of blood still: all the perfumes of Aribia will not sweeten this little hand. (SINKS) Oh! Oh! Oh!"

SPADE:      Hey, Mrs. Delafield, are you all right. Should I get you a doctor?

IRENE:      Flatterer. But, they loved me in Sydney.

SPADE:      I wasn't kidding about that, Mrs. Delafield. How would you like to make a comeback right here in San Francisco?

IRENE:      Benefit? Oh but so soon after poor Russell . . .

SPADE:      This would be sort of private benefit. A small but select
            audience.

IRENE:      Tell me more, Mr. Spade . . . You interest me strangely.

(MUSIC:     (BRIDGE AND TO B.G.)

SPADE:      I gave her her lines and told her what I wanted her to
            do with them. She fainted. And, when he came to, she
            agreed. Then I phoned Dundy. I don't know whether he
            fainted or not. There was a long silence on the other end
            of the phone. When he came back he called me a tin-star,
            a cheap shamus, a snoop-hound, a snouter, a soft heel, a
            weasel, and a sloose. I called him a harness-bull, a chair-
            barnacle, a flat arch, a Joe Goss, a beagle, a side-walk snail,
            and no wonder he never got promoted. Then he sued for
            a separate peace and we started all over again. He finally
            said he would, but if it didn't work it would be my license
            and not his badge. They arrested your mother-in-law at
            four o'clock that afternoon. I waited twenty minutes after
            the extras hit the streets and then I went upstairs to my
            apartment. You were standing with your chin up and your
            hair down.

TERRY:      Sam, Sam Darling. It's all too ghastly. I can't believe it.
            Why did she do it?

SOUND:      (DOOR CLOSE)

SPADE:      Why did she do what?

TERRY:      Let herself be arrested like that. What is this statement
            the police say they're going to get out of her?

SPADE:      I don't know. It might be a confession.

TERRY:      It couldn't be.

SPADE:      Why not? You told the cops you didn't actually see your husband shoot himself.

TERRY:      But, poor old Boody, she was so gentle, so sweet. She's strange of course. Eccentric . . . She always did say she'd rather see Russell dead than in a sanitarium. Her own son . . .

SPADE:      It happens.

TERRY:      Do you think they can get a conviction against her?

SPADE:      If it was murder. And, if they can make her talk.

TERRY:      But it's impossible. How could she have gotten out of the house and down to the potting shed without our seeing her?

SPADE:      She told me she had a secret path around back of the hedge.

TERRY:      (GASPS)

SPADE:      Hey, take it easy.

TERRY:      If they make me go down there . . . to the police station. I don't want to see her. I don't want to see her. And she's so strange. Sometimes she imagines things. There's no telling what she'd say.

SPADE:      It'll be okay, Sweetheart. I'll be right there with you.

MUSIC:      (BRIDGE INTO B.G.)

SPADE:      Now here's what you've got to believe, Terry. I really didn't know. On the way over to the hall I began wishing I'd let well enough alone. But it was too late for that. It was too late for everything, but what was waiting for us down at headquarters. It was an ugly little scene. Your mother-in-law had the whole stage to herself, but, I don't think she liked it. The lights were too bright, and too hot, and too close to her. Lt. Dundy and Sgt. Polhaus, in shirt-sleeves and ties loosened, jumbo-size leather snaps hanging out of their hip pockets, were looming over her, their faces showing beet-red and brutal in the reflected light. They didn't look as though they were acting.

BIZ:        (SCENE ON SLIGHT ECHO)

SOUND:      (AD LIB STEPS UNDER:)

DUNDY:      All right Mrs. Delafield. Let's start again. Way back at the beginning.

IRENE:      But, I've already told you, over and over again . . .

POLHAUS:    And you're going to tell it again, and again, and again. Ten times, a hundred times, a thousand times.

IRENE:      I'm so tired. If you'd only let me have a little sleep. Those lights. Sleep, that knits up the raveled sleeve of care (A GROANING GASP)

TERRY:      (SOFTLY: WHISPERING) Poor Boody. Do they have to be so cruel?

SPADE:      Yeah.

POLHAUS:    Wake up. Wake up. Hold your head up.

DUNDY:      Let me handle this. Now Mrs. Delafield. Nobody wants to hurt you. Me and the sergeant want to sleep too. We can't!! Not till you tell the truth!

IRENE:      But . . . I . . . but I . . .

DUNDY:        Why did you lie about the secret path? Why are you ly-
              ing now about your daughter-in-law? You're shielding her.
              Aren't you. (RISING INFLECTION) Aren't you. Aren't
              you.

POLHAUS:      Come on talk! Pour it on Lt. I think she's ready to crack.
              Shall I give her treatment number three?

IRENE:        No. No, no. Not again. I'll talk, I'll tell you everything,
              everything.

TERRY:        Sam, you've got to stop her.

SPADE:        Too late, gorgeous.

POLHAUS:      Come on you. Stop bawling and spit it out.

IRENE:        I'd taken the little gun away from him, earlier in the day,
              and then when my husband said he was going to have him
              taken away in a straitjacket . . .

TERRY:        No, no! Don't listen to her.

SPADE:        Shut up!

IRENE:        (CONTINUES) . . . I went crazy. I didn't know what I was
              doing. I ran down to the shed.

TERRY:        (SCREAMS) Boody, no! She's lying. I shot him. I did it! I
              killed him! Can't you hear me? (GASPS)

SOUND:        (REGISTER:     SLOW    HEAVY    FOOTSTEPS    AP-
              PROACHING AND OUT)

DUNDY:        Yes, I hear you, Miss.

TERRY:        Well . . . aren't you going to arrest me?

DUNDY:        Don't be impatient; we'll take your statement in a minute.
              First I want to thank Mr. Spade for his cooperation. Good
              work, Sam. The department appreciates it.

IRENE:      Terry. Terry, dear. I'm so sorry. Mr. Spade assured me I was doing it for your own good.

TERRY:      Then, I better thank him.

SPADE:      Look Terry, I . . .

SOUND:      (SLAP)

TERRY:      Thank you very much. (SOUND: SLAP) Thank you for everything. (SOUND: SLAP) (SOBS) Oh, Sam. How could you?

MUSIC:      (BRIDGE)

SPADE:      Period. End of report. Type it up Effie.

EFFIE:      I'm sorry, Sam. I can't.

SPADE:      Effie, don't you be mad at me too.

EFFIE:      Don't touch me . . . you . . . you, monster. And that girl loved you. And, and, you betrayed her. You, you Judas. (SOBS FADING)

SOUND:      (EFFIE'S STEPS RUNNING: DOOR OPENED THEN SLAMMED)

            (DRINK POURED: SPADE DRINKS: GLASS SET DOWN HARD)

SPADE:      Sour racket. (FADE) Effie! Effie! Come back. Don't leave me.

SOUND:      (HIS STEPS FADE UNDER LINE

EFFIE:      (FADE ON: SNIFFING) Well, Sam. Here it is. I hope it's all right.

SPADE:      What is it?

EFFIE:      The report, Sam. I decided to do it after all, and leave my desk in order. (WAILS) I'll need a reference..!

SPADE:      Sit down. I'll dictate it.

EFFIE:      (RISING WAIL)

SPADE:      To whom it may concern:   Miss Effie Perine has been in my employ for the past – how many years? Fill it in. She is capable, honest, efficient and understanding . . .

EFFIE:      That's true, Sam. And, if you can only think up some explanation for the way you treated that poor girl . . .

SPADE:      Look, Sweetheart. First off, we're in the detective business, remember. We can't make up our own rules as we go along. But I want you to know, this is one time I might have done just that, only one reason I didn't . . .

EFFIE:      Yes, Sam?

SPADE:      I was hoping I'd prove her innocent. But, that's not the point. Whoever had killed Russell Delafield. His mother, his father, or his wife. It was justifiable homicide in my book, and in Terry's case it was justifiable homicide in anyone's book. He made repeated attempts on her life. And, her story that she killed him in self-defense will stick. If, I have to bribe every member of the jury myself. Period. End of explanation. You can take it or leave it.

EFFIE:      Well . . . I'll think it over. Goodnight, Sam.

SPADE:      Goodnight, Sweetheart.

MUSIC:      (UP TO CURTAIN)

# THE ADVENTURES OF SAM SPADE
## "THE COMMONWEALTH TANKARD"

SUNDAY, AUGUST 10, 1947    #46
4:00 - 4:30 PM PST
9:00 - 9:30 PM EST

ANNCR: The Adventures of Sam Spade, detective- brought to you by Wildroot Cream-Oil, the non-alcoholic hair tonic that contains Lanolin . . . Wildroot Cream-Oil "again and again the choice of men who put good grooming first."

MUSIC: PUNCTUATION . . . UP INTO TRILL INTO PHONE BELL

SOUND: PHONE BELL

SOUND: TELEPHONE ON FILTER MIKE LIFT RECEIVER

EFFIE: Sam Spade Detective Agency.

SPADE: (ON FILTER) Me, Sweetheart.

EFFIE: Oh, Sam. Lieutenant Dundy of Homicide called. He wants to know whether-whether to send his men after you or whether you're going to-(BREAKS) give yourself up!

|  | (WAILS) Ohhhhh, Sam. |
|---|---|
| SPADE: | Dry those tears, Sweetheart. Everything is back where it belongs- including the Cromwell family. |
| EFFIE: | Oh, Sam. Then- then everything's all right? You've beaten the rap? |
| SPADE: | Don't I always? |
| EFFIE: | I know, Sam. I shouldn't worry so much. But every time I think this may be- Ohhhh . . . .Sam . . . . |
| SPADE: | That's enough, Effie. Dry the phone and hang up. I'll be right down to dictate my report on the Commonwealth Tankard. |
| MUSIC: | (THEME AND TO B.G.) |
| ANNCR: | Dashiell Hammett, America's leading detective fiction writer, and creator of Sam Spade, the hard-boiled private eye, and William Spier, radio's outstanding producer-director of mystery and crime drama, join their talents to make your hair stand on end with Adventures of Sam Spade . . . (MUSIC: ACCENTS) Say, men, if you want the girls to make you their choice, better make Wildroot Cream-Oil your choice! Wildroot Cream-Oil is "again and again the choice of men who put good grooming first." And it's especially popular right now, during summer- because it has what it takes to keep your hair neatly in place, despite summer sun, wind and water! Wildroot Cream-Oil is extra soothing. It contains soothing LANOLIN! So get a bottle- or tube- of Wildroot Cream-Oil at your drug or toilet goods counter. And ask your barber to use Wildroot Cream-Oil on your hair. |
| MUSIC: | SNEAK UNDER |

| | |
|---|---|
| ANNCR: | And now, Wildroot brings to the air, the greatest private detective of 'em all . . . in the Adventures of Sam Spade! |
| MUSIC: | (UP TO SHOW) |
| SOUND: | (DOOR OPENED STEPS) |
| EFFIE: | (FADE ON) Sam! Oh, look at you! Your face! |
| SPADE: | A mere scratch, Effie. |
| EFFIE: | Scratch indeed! |
| SPADE: | Oh, that. Lipstick. |
| EFFIE: | Might I inquire whose? |
| SPADE: | Come on in, Sweetheart, I'll tell you all about it. |
| SOUND: | (STEPS:    CHAIR: DRAWER:    ETC.) |
| EFFIE: | (FADES ON) What was she like, Sam? Very pretty? |
| SPADE: | Pretty as a coral snake and twice as deadly. |
| EFFIE: | Oh. One of those. What was her name? |
| SPADE: | Patience. |
| EFFIE: | Hmmm. Pretty name. Patience. She must have been at the end of it when she met you. |
| SPADE: | Date: August 3rd, 1947. To: Mrs. Oliver H. Cromwell. From: Samuel Spade, License number 137596. Subject: The Commonwealth Tankard. |
| EFFIE: | Tanker, Sam? Like an oil tanker? |
| SPADE: | Tankard, Sweetheart. T-A-N-K-A-R-D. As in beer-mug. |
| EFFIE: | You mean all that fuss over an old beer-mug? |

SPADE:         Dear Mrs. Cromwell: (MUSIC SNEAK) The first time I
               ever heard of the Commonwealth Tankard was yesterday
               afternoon when I was summoned to the office of Mr. Mer-
               rill Janeway, dealer in antiques and objects of art. When
               I walked into Mr. Janeway's reception room, I thought
               I was going to like the job. The décor looked like easy
               money, and the blond behind the desk was easy to look
               at- honey-colored hair, forest green eyes, the kind you
               can get lost in, and a smile that told you she understood
               just how you felt. (MUSIC: ACCENT & OUT)

PATIENCE:      Yes, sir? What can I do for you?

SPADE:         Sorry, I'm here on business.

PATIENCE:      You don't look like a businessman.

SPADE:         If you mean that as a compliment- Thanks.

PATIENCE:      I do. Did Mr. Janeway send for you?

SPADE:         He did. Spade's the name. Private detective.

PATIENCE:      Oh? What's it all about, Mr. Spade?

SPADE:         I don't know. Do you?

PATIENCE:      I'm not his regular secretary. I'm just sitting in for my
               room-mate; she had some shopping to do. But don't tell
               Mr. Janeway, will you? He might be annoyed.

SPADE:         I don't think he would be. He in there now?

PATIENCE:      Sure. Go on in.

SPADE:         I'm in no hurry.

PATIENCE:      Thanks. But Mr. Janeway's always in a hurry.

SPADE:         Who's Mr. Janeway?

PATIENCE:   Oh, stop it; I'll be here when you come out. (FADE) Door on the left.

SOUND:   (STEPS: DOOR OPENED)

JANEWAY:   (FADES ON) Ah, you're Spade, aren't you? Come in, come in! (SOUND:DOOR CLOSES) (STEPS) Sit down.

SPADE:   Thanks.

JANEWAY:   This is a simple assignment, Mr. Spade; it won't take much of your time. I have just sold one of the most valuable antiques that has ever passed through my hands. You've heard of the Commonwealth Tankard?

SPADE:   No, I'm afraid I haven't, Mr. Janeway.

JANEWAY:   Indeed? I thought you had considerable knowledge of the antiquities.

SPADE:   What made you think that?

JANEWAY:   Your reputation, sir! I refer specifically to your magnificent work in the affair of the Maltese Falcon.

SPADE:   (SOUND: CHAIR SCRAPE) Thanks very much, Mr. Janeway, but if it's that kind of a caper, I'm not interested.

JANEWAY:   Now wait one minute, please, Mr. Spade. Allow me to finish. It is true that the Commonwealth Tankard bears the device of a Falcon. But it is no such troublesome object as your Maltese bird. Now here is all I want you to do, Mr. Spade.

(SOUND: HEAVY DESK DRAWER OPENED: PARCEL SET ON DESK)

This parcel contains your precious burden- the Commonwealth Tankard. You are to deliver this into the hand of my client, Dr. Jan Duroc, 1221 ½ Leavenworth Street, City, who will place in your hands an envelope addressed to me. This envelope will contain a not inconsiderable sum of money. Three hundred and twenty-five thousand dollars, to be exact. See that you count it.

SPADE: That's a lot of cash. Is this thing hot?

JANEWAY: My dear fellow, Janeway and company is no fly-by-night concern. This piece was purchased by me from the collection of the late Oliver H. Cromwell of this city. I can show you the bill of sale, signed by his daughter, Miss Patience Cromwell.

SPADE: I'd rather see what's in that package.

JANEWAY: Egad, sir, you are the cautious one! Very well, you shall feast you eyes on it.

(SOUND: PACKAGE UNWRAPPED) (TANKARD LIFTED FROM BOX AND SET ON TABLE)

There! There you are, Sir! The Commonwealth Tankard!

SPADE: (MUSIC SIMULTANEOUS) It didn't look like three hundred grand, but I'm no expert on antiques. It was a hunk of heavy, crudely carved silver, with a fancy handle, a hinged cover with a figure of a falcon about an inch and a half high perched on the edge of it. The tankard rested on three claw-shaped feet with the talons extended. I guessed it would hold about a quart and a half of beer or a fair-sized geranium plant, but it still didn't look like three hundred grand. Janeway picked it up as if it were a basket of eggs and held it over to the light. (ACCENT AND OUT)

JANEWAY: Here, sir! Here you see one of the reasons for its not inconsiderable value. The inscription- faint but still legible: "To O.C., Lord Protector of the Commonwealth, Upon the Occasion of His Accession to Power, from his loyal subject and loving kinsman, John Hampden, A.D. 1653. Have you any idea of the significance of that inscription, sir!

SPADE:      I'll take your word for it.

JANEWAY:    You need not! Leaf through the pages of history, and there you will find, writ high, the name of Oliver Cromwell, Lord Protector of the British Commonwealth. But that is only part of the history of this historic- er- (SEARCHES FOR WORD)

SPADE:      Beer mug. I'll just wrap this up again and get along with it, Mr. Janeway. (SOUND: PACKAGE BEING WRAPPED)

JANEWAY:    You understand, sir, that this is authentic, beyond the shadow of a doubt. The late Oliver H. Cromwell of this city, from whose collection it was taken, was a direct descendant of the illustrious Protector of the Commonwealth.

SPADE:      Very interesting, Mr. Janeway. Will you just hold your finger here while I tie this knot?

JANEWAY:    Oh, yes indeed. (SOUND: KNOT TIED) You might be interested in the history of this tankard before it fell into the possession of the Lord Protector.

SPADE:      Yeah, yeah, I'll just run this package on up the hill, and-

JANEWAY:    (EYES CLOSED) That priceless tankard, sir, was fashioned by the great 16th-century Chinese craftsman Chen Shu, (START SLOW FADE) (SOUND SPADES STEPS TIPTOE-ING OUT) who was brought to England in irons, in the year 1595. In irons, sir! They were struck off at Plymouth

in the royal presence, by His Majesty" Master of Horse-
(DOOR QUIETLY OPENED UNDER AND CLOSED
CUTTING OFF THE SPEECH)

PATIENCE:    Well, you made it faster than I expected!

SPADE:    Does he always go on like that?

PATIENCE:    He's good for a couple of hours before he even realizes
you sneaked out on him.

SPADE:    I sensed that.

PATIENCE:    (EFFORT) These typewriter desks. Always jammed up.
Lend me some muscle, will you, Mr. Spade. I'll clear a
space here for your package. (BIZ)

SPADE:    Hmmm. Nice gadget. Have to buy one for my secretary.
(SOUND: TYPEWRITER DESK:    HINGES, SPRINGS,
SNAPS INTO PLACE) There you are!

PATIENCE:    Thanks. Men are so useful. No office should be without one.

SPADE:    We also carry the large economy size for restaurants and
bar-rooms. Would you care to join me in a short beer?

PATIENCE:    I can't right now, but I'm here everyday, nine to five.
Here, don't forget your package. My regular department
is stock. Just ask the forelady for Cathy.

SPADE:    I'll remember that, Sweetheart.

PATIENCE:    I know you will.

SPADE:    (MUSIC: SIMULTANEOUS:) She gave me her "Must you
really go" Look Number 24A for warm afternoons, I gave
her "Will you kiss me now or later" Number 137596, and
if I hadn't been holding the package, I don't know what
would have happened. I fell out of the door and floated

up the hill to 1221 ½ Leavenworth. Dr. Andre Duroc met me at the door of his apartment. He was wearing a Chinese silk dressing gown, an expensive coat of tan, and a smile full of anxiety.

DUROC:    You have it! At last! The Commonwealth Tankard! Sit down, excuse me, I cannot wait to see it.

SPADE:    Take it easy, Doctor. That package is C.O.D.

DUROC:    (SOUND: PACKAGE UNWRAPPED) Of course. I have the money for you. Ah, now we shall se . . . (SOUND: TANKARD LIFTED FROM PACKAGE: SET DOWN) Snap on the light there. Mr. Spade, will you?

SOUND:    (LIGHT SWITCH)

MUSIC:    (STING AND UNDER)

SPADE:    It didn't take much light to see what had happened. The honey-headed little number in January's outer office had switched packages on me while I was helping her with the typewriter. The beer-mug I'd brought to Dr. Duroc was the same size and weight as the Commonwealth Tankard, but instead of the falcon of the cover and the date 1625, there was a bubble dancer done in plastic and the inscription read: "Yippee Milwaukee, Souvenir Beer Salesman's CONVENTION, 1945." The color drained out of Duroc's face, leaving a sticky yellow in place of his healthy tan. He stood speechless for a moment with the Milwaukee mug in his hands, then he exploded. (DUROC: "LIAR! THIEF! IMPOSTOR!") (SOUND: TANKARD THROWN: CRASHES: UPSETS A LAMP) I ducked just in time, and the phony tankard landed across the room. He stumbled towards me, grabbed me by the lapels, and hung there, drooling and jibbering.

DUROC:      Who are you? What is he trying to do to me? It's all the money I have. He agreed. What more does he want? Tell me! Tell me!

SPADE:      Doctor, what you need is a sedative. You've still got your dough. What are you losing?

DUROC:      The tankard, the tankard. I must have that tankard, do you hear me?

SPADE:      Yeah, it sounded like you said something about a tankard!

DUROC:      (WEEPS) He promised it to me. He promised. (SOBS)

SPADE:      Please, doctor. My suit. You're getting it all wet.

DUROC:      I don't care. I don't care whether I live or die, I want my tankard.

SPADE:      Doctor, I can't stand it. Don't cry like that. I'll try and find your tankard.

DUROC:      (STOPS CRYING) You will? You will find it? Oh, you are a nice man. You are not a liar, you are not an imposter, perhaps you are not even a thief!

MUSIC:      (BRIDGE AND TO B.G.)

SPADE:      I accepted Dr. Andre Duroc's apologies and left. When I got back to the Janeway Building, it was a little after five and the office workers were streaming out on their way home. In the lobby I punched the button for the automatic elevator and watched the lights blink on and off as it came down from the eighth floor.

(SOUND:     ELEVATOR DOORS OPEN) (BIZ: GIRLS EMERGE CHATTERING) Five girls go out of it. I let four of them brush past me. The fifth was carrying a package. I grabbed her by the arm and shoved her back in the elevator.

PATIENCE:    (LOW) Let go of me. Let me go.

SPADE:       I'll let you go. Back upstairs with me.

SOUND:       (ELEVATOR DOORS CLOSE: HUM OF ELEVATORS)

PATIENCE:    I won't go back there, do you hear me. I'll- (SOUND SCUFFLE)

SPADE:       Keep away from those buttons. I'm running this car.

PATIENCE:    You don't know you're doing. I've got to get out of here. I'll kill you I'll- (SCUFFLE)

SPADE:       Ouch! You bit me. That's not fair.

PATIENCE:    Will you stop this elevator!

SPADE:       Okay. (SOUND: EMERGENCY BUTTON: ELEVATOR STOPS ABRUPTLY)

PATIENCE:    That's the emergency button!

SPADE:       This is an emergency, Sweetheart. Now be a good girl and hand over the package.

PATIENCE:    No!

SPADE:       Okay, we'll just stay here for awhile.

SOUND:       (BUZZER AT IRREGULAR INTERVALS)

PATIENCE:    You'll have to kill me to get it.

SPADE:       I hope I don't have to. You're so young, you showed such great promise . . . .

PATIENCE:    I think you're really capable of it. But you wouldn't get away with it- not like this.

SPADE:       You're a thief, you're resisting arrest. I'd get away with it.

PATIENCE:     You seem very sure of that.

SPADE:         License Number 137596.

PATIENCE:     No! No! I'll scream. They'll hear me all over the building
              . . .

SPADE:         Come here . . .

PATIENCE:     (STARTS TO SCREAM. SMOTHERED AS SPADE KISSES
              HER)

(MUSIC SNEAK) (THEN: "MMMMMMM")

SPADE:         (MUSIC UNDER) It was a great love scene. We both en-
              joyed it a lot. I didn't know till we passed the fourth floor
              that part of that feeling on the pit of my stomach was the
              downward movement of the elevator. While I was get-
              ting a grip on the package, she'd managed to get at the
              automatic control panel and push the main floor button.
              (SOUND: ELEVATOR DOORS OPENED) When the el-
              evator stopped and the doors opened on the main floor
              lobby, I yanked the package away from her with one hand
              pushed her out of the car with the other.

(MUSIC:        ACCENT) (BIZ: PATIENCE REACTS) Before she even
              had time to look started (SOUND: ELEVATOR DOORS
              CLOSED), the package and I were on our way up to Mr.
              Janeway's office. (SOUND:REGISTER ELEVATOR HUM
              THEN OUT AND DOORS OPENED: STEPS ON COM-
              POSITION FLOOR: THEN OUT) I started down the
              corridor, but I stopped short of Janeway's door. Because
              then is when it opened and a white uniformed man came
              out, followed by a basket, followed by another white-
              uniformed man who was holding onto the other end of
              the basket. All four of them, the men, the basket, and

the corpse in the basket, were obviously headed for the morgue.

MUSIC:    (UP TO FIRST ACT CURTAIN)

ANNCR:    The makers of Wildroot Cream-Oil are presenting the weekly Sunday adventure of Dashiell Hammett's famous private detective . . . SAM SPADE!

MUSIC:    UP AND RESOLVES OUT

ANNCR:    Now! Here's important news on good grooming! Better than four out of five users of Wildroot Cream-Oil say they prefer Wildroot Cream-Oil to all other hair tonics. Here is new and even more conclusive evidence that Wildroot Cream-Oil is . . . "again and again . . . the choice of men . . . who put good grooming first." So if you want the well-groomed look that helps you get ahead, socially and on the job, listen: Recently, thousands of people from coast to coast who brought Wildroot Cream-Oil for the first time were asked: "How does Wildroot CREAM-Oil compare with the hair tonic you previously used?" The results were amazing. Better than four out of five said they preferred Wildroot Cream-Oil. And no wonder. It gives you the advantages that men consider most important Wildroot Cream-Oil grooms your hair neatly and naturally, relieves annoying dryness . . . and removes loose dandruff . . . What's more, non-alcoholic Wildroot Cream-Oil is the only leading hair tonic that contains soothing LANOLIN, that's like the oil of your skin. So ask for Wildroot Cream-Oil . . . "again and again the choice of men who put good grooming first."

MUSIC:    ACCENT AND HOLD

ANNCR:     And now back to "The Commonwealth Tankard" . . .
           tonight's adventure with SAM SPADE.

MUSIC:     UP INTO SECOND OVERTURE

MUSIC:     (SECOND OVERTURE AND TO B.G.)

SPADE:     The boys from the morgue loaded their stiff into the
           freight elevator, and went on their way. I took one peek
           through the door of Janeway's office and beat a hasty re-
           treat into a nearby broom closet. The office was swarm-
           ing with cops, and I assumed that Mr. Janeway had been
           the victim of foul play. I waited till the homicide boys had
           drifted out before I drifted in. The place was a shambles-
           paneling pried loose from the walls, filing cabinets over-
           turned, carpets ripped up, stuffing pulled out of furniture.
           The only thing they hadn't broken was the cooler, and
           that was transparent. None of it looked like police work
           except the fingerprint powder that was spread all over ev-
           erything and gave it an eerie look- like a bunch of ruins af-
           ter a light snowfall. While I stood there looking at it, that
           eerie feeling began to grow on me. The thing Janeway's
           office had been frisked for- the reason for the corpse I'd
           seen carried out in that morgue basket- was still in the
           package under my arm. I shifted it uneasily from one arm
           to the other, half-expecting the brown wrapping paper to
           burst into flames. The Commonwealth Tankard was get-
           ting hotter by the minute.

MUSIC:     (UP AND DOWN)

SPADE:     I went back to my apartment, locked myself in, shoved
           the bureau against the door, hung blankets over the win-
           dow blinds, turned out the lights, and unwrapped the
           tankard by the feeble glow of my Buck Rogers combined

pen, pencil, flashlight and aspirin-holder. There was nothing inside of the tankard, the falcon on the lid was all one piece, the handle was solid, and nothing was wrong with the claw-feet except they were kind of ugly. I held it to my ear like a seashell, it didn't even sound like a seashell. So I filled it with bourbon and sat down to think. There were no secret poison receptacles in it either, but after an hour or so, I felt more like King Charles the First's Master of Horse than the greatest private detective of them all. I swaggered over to the kitchenette, rinsed out the tankard, dried it carefully, and put it away in a diabolically clever hiding place- behind my dirty laundry in the oven of the gas stove.

MUSIC:      (UP & DOWN)

SPADE:      Up bedtimes, and fetched in the Chronicle from my doorstep. The headlines told me all I need to know:
They said: Art Dealer Murdered; Police Seek Blonde Mystery Woman; Theft of Commonwealth Tankard, Historic Relic, Believed Motive. According to the story, Merrill Janeway's body was lying unclaimed at the morgue. I decided to return the tankard to its rightful owner.

MUSIC:      (UP AND OUT)

SOUND:      (MORGUE FOOTSTEPS)

MAXIE:      (FADES ON) Ah, Sammy! Long time no see! Looking for a friend?

SPADE; Yeah, I've always got friends in the morgue, Maxie.

MAXIE:      What's the tag on this one?

SPADE:      Janeway

MAXIE:    Janeway. The one they took out of that office on Sutter Street?

SPADE:    The same, Maxie, the same. Anybody claim him yet?

MAXIE:    No, and don't look like they will.

SPADE:    Do me a favor, Maxie, put this with his things. It belonged to him.

MAXIE:    Sure. (FADES OFF A LITTLE) You know, Sam, I should have known you had something to do with this one. (FADES BACK ON) Boy, can you pick 'em.

SPADE:    I don't pick 'em Maxie, they pick me.

MAXIE:    I been handling stiffs fifteen-sixteen years, Sam, and I never seen the like of this one.

SPADE:    How's that? Bad shape?

MAXIE:    Bad! Listen, Sam, they bring this guy in, and we put him up on the slab, see? He looks pretty good for multiple contusions. Seemed like awful quick rigor, but we get 'em like that. So we get out the pump, you know- and I'm looking through the racing form, waiting for him to drain, and all of a sudden out of the corner of my eye I notice, and I get this whiff of formaldehyde. What do you think come out of him, Sam?

SPADE:    Napoleon brandy?

MAXIE:    Naw! Embalming fluid!

SPADE:    Huh?

MAXIE:    That's what I said. No blood, Sam. Embalming fluid. Now I ask you, how could a man carry on a business in that condition?

SPADE:     Let me see him, Maxie, will you?

MAXIE:     Sure. Come on in. (SOUND: STEPS ON SLIGHT ECHO: RUNNING WATER BACKGROUND) Lessee- G-H-I-yeah, here it is- right between Jason and James. Merrill Janeway. (SOUND: DRAWER PULLED OUT) Hiya, Merrill, ya spook! Looks real cute, don't he, Sam?

SPADE:     You don't know how cute, Maxie.

MAXIE:     I dunno, Sammy. I made a real study of this one. Lookit there. Right there by the left temple. Whaddaya see?

SPADE:     Nothing.

MAXIE:     That's what's cute. Now watch here. Pardon me, Merrill. There! Now I ask you, Sam. Full of embalming fluid, and a hole in his head an inch deep. Does that make sense?

MUSIC:     (IN AND TO B.G.)

SPADE:     It was beginning to, in a gruesome sort of way. The wax plug that Maxie had removed from the head wound was shaped like a falcon's claw. (MUSIC ACCENT) I didn't touch it. I had Maxie put it in an envelope and I carried it out with me. My next stop was the newspaper files of the Chronicle, where I spent the next couple of hours looking over the clips on your illustrious family, Mrs. Cromwell . . . The pictures of your husband, Oliver H. Cromwell, looked about the way I expected they would. The society pages carried some pictures of you (retouched)

And of your daughter Patience Cromwell. (unretouched) I spend a fascinating half-hour reading between the lines of your husband's obituary. It said he was a philanthropist, a vivid and forceful personality, and would be mourned by the thousands of loyal employees of the Cromwell Industries. By which they meant that he was a hypocritical ill-tempered old miser whose factories were all sweatshops. It also said he had died of a heart attack while climbing the stairs in his Burlingame mansion. That's where I left him and called you, Mrs. Cromwell. Then I went back to my apartment.

SOUND:     (DOOR UNLOCKED)

MUSIC:     (ACCENT AND OUT)

PATIENCE:  Sam, I-. Please, Sam, don't turn me away until-

SOUND:     (DOOR KICKED SHUT)

SPADE:     How did you get in here?

PATIENCE:  The janitor. I told him I was your sister.

SPADE:     (LAUGHS)

PATIENCE:  What's so funny?

SPADE:     Me as you brother. I knew I'd make the social register sooner or later.

PATIENCE:  What do you mean by that?

SPADE:     You never did look like anybody's secretary to me, Sweetheart, and when you bit me in the elevator I knew you'd been to Finishing School.

PATIENCE:  All right, I'll tell you everything. I'm Patience Cromwell.

SPADE:     You admit it. I admire your courage.

PATIENCE:  Please, Sam, don't. Don't you try to hurt me, too. I know I've lied to you and gotten you in a lot of trouble. But this is the truth. There's nowhere I can go, no one I can trust. Please let me stay here.

SPADE:        Can you cook?

PATIENCE:     I'd be willing to try. You won't believe this, but I'd do almost anything for you.

SPADE:        This joint needs a woman's touch. They all tell me that.

PATIENCE:     I'm not as useless as I look.

SPADE:        I know that, Sweetheart. But if we're going to play house, we've got to start with a clean one.

PATIENCE:     All right, Sam.

SPADE:        There's a lot of dirty dishes in the sink. Let's start with the tankard.

PATIENCE:     I had to get it back, Sam. My mother found out that I stole it from Father's collection and sold it to Mr. Janeway.

SPADE:        When was that?

PATIENCE:     Right after Father- right after Father's death, that is. I had to have the money. Mother wouldn't help me. Father was an elderly man-we were never very close- I never felt it was irreverent or anything. But when mother found out, she was furious. She threatened to have me thrown into jail if I didn't get the tankard back. I didn't have the money- so the only way I could get it was to steal it. And that's the true story about the Commonwealth Tankard.

SPADE:        I like it. You tell it very well, Sweetheart. Now let's have the true story about the Commonwealth Tankard.

PATIENCE:     You don't believe me?

SPADE:        Sure I believe you- just like I believe that your father had a heart attack and merely fell down the stairs, just like I believe that Dr. Duroc never got paid off for the death certificate.

PATIENCE:    You're guessing. You're playing at being a detective. Things aren't always what they look like on the surface.

SPADE:       I know just what you mean, Sweetheart. Here. Here's what you're trying to tell me, isn't it?

PATIENCE:    What-? What is that?

SPADE:       That's a hunk of a special kind of wax. Undertakers use it sometimes to make a stiff look pretty for the funeral. Funny shape isn't it. Like a falcon's claw. Matches the legs on that tankard.

PATIENCE:    What are you going to do with it?

SPADE:       Keep it- for evidence if I need it.

PATIENCE:    I was afraid you were going to see that. And I'm sorry you did, because now I'll have to try and make you give it back to me.

SOUND:       (SAFETY CATCH ON GUN)

SPADE:       Now wait a minute, angel. On you that gun looks terrible. Put it away.

PATIENCE:    Sam, I mean it.

SPADE:       They're looking for you for one murder. Another one isn't going to help you any. Especially with that story you tell-the true story of the Commonwealth Tankard, authorized version.

PATIENCE:    I didn't kill Mr. Janeway.

SPADE:       I know that. I'm trying to help you.

PATIENCE:    How can I believe you? How can I know it isn't just an-other trick?

SPADE:    You can't. I'm a detective, Sweetheart.

PATIENCE:    Stop! You're asking for it.

SPADE:    Drop it, angel.

PATIENCE:    No. No, I- (BREAKS) (SOUND:   GUN   DROPPED) Oh, Sam, Sam! I couldn't. No matter what happens. Hold me close, Sam. I'm so scared. Hold me close.

SPADE:    (COMING OUT OF CLINCH) That's better.

PATIENCE:    I know now I can trust you, can't I, Sam? (PAUSE) Can't I, darling?

SOUND:    DOOR BUZZER

PATIENCE:    Sam, don't answer. Please don't answer it, darling.

SPADE:    If it's the cops they'll bust in anyway.

PATIENCE:    You! The janitor told you I was here. You called them from downstairs. You let me think- (SOBS)

SPADE:    Shut up. I didn't call the cops. It's your mother.

PATIENCE:    Why? You haven't found out-anything, have you?

SPADE:    Get out of sight. There's a closet behind the wall-bed.

PATIENCE:    But-

SPADE:    And don't make any noise. (SOUND: STEPS: DOOR OPENED)

MRS. CROMWELL:    Mr. Spade?

SPADE:    Come on in, Mrs. Cromwell.

SOUND:     (DOOR CLOSED: STEPS)

MRS. C:    I've been to the morgue, Mr. Spade. I've claimed my hus-
           band's body. I can never thank you enough.

SPADE:     Mrs. Cromwell, do you know that your daughter is in a
           very bad spot?

MRS. C:    Isn't there anything we can do, Mr. Spade? If I could only
           find her, talk to her . . .

SPADE:     Nuts. You saw her this afternoon and the two of you
           fixed up a story to tell me. I've already heard it, I don't
           believe it, so don't tell it to me again.

MRS. C:    How much of the truth do you know?

SPADE:     That your husband was murdered by a blow on the head
           from the Commonwealth Tankard and that either you or
           your daughter or the two of you together hit him.

MRS. C:    Well . . . you don't leave me much to tell. Only this, Mr.
           Spade. I did it. Patience had nothing whatever to-

PATIENCE:  (OFF) Mother!

MRS. C:    Patience! What are you doing here?

PATIENCE:  (FADE ON) I'm not going to let you take the blame alone.
           Mother.

MRS. C:    My poor foolish darling. You're young, you have your
           whole life ahead of you, my dear. Please let me handle
           this in my own way.

SPADE:     How about a little truth telling from both of you? I can't
           really help you without it.

PATIENCE:  I think he really does want to help us, mother.

SPADE:        Thanks, Sweetheart.

MRS. C:       Well, the night it happened, Patience was having one of her quarrels with her father. I heard their voices in his study. It was over her infatuation for Andre-Dr. Duroc. They spoke such violent words that I became frightened and tried to intervene. My husband had an uncontrollable temper. He was-hurting Patience. I tried to separate them and he flew into an insane rage. He picked up the poker from the fireplace and raised it to strike me. The Commonwealth Tankard was just behind me on the mantelpiece. I reached for it and threw it at him to stop him. It hit him in the head. Then I ran out of the room. He came after me. I ran down the stairs. He must have stumbled-anyway he fell.

SPADE:        Why didn't you tell the story before? That isn't murder-it isn't even manslaughter.

MRS. C:       I'm afraid it is, Mr. Spade. The doctor arrived a little before he died . . . He said the blow from the tankard was definitely what killed him.

SPADE:        What did he charge for calling it heart failure on the death certificate?

PATIENCE:     What does it matter? What does any of it matter now?

SPADE:        Why did you sell that tankard to Janeway?

PATIENCE:     He said he had a customer in England for it. I thought it was the best way to get it far, far away. Then I read on the paper that it was being sold in San Francisco for ten times its actual value. I suspected the buyer was Andre Duroc.

SPADE:        Why?

PATIENCE:     You asked what his price was for that death certificate. Well, I agreed to marry him. But Mother-

MRS. C:        I told him Patience had no intention of marrying him. That's when he bought the Tankard with the idea of blackmailing us.

SPADE:         Who snatched your husband's body and why?

MRS. C:        Mr. Janeway helped me.

PATIENCE:     Mother! How could Mr. Janeway-?

SOUND:         (DOOR BUZZER)

SPADE:         Pardon me.

SOUND:         (STEPS DOOR OPEN)

JANEWAY:      (COMING ON) Ah, Mr. Spade! I find you in! Egad, and here's that courageous little woman, Mrs. Cromwell. And that naughty- but lovely-young woman, Patience. So ineptly named. Ah, what a lot of trouble you've caused young lady.

PATIENCE:     Mother, I think you owe us an explanation.

MRS. C:        I started to tell you, Patience . . .

JANEWAY:      Allow me, Mrs. Cromwell. Your mother has told me everything Patience. She came to me yesterday, and told me what a mistake I had made in selling the tankard to that young sawbones, Dr. Duroc. I admired her courage as well as her- ah-ah-

SPADE:         Money?

JANEWAY:      Personality, Mr. Spade. I believe that is the word. Well to make a long story short. I felt I must do something to make amends. It occurred to me that the tankard was no threat at all without the body it had left its mark upon. So Penelope- Mrs. Cromwell- and I- went to the- er- cemetery- with my station wagon- and her shovel and- well- then there was the question of what to do with it. So I hit my capital idea as passing it off as me. That way it would stay in a morgue icebox until we could manage to get the tankard back. As a detective what do you think of that, Mr. Spade?

SPADE: As a detective, I don't get it. How did you hope to fool anyone into thinking that was a fresh corpse?

JANEWAY: Well it was embalmed.

SPADE: That's what I mean. Embalming fluid in it.

JANEWAY: I say, that was an oversight, eh, Penelope? But by gad, we put it over, didn't we? Ho ho. Ho ho ho. Ho ho- (STOPS ON SOUND CUE)

SOUND: (DOOR CLOSED OFFSTAGE)

DUROC: (FADES ON) So you think you put it over. Janeway?

PATIENCE: Andre!

JANEWAY: Now look here, Duroc.

SPADE: You're late, Doctor.

DUROC: I wouldn't have missed this little comedy for anything. Thank you for leaving the door open for me, Mr. Spade.

PATIENCE: Sam, you knew he was coming!

SPADE: Now don't start that again, Sweetheart. Go get yourself a glass of milk.

DUROC:      No! Everyone will please stay in this room. Yes, you too, Spade. I'm holding the gun now.

SPADE:      What do you want?

DUROC:      The tankard- and the body. And no one leaves here till I have both of them.

SPADE:      Did you bring the money?

DUROC:      I've got it.

SPADE:      Okay. Mrs. Cromwell, get on that phone. Call the morgue. The tankard's there, too.

MRS. C:     Mr. Spade, I trusted you.

SPADE:      Stop mouthing. Get on that phone.

DUROC:      You're a nice man, an honest man, Mr. Spade. The only person here who has kept his word.

MUSIC:      (PUNCTUATES UNDER)

SPADE:      After you had made your phone call, Mrs. Cromwell, we sat and waited. We didn't have to wait long. Maxie was prompt. (SOUND BUZZER: STEPS DOOR OPENED)

MAXIE:      Here's the package, Sam. Just like you ordered it.

SPADE:      Thanks, Maxie.

MAXIE:      Well, I'll be getting back to the shop now . . .

DUROC:      One moment!

MAXIE:      Yeah?

DUROC:      Where is that body? I must have Cromwell's body!

MAXIE:      Hey, Sam, who is this guy, some ghoul or something?

SPADE:      Nah, just a medical student. See you around, Maxie.

MAXIE:      Okay, they're your clients; I'll get 'em later. Goodbye, all, see you at the morgue, (FADE) and I ain't kiddin!

SOUND:      (STEPS:    DOOR CLOSED)

DUROC:      I said you were a man of your word, Mr. Spade. I was wrong.

SPADE:      No you weren't. Here. I'll take the wraps off of it. (SOUND: PACKAGE UNWRAPPED) (TANKARD SET ON TABLE) There you are, Duroc. The Commonwealth Tankard.

DUROC:      Yes. That is good! Now when do I get the body?

SPADE:      You're got it now . . . That's Cromwell's body inside the tankard. Mrs. Cromwell ordered the body cremated . . . at my suggestion, Duroc. So much more-portable that way.

SOUND:      TANKARD POUNDED ON TABLE.

DUROC:      Ashes- nothing but ashes! It's worthless now. You are all thieves, imposters, liars!

PATIENCE:   (LAUGHS) Oh, Sam, I just can't help it. If he weren't so wicked he'd be funny.

DUROC:      Go ahead, laugh. You would pay me anyway if you had any decency. I ridded you of that tyrant, whom you both hated. He would have killed you if he lived long enough. I saved your lives.

PATIENCE:   You-you killed father?

DUROC:      Yes, yes, I am the one that made you rich. I! I! Why do you think I sent you out of the room while I examined the body? Because he was not dead enough. I made sure he would not stand any longer between you and me, my darling. I took the tankard, and hit him again. (SOBS) And look what you are doing to me. You owe me. You must pay. (BREAKS DOWN COMPLETELY)

JANEWAY:     Egad, the fellow's mad! Come Penelope.

MRS. C:     Oh, Merrill, how can we ever thank you.

JANEWAY:     Nonsense, all in a day's work, m'dear. Come, I'll escort you home. Oh. Don't forget Oliver.

MRS. C:     Oliver?

JANEWAY:     In the tankard, my dear, remember?

MRS. C:     Oh, but really, don't you think it would be rather-?

JANEWAY:     Quite right. Three's a crowd. Patience!

PATIENCE:     Yes, Mr. Janeway?

JANEWAY:     Look after your father. Your mother's had a hard day.

MUSIC:     BRIDGE & TO B.G.

SPADE:     And that Mrs. Cromwell is the crop. You know by this time that Duroc went quickly when the cops came after him; Patience went quickly home a little later. She's still a little mixed about things in general. Frankly, I think she still doesn't trust me. And frankly I don't blame her. Period. End of Report.

MUSIC:     (THEME AND TO B.G.)

ANNCR:     Wouldn't it be great if you could be absolutely sure about your appearance- especially the appearance of your hair and scalp? There's a way, you know- Wildroot's famous

Close-Up Test. Stand in front of your mirror, and take a close-up look at your hair and scalp. You may be startled by what you see! Signs of truly unruly hair, dryness or loose dandruff tell you, you need Wildroot Cream-Oil right away! Wildroot Cream-Oil grooms your hair neatly and naturally- keeps it handsomely in place, all summer long. You see, Wildroot Cream-Oil is non-alcoholic and contains soothing LANOLIN . . . And by the way, remember: Now you can get Wildroot Cream-Oil in handy tubes. Up till recently Wildroot Cream-Oil in tube form is economical to use, easy to pack . . . just right for that summer vacation trip or the bathroom cabinet. So get a tube or bottle of famous non-alcoholic Wildroot Cream-Oil.

MUSIC:     THEME

ANNCR:     The Adventures of Sam Spade . . . Dashiell Hammett's famous private detective is produced and directed by William Spier; Sam Spade is played by Howard Duff. "The Adventures of Sam Spade" is written for radio by Bob Tallman and Gil Doud, with musical direction by Lud Gluskin. This is Dick Joy reminding you that next Sunday author Dashiell Hammett and producer William Spier join forces for another adventure with Sam Spade brought to you by Wildroot Cream-Oil . . . again and again . . . the choice of men who put good grooming first.

MUSIC:     (GOODNIGHT SWEETHEART TO:)

ANNCR:     Smart girls use Wildroot Cream-Oil too- for quick good grooming and to relieve dryness between permanents. Mother's say it's a grand for training children's hair-

THIS IS CBS . . . THE COLUMBIA . . . BROADCASTING SYSTEM . . .

# THE ADVENTURES OF SAM SPADE
## "CAPER WITH TEN CLUES"

PROGRAM #3
5:00 – 5:30 PM
SUNDAY, OCTOBER 13, 1945
9:00 – 9:30 PM

ANNCR:    The hair-raising adventures of Sam Spade, detective, brought to you by the makers of Wildroot Cream-Oil for the hair.

MUSIC:    (PUNCTUATION . . . UP INTO TRILL . . . INTO)

SOUND:    PHONE BELL . . . LIFT RECEIVER

EFFIE:    Sam Spade, Detective Agency.

SPADE:    (FILTER) Hello, Sweetheart.

EFFIE:    Sam! My, you sound tired!

SPADE:    I am. Tough caper, Sweetheart. All those clues to follow up.

EFFIE:    I counted them. Nine. Which one paid off?

SPADE:    The tenth.

EFFIE:     Oh. I thought there were only nine.

SPADE:     Nine that didn't pay off. That was the tenth clue.

EFFIE:     I don't understand . . .

SPADE:     You will, Sweetheart, you will. I'm coming right over to dictate my report.

MUSIC:     (THEME)

ANNCR:     Dashiell Hammett, America's leading detective fiction writer and creator of Sam Spade, the hard-boiled private eye, and William Spier, radio's outstanding producer-director of mystery and crime drama, join their talents to make your hair stand on end with the Adventures of Sam Spade . . .

MUSIC:     (ACCENT)

ANNCR:     . . . presented each Sunday by Wildroot Cream-Oil, the non-alcoholic hair tonic that will put your hair back in place again, grooming it neatly, naturally, the way you want it. Men, why take a chance of displeasing the lady in your life? 97 out of a hundred girls, according to a recent survey, dislike a man whose hair is unkempt or slicked down looking. So let Wildroot Cream-Oil groom yours neatly and naturally, which, as our survey shows- is just the way girls like to see it. At the same time, Wildroot Cream-Oil relieves dryness and removes loose ugly dandruff. There's not a drop of alcohol in Wildroot Cream-Oil. What's more, it contains soothing LANOLIN. So ask for Wildroot Cream-Oil at your drug or toilet goods counter.

MUSIC:     (SNEAK UNDER)

| ANNCR: | And now, Wildroot brings to the air the greatest private detective of 'em all . . . .in . . . The Adventures of Sam Spade. |
|---|---|
| MUSIC: | (UP TO OVERTURE) |
| MUSIC: | (OVERTURE) |
| SOUND: | DOOR . . . .STEPS |
| EFFIE: | (FADING IN) Oh, Sam. Just a minute. |
| SPADE: | What are you doing? |
| EFFIE: | Feeding the ants. |
| SPADE: | Feeding what? |
| EFFIE: | The ants. It's an ant palace. A man sold it to me, isn't it cute? |
| SPADE: | No, but he must have been. What's it for? |
| EFFIE: | It's educational. You watch the ants through the glass and you learn a lot. You see. These big ones with the sharp jaws are soldier ants, and ones that are carrying things are the slaves. |
| SPADE: | Is that so? |
| EFFIE: | Ow! Sam, what are you doing? |
| SPADE: | I am a soldier ant. Get your book and carry it into my office. |
| EFFIE: | Yes, master. |
| SOUND: | STEPS CHAIR DRAWER . . . BOTTLES |
| SPADE: | Date: October 13th, 1946. To: Mrs. Creda Dexter Gantvoort. From: Samuel Spade: License Number 137596. Dear Creda: |

EFFIE:      Hmmmmm.

SPADE:      The following report will explain the items on the enclosed bill for services rendered. If you'd rather not pay same, I will sell this to Daffling Detective Magazine, to cover my losses. (MUSIC: SNEAK) As you well remember, it was a little over a week ago that my secretary, Miss Effie Perine, came into my private office, and with a leer on her face, announced that a Miss Dexter was outside clamoring for an interview. I told her to show you in. She did.

MUSIC:      (SWELLS VERY BRIEFLY AND OUT)

CREDA:      I hardly know where to begin, Mr. Spade. It's all rather embarrassing.

SPADE:      It always is when people come to me, Miss Dexter. Go ahead.

CREDA:      Well, it's about my father.

SPADE:      What is?

CREDA:      You may have read in the papers . . . I'm to be married to Jacob Gantvoort tomorrow afternoon.

SPADE:      Is there a Jacob Gantvoort, Junior?

CREDA:      No, there's only one. He's-my fiancé.

SPADE:      And the wedding's tomorrow. Think he'll last that long?

CREDA:      I know many people think it's odd- the- discrepancy in our ages. That's why my father has been such a problem. He says he won't permit me to marry a man older than he is. He says I'm throwing away my youth for-

SPADE:      For twenty-five million bucks?

CREDA:     I see you understand my problem, Mr. Spade.

SPADE:     Just what do you want me to do?

CREDA:     I want you to keep your eye on my father- see that he doesn't do anything rash.

SPADE:     Such as?

CREDA:     Such as this.

SOUND:     PAPER HANDLED

SPADE:     Poison pen letter?

CREDA:     Read it.

SPADE:     "You old goat. If you go through with this farcical wedding to my daughter, I will beat your brains out with the typewriter this note is written on. Signed, Madden Dexter." Hmmm.

CREDA:     Daddy has a nasty temper.

SPADE:     He has indeed. Any other exhibits.

CREDA:     Yes, this telegram. Daddy's on his way here New York now. The train arrives in Oakland at ten o'clock tonight.

SPADE:     And you want me to pick him up there and tail him?

CREDA:     I hate the idea of having him followed, somehow. Perhaps you could get on the train at Sacramento and get acquainted with him. He's quite fond of drinking, you know . . .

SPADE:     You want me to get him plastered and keep him that way until after the wedding. That it?

CREDA:     I'll leave the method to your discretion, Mr. Spade.

SPADE:     How much money do you have with you?

CREDA:      A hundred dollars or so . . .

SPADE:      You can leave that to my discretion, too.

MUSIC:      BRIDGES TO B.G.

SPADE:      That evening I hopped a plane to Sacramento and arrived in plenty of time to meet the Transcon from Chicago. (SOUND: TRAIN IN STATION) I found Car 120 and walked down the corridor to Drawing Room B, where your father's wire said he'd be traveling. (SOUND: RAPPING ON DOOR) Rapped on the door, and-

SOUND:      (COMPARTMENT DOOR OPENED)

BONFILS:    Eh? Who are you, sir?

SPADE:      You Madden Dexter?

BONFILS:    No, but come in, sir, come in!

SPADE:      Thanks.

SOUND:      DOOR CLOSED

BONFILS:    Gets dashed lonesome traveling. Three thousand miles, you know. Have a drink, sir. I don't recall seeing you before on the trip. Come all the way across?

SPADE:      I just got on.

BONFILS:    Looking for this chap Dexter, eh? Drink?

SPADE:      Thanks.

SOUND:      DRINK POURED . . . SELTZER BOTTLE

SPADE:      No fizz in mine.

BONFILS:    As you wish. Ah, nothing like whiskey to take the edge off these beastly accommodations they give you on American trains.

SPADE:      You English?

BONFILS:    Bonfils is my name. Emil Bonfils. A citizen of the world, sir. Another drink; Say when, sir.

SPADE:      Just to the top off the glass.

SOUND:      DRINK POURED

BONFILS:    So! You're a detective.

SPADE:      Does it show?

BONFILS:    Come, sir! Why else does a man get on a train at Sacramento to meet a man who's going to San Francisco?

SPADE:      You tell me!

BONFILS:    (LAUGHS) A drink, sir?

SPADE:      I really shouldn't. My kidneys, you know.

BONFILS:    Ah, this Dexter chap . . . What's he wanted for, Eh? Hmmm?

SPADE:      The way I got it, he's not wanted.

BONFILS:    Nuisance, eh?

SPADE:      His daughter asked me to look after him. He drinks, it seems.

BONFILS:    (EXPLODES INTO LAUGHTER:    CHOKING ON HIS DRINK) I say, that's capital. Used to be fathers sent detectives to look after their daughter on trains. And now—another drink, sir!

SPADE:      (WOOZILY) Okay. Good whisky . . . capital . . .

BONFILS:    (CHUCKLES) I recall an indecent that occurred many years ago. I was on the Stamboul train on my way to . . .

(SOUND:    GLASS DROPS: BREAKS) (MUSIC  UNDER:)

I say, what's the matter, old chap? Getting sleepy? Bless my soul, the man's passed out!

SPADE:    I could still see his face dimly across the compartment. He was still talking, but the sound of his words had faded away. Then he faded away, too.

MUSIC:    (PUNCTUATES AND TO B.G.)

SPADE:    Two conductors shook me into semi-consciousness four hours later and helped me stagger off the train at Oakland. I was still groggy when I got off the ferry across the bay in San Francisco. I was mad, when I got to your place, Creda. The great Spade laid low by knock-out drops! When I rang your buzzer (SOUND: BUZZER HONKS INSIDE), the noise it made sounded like the razzberry I was giving myself for my brilliant night's work.

SOUND:    STEPS WITHIN: DOOR OPENS

CREDA:    Oh, Mr. Spade. Come in.

SOUND:    DOOR CLOSED . . . STEPS

SPADE:    Here's your hundred dollars, Miss Dexter, less the price of transportation.

CREDA:    Don't be silly. Keep it. It's not your fault.

SPADE:    What isn't my fault?

CREDA:    That you . . . couldn't find father on the train. He wasn't on it.

SPADE:    Oh?

CREDA:    Here's a wire from him. It was delivered just an hour ago. Dad's still in New York.

SPADE:      Well, it looks like he's not going to beat anybody to death with a typewriter . . . or anything else. (PAUSE) What's the caper, Sweetheart?

CREDA:      I don't understand you.

SPADE:      I think you do. Is Bonfils in it with you?

CREDA:      I never heard of anybody named Bonfils.

SPADE:      Creda, I think you're a suspicious character.

CREDA:      Why does everybody treat me as a criminal simply because I'm going to marry Jacob Gantvoort? My father, Charles- even you, a stranger.

SPADE:      Who's Charles?

CREDA:      His son. Oh, I can see his point . . . I'll be his stepmother and he's a year older than I am. Silly, isn't it?

SPADE:      I wouldn't like you for my stepmother . . . I don't think.

CREDA:      (LAUGHS) Would you like some coffee?

SPADE:      Yeah.

CREDA:      I don't know what happened tonight, Mr. Spade, but if it was because of me, I'd like to make it up to you somehow.

SPADE:      Make that coffee. Then we'll discuss how.

MUSIC:      (BRIDGE AND TO B.G.)

SPADE:      When I left your place it must have been around four a.m. My watch had stopped, and I'd fallen asleep at least once. I walked down the hill to my office. There was a big car- a Hispanic suiza- parked outside the building, and there was a light on up in my shop.

| | |
|---|---|
| SOUND: | STEPS UP STAIRS AND DOWN CORRIDOR |
| SPADE: | I went up the stairs and down the corridor to my door. I opened it, and- (MUSIC: PUNCTUATE) I'll spare you the details. My impression was of something that had once been a rather frail, grey-haired old man. It was hard to make out what his face looked like. On the back of his head- well, those things weren't the worst of it anyway. The worst of it was- he was still alive- and still conscious. |
| GANTVOORT: | (IN PAIN) Creda- said she- came here- couldn't get- farther. |
| SPADE: | You're Jacob Gantvoort? |
| GANTVOORT: | Yes- Yes . . . |
| SPADE: | Who did this to you? |
| GANTVOORT: | Dexter. |
| SPADE: | Madden Dexter? Creda's father? |
| GANTVOORT: | Mmmmm-Dexter. (PANICKY) Creda! Creda! (GASPS: GROANS) |
| MUSIC: | (PUNCTUATES) |
| SOUND: | STEPS . . . PHONE DIALED |
| DUNDY: | Homicide. |
| SPADE: | Dundy? This is Sam Spade. There's a man named Jacob Gantvoort here in my office. He's dead. I think he was beaten to death with a typewriter. |
| MUSIC: | (UP TO FIRST ACT CURTAIN) |
| MUSIC: | (ACCENT AND HOLD) |

ANNCR:      And now back to "Caper with Ten Clues" tonight's ad-
            venture with . . . SAM SPADE.

MUSIC:      (UP INTO SECOND OVERTURE AND TO B.G.)

SPADE:      While Dundy and the homicide boys were on the way
            over, I sat in my outer office. I'm not usually squeamish
            about such things, but I didn't like being reminded of what
            Jacob Gantvoort's killer had done to him. An hour later, af-
            ter Dundy had asked me all the questions I cared to answer
            and a few others I didn't hear, Gantvoort Junior, young
            Charles, arrived to identify the body. The typical Holly-
            wood version of a pampered rich man's son, a little too
            handsome, a little too blue-eyed, a little too graceful, a little
            too much grip to his handshake. Sergeant Polhaus pulled
            the sheet off the body, and the young men stuck a cigarette
            between his lips as be bent over to get a closer look.

CHARLES:    Hmmm? Yeah. Yeah, that's father all right. I say, sir, do
            you have a light?

SOUND:      MATCH STRUCK

DUNDY:      I think you might at least take your hat off, sonny. What's
            the matter? Didn't you and the old gentleman get along?

CHARLES:    That's an impertinent question. I suppose you have to ask
            it. No, we didn't. We haven't spoken for the last two
            years. Anything more you want me to identify?

DUNDY:      Yeah, this stuff- we took it off the body and out of his car,
            where it happened.

CHARLES:    You mean you want me to tell you whether these things
            belonged to or had any connection with my father?

DUNDY:      That's the idea.

CHARLES:    One: The typewriter- not his- definitely not. Two: That wallet- not his. Three: Gold cigar-cutter-preposterous-didn't smoke. Four: A derby hat? Are you kidding?

DUNDY:    Well, well - you've a very alert young man, Mr. Gantvoort.

CHARLES:    Maybe it would be more help if I told you what's not here that should be. (RAPIDLY) One: Right shoe is missing. Two: His hearing aid-deaf as a post. Three: His shirt studs-rubies. Four: Woolen vest-always cold. Five: Pill box- with pepsin tablets- took 'em after every meal- indigestion . . . Hmmmm. That's all.

DUNDY:    Well, that's a great deal. We have nine valuable clues!

CHARLES:    Yes. And you're sure Madden Dexter is in New York?

DUNDY:    Positive. We checked by phone. (CLEARS THROAT) Well, I guess we've finished here. Sam. Take it out, boys. Coming along, Mr. Gantvoort? Not that you need to-

CHARLES:    No, thank you, Lieutenant. I'm a little tired from all this. I think I'll just sit here for a minute if this gentleman doesn't mind.

DUNDY:    Well . . . goodbye again, then.

SPADE:    Goodbye to you, Lieutenant Dundy!

SOUND:    DOOR CLOSED

CHARLES:    (SUDDENLY) Now, Mr. Spade, I want to know what your connection is with Creda Dexter!

SPADE:    (CHUCKLES) She's my client.

CHARLES:    Accomplice is more like it!

SPADE:    How did you guess?

CHARLES:    Pretty smart apple, aren't you. Well, I know all about it. I know she came to your office and I know you went to her house. I followed her here and you there.

SPADE:    Everybody wants to get into the act.

CHARLES:    She murdered my father and you helped her.

SPADE:    Look, sonny, you've got some wrong ideas about Creda. She doesn't kill the goose that lays the golden eggs- not before the eggs are laid. Not Creda.

CHARLES:    Are you trying to tell me you didn't know my old man was secretly married to her yesterday afternoon- that he signed over his entire fortune to her- lock, stock and barrel?

SPADE:    Pardon me while I drop dead.

CHARLES:    I'm going to prosecute you, Spade. Put that in your pipe and smoke it!

SPADE:    Well, since you've been so nice to me, I'm gonna give you a little tip.

CHARLES:    Yeah, what?

SPADE:    Those nine clues of yours. Uh- uh. It's the tenth clue that's going the break the caper.

CHARLES:    Tenth clue?

SPADE:    Yes. That fact that those nine are phonies. You see? That's the tenth clue!

MUSIC:    (BRIDGE)

SOUND:    DOOR SLAMMED

CREDA:    Sam- what-?

SPADE:      I've seen Charles, Creda. You're going to do some talking.

CREDA:      What did he tell you? Sam, darling, I swear-

SPADE:      Stop acting and talk! (FURIOUS) I don't like it. I don't
            mind being sent on a goose chase and being given knock-
            out drops if I was stupid enough to- But I don't like to
            see a frail old man with his head beaten to a pulp- dying
            with your name on his lips when you're the one that was
            responsible for all his misery.

CREDA:      How could I have known it would end like that? How
            could I have known? (SOBS)

SPADE:      Stop that. (SLAP) Stop bawling.

CREDA:      (GASPS) You struck me.

SPADE:      That's right.

CREDA:      (FRIGHTENED) We didn't kill him. We never intended
            to. I swear we didn't.

SPADE:      What did you do?

CREDA:      Well, it was Charles's idea. I was to flirt with the old man
            and talk him into signing over the estate to me- before the
            marriage if possible. But Jacob was so kind . . . I had to go
            through with it . . . I couldn't have borne hurting him like
            that. Charles was furious, of course, thought I was trying
            to double cross him.

SPADE:      You must be quite a talker- twenty five million bucks just
            like that.

CREDA:      Oh, it was easy. You see he was so determined that
            Charles shouldn't inherit anything from him . . . if he
            signed the whole thing over to me, legally, while he was

still alive, he thought it would be out of Charles's reach forever- no wills to be contested or anything. That's all, Sam- honestly.

SPADE:      I fell asleep while you were making coffee this morning. You must have gone out. Where did you go?

CREDA:      I can't tell you that.

SPADE:      Not even if you die for Gantvoort's murder?

CREDA:      Not even then.

MUSIC:      (BRIDGE AND TO BACKGROUND)

SPADE:      I found a slip of paper on her telephone pad. It said: E.B. St. Mark. Ten minutes later I was at the St. Mark and mushing across a carpet with a nap three inches thick in Bonfils' penthouse suite. He was standing in the middle of it like a becalmed schooner.

BONFILS:    Well, sir! So we meet again! I owe you an apology.

SPADE:      Shut up!

BONFILS:    Well, sir, you needn't take umbrage. You came here! I didn't send for you. Mr. Spade, you persist in stupidly believing that I am Madden Dexter, traveling incognito- I assure you that this is not the case. Since you believed that I was Dexter and you had been employed to look after Dexter, I should have had the nuisance of being followed around by you all that evening. Nobody likes that.

SPADE:      Especially if he has a murder to commit. You did kill Gantvoort didn't you?

BONFILS:    I mean to talk to you about that. I've a proposition to lay before you. Hear me out.

SPADE:      I'm listening.

BONFILS:    Last week I was on my way to New York from San Fran-
            cisco, and had an hour to kill in Chicago- no pun intended,
            sir! –before making my connections at the other station.
            So I went into a saloon. There was a man there- very
            drunk- oh, pathetically drunk, Mr. Spade. I like drunks-
            in vino veratas, you know. So I listened to his story. His
            daughter was about to marry aged-tycoon for his gold,
            and he was going to the wedding in San Francisco. He
            seemed to dislike his daughter's fiancé and several times
            expressed a desire to kill him. This led to a general discus-
            sion of murder- favorite topic of mine, did you know- and
            the fact that every man has at least one murder he would
            commit if he could get away with it. I for instance was
            going to New York for a business conference with a man
            whom I simply must kill, come what may. A quite horrid,
            a leprously horrid old miser named (WITH LOATHING)
            Mervin Studge. Studge was holding some notes of mine
            which I was not prepared to meet, and killing him was the
            only way I could get an extension of time to enable me to
            do so. Logical?

SPADE:      So- you and Madden Dexter exchanged crimes.

BONFILS:    Precisely, sir. I went back to San Francisco on his train
            and he went back to New York on mine. I was to kill
            old Gantvoort and he was to kill Studge. Since neither
            of us had any connection with our prospective victims,
            the chances were we'd get away with it. And we did. Or
            rather I did. That fool Dexter didn't keep his part of the
            bargain.

SPADE:      He didn't, eh?

BONFILS:    Fancy! He had the efficiency to send me a wire calling the deal off- an hour after I'd beaten Gantvoort's brains out. And now I believe he's on the way to San Francisco again. You see the difficulty he placed me in.

SPADE:    Oh, I don't know. Creda ought to be willing to give you more than enough to cover the notes. After all, if you're caught, her father is an accessory.

BONFILS:    Oh, yes- Creda! Tsk! Tsk! I talked with the girl last night. Most uncooperative. No sense of honor- no ethics- might have known- met the father. Now, you sir- a proposition. You, I take it, are a man of- shall we say, elastic scruples?

SPADE:    Trying flattery now, eh?

BONFILS:    Ho! Very Good! Well, there's no need of a man of your caliber to impress upon old Dexter the utter necessity of honoring his word! He's arriving tonight, you know- and . . . .

SPADE:    No dice- besides . . . I'm retiring from the case.

MUSIC:    (BRIDGE AND TO B.G.)

SPADE:    So I was lying. I called Creda and told her to meet me at the Ferry Building, in a couple of hours. Then I walked down to the Embarcadero, and headed for a little hole in the wall with a big sign on it- "headline Harry" –Job Printing, Jokes and Novelties." (SOUND: SHOP BELL) (SOUND: PRINTING PRESS) Headline Harry was in there printing joke money on elastic paper.

HARRY:    (COMING ON) Hi, Mr. S. How's your metab, this P.M."

SPADE:    Fine, Harry. Look, how long would it take you to eradicate the ink from the headline and lead article of these two newspapers, and print something else in the blank spaces.

HARRY:     Touchy job, pulp paper don't take ink herald. None too well. Take couple hours. Want this kept on the Q.T.?

SPADE:     Yeah. Print it the way I've written it out here.

HARRY:     Itals. And Rom. Caps? Maybe a two-color job?

SPADE:     Make it look like it belongs there.

HARRY:     Gotch! You wanna fool somebody- not kidding, but fooling. Sure. Natch.

SPADE:     Perf! Now I want you to send one copy up to the St. Mark Hotel. Tell the boy to give it to the house dick there and tell him I want it delivered to Emil Bonfil's room in place of his regular evening paper. I'll wait for the other one and take it with me. Got all that straight?

HARRY:     Bonfils. St. M., House D., Gotch!

SPADE:     (MUSIC: SIMULTANEOUS) (SOUND: FOG HORNS: HARBOR SOUNDS) Creda was waiting when I got back to the Ferry Building. The fog was rolling in. We got aboard and on the way over we talked. I asked her: Just how badly do you want Bonfils to pay for the killing of Gantvoort?

CREDA:     More than anything. The way he took advantage of my father! Daddy must have been very drunk to have agreed to such a thing.

SPADE:     But he did agree to it, Creda. He's guilty right along with Bonfils.

CREDA:     Sam- what are you thinking of?

SPADE:     Here- read this.

CREDA:     ("CREDA GANTVOORT INDICTED FOR MURDER OF

HUSBAND": Bride of few hours sought for slaying of aged tycoon.") What is this?

SPADE:    I had it printed. If you play along, your father will confess when he reads it, to save you.

CREDA:    I won't hear of it.

SPADE:    It'll be better for him if he does confess. There's a chance the jury will see things our way.

CREDA:    You really think so, Sam?

SPADE:    I really do, Sweetheart. Well, how about it? Will you go that far with me?

CREDA:    Okay, Sam.

SPADE:    (MUSIC: SIMULTANEOUS) We got off the boat on the other side and walked up to meet the train. Madden Dexter looked at the headline I showed him, and without a word sat down and wrote a confession. I stuck it in my pocket and the three of us walked back to the ship. By now the fog was so thick you couldn't see from one end of the ferry boat to the other, and so cold that the few passengers were all inside at the coffee counter. Old Dexter and Creda and I went in.

DEXTER:    Coffee! Nothing but coffee! Isn't there a place on this boat where a man can get an honest drink?

CREDA:    Stop yelling, Father, everybody's looking.

DEXTER:    Let 'em look. They'll see plenty in the newspapers tomorrow.

SPADE:    Psst! Mr. Dexter?

DEXTER:    Yes, lad! What is it?

SPADE:      I've got a bottle in my pocket . . . if you'll come out on deck . . .

CREDA:      Sam, I don't want him to have a drink. He's got to be sober when we talk to the police.

DEXTER:     Yes. Yes, she's right, lad. But Creda, just one might-

SPADE:      Well, I'll be out on deck if you change your mind.

SOUND:      DOOR: CROWD NOISE OUT FOG HORNS: WATER, ETC

SPADE:      (MUSIC:  SIMULTANEOUS) I saw it out of the corner of my eye as I walked out on deck. By a lifeboat. The shape of a man- the general shape of a man, I should say. Even though the fog it reminded me of a penguin. I walked straight over to the rail, lit a cigarette, and waited. Then it happened.

BONFILS:    Sorry I'm forced to do this, Mr. Spade, but-

SOUND:      WHOP! BODY FALLS- SPADE GROANS LOUDLY

MUSIC:      (PUNCTUATE)

SPADE:      I rolled my head with it almost as fast as it came at me. The sap caught me behind the left ear- not hard enough to knock me out- not hard enough to stun me- just hard enough to hurt. I dropped like a dead man and lay very, very still. I figured Dexter would hold out against the temptation of the drink I'd offered him for anyway three minutes. It wasn't that long. Bonfils saw him coming and took up an ambush beside the door. Dexter pushed the door part way open, hesitated, then opened it all the way and stepped out on the desk.

DEXTER:     Mr. Spade! Where are you? I-

| | |
|---|---|
| SOUND: | BOAT WHISTLE AND SHOT FIRED BODY FALLS . . . SCRIMMAGE |
| SPADE: | The muzzle of Bonfil's gun spat fire and Dexter fell. I was on top of Bonfils before he threw the rod into the water. Nobody inside had heard the shot. We fought it out alone. I had little trouble pinning him down. He was round but solid. I couldn't get a grip on him. I might have gone on longer than it did, but suddenly he stopped struggling, He was shaking like jelly. |
| BONFILS: | Really, Mr. Spade! This is absurd. Rolling about like guttersnipes. Let's stand on our feet like men! Do you agree? |
| SPADE: | I agree, Mr. Bonfils. |
| BIZ: | THEY GET UP PUFFING |
| SOUND: | DOOR OPENS |
| CREDA: | (COMING ON) Sam, did you see father-? Oh! |
| SPADE: | He's dead, Creda. |
| CREDA: | You did it. You deliberately lured him out here to his death. |
| SPADE: | You're right, Creda. That's exactly what I did! |
| CREDA: | But why? Why, when he was willing to stand trial? |
| BONFILS: | He confessed? That scoundrel turned State's evidence. |
| CREDA: | (SOBS) |
| SPADE: | Shut up, Bonfils. Look, Creda. This is blood I'm mopping off my head. I tried to prevent your father getting knocked off. But I had to risk his life to nail Bonfils . . . |
| CREDA: | But the confession . . . |

SPADE:      It might have been enough. It might not.

BONFILS:    Well, Mr. Spade, it's been a fascinating experience. You've handled it well, sir! I congratulate you.

CREDA:      Go on. Congratulate each other! The men who killed my father!

SPADE:      Stop it, Creda.

CREDA:      A poor gentle old man that never hurt a fly.

SPADE:      (GETTING MAD) A poor gentle old man that plotted a cold blooded murder! He's a guilty as Bonfils, can't you see that?

CREDA:      No- no- no . . .

SPADE:      In fact, he was worse than Bonfils. Bonfils at least kept his part of the bargain.

MUSIC:      (BRIDGE AND TO B.G.)

SPADE:      And that, Creda, darling, is the crop. Emil Bonfils will stand trial next month, if one can believe what one reads in the papers. And I understand the attorneys' for Gantvoort's estate are charging you and Charles with conspiracy to defraud. I don't suppose you'll understand what I mean when I say you're the warmest-hearted coldest-blooded woman I ever met. I case you don't, I mean it as a compliment. Period. End of report.

EFFIE:      That all, Sam?

SPADE:      Yeah. Type it up and mail it. What's the matter? Why are you fidgeting like that?

EFFIE:      I don't know. I've never had a case report of yours get under my skin the way this one- the last ten minutes . . . I'm just tingling all over . . . I just . . . Sam- the ants! They're all over me! The palace has sprung a leak!

SPADE:     Don't worry the slave ants are carrying the soldier ants away. Besides, they're educational.

EFFIE:     You're educated enough, already. I've got to go and do something about this. Goodnight, Sam.

SPADE:     Goodnight, Sweetheart.

MUSIC:     (UP TO CURTAIN)

# THE ADVENTURES OF SAM SPADE
## #153 "THE SILVER KEY CAPER"

SUNDAY, AUGUST 21, 1949 (REVISED)
4:00 – 4:30 PM PST
9:00 – 9:30 PM PST

| | |
|---|---|
| ANNCR: | The Adventures of Sam Spade, detective- brought to you by Wildroot Cream-Oil Hair Tonic, the non-alcoholic hair tonic that contains Lanolin. Wildroot Cream-Oil, "again and again the choice of men, and women and children, too." |
| MUSIC: | (UP INTO TRILL, PHONE BELL) |
| SOUND: | PHONE RINGS, RECEIVER LIFTED. |
| EFFIE: | Sam Spade Detective Agency. Hello, Sam. |
| SPADE: | It's me, swee . . . Hey, wait a minute. How'd you know it was me? |
| EFFIE: | Figured the percentages. |
| SPADE: | A form player, yet. What d'you mean, percentages? |
| EFFIE: | Well, Sam . . . the only other reason for the phone ringing would be a client and you know how . . . |

SPADE:      I see, I see. It figures, Ef, but there is no further need to reflect on the state of business. There are far more important things to do and wait till you see tomorrow's papers.

EFFIE:      Really, Sam?

SPADE:      Let me give you the lead.

EFFIE:      The lead, indeed.

SPADE:      Newspaper parlance. Here it is, quote: "Samuel Spade, private investigator and idol of millions was picked up bruised and bleeding . . . "

EFFIE:      Ohhhh, Sammm . . .

SPADE:      " . . . bruised and bleeding this morning at an impossible hour, babbling incoherently about something he persisted in calling 'THE SILVER KEY CAPER.'" Stop the presses, have that set up for page one, and I'll be right down to dictate my reporter's report on same.

MUSIC:      (THEME AND TO BACKGROUND)

MUSIC:      (OVERTURE)

SOUND:      DOOR CLOSED, STEPS IN.

SPADE:      (HUMMING)

EFFIE:      (FADES IN) Oh, Sam, I've got it all ready:    arnica    and aromatic ammonia and iodine and . . . Sam!

SPADE:      (POURING) What's the matter, Sweetheart?

EFFIE:      You . . . you're not hurt at all.

SPADE:      Disappointed?

EFFIE:      Well, well no, Sam. But gee whillikens, I got out my nursing manual from the war and my first aid book and . . .

SPADE:      (DRINKS) Hahh. Feel like my old self now.

EFFIE:      But you said you were bruised and bleeding.

SPADE:      Aw, you know how newspapermen are, Ef. Give the yarn a boost here and there. Helps sell papers.

EFFIE:      Well I'm really glad, Sam.

SPADE:      Good to hear you say so, Ef.

EFFIE:      Then . . . nothing happened?

SPADE:      Well, let's not write it off as a pink tea. After all, didn't I hafta stand in a barrel down at a while-you-wait cleaning shop while the guy pressed my only suit? Didn't I? And didn't I nearly drown in a rain-filled gutter on Sacramento Street? Didn't I?

EFFIE:      Well . . .

SPADE:      That's better. Date:

EFFIE:      Fill it in. To:

SPADE:      To: Mr. Benjamin Larkin, City Editor, San Francisco Post. From Samuel Spade, License Number 137596. Subject: The Silver Key Caper. Dear Benjamin:

MUSIC:      (SNEAKS IN AND UNDER . . . )

SPADE:      The story was one of the kind even a bored commuter overlooks: eight lines at the bottom of Page 16 in your own newspaper, reporting that one Chloe Andrews, a young newspaperwoman, had been struck and killed by a hit-and-run driver on Mission Street. But you who had prescribed that kind of treatment for the item, considered it of sufficient importance to call me into your office and pay money out of your own pocket for additional details:

LARKIN:    I know, I know, Sam. But there's more to this than just a hit-and-run.

SPADE:    How much more?

LARKIN:    I'm hoping you'll find that out. Chloe was a feature writer and a darn good one; so good, in fact, that she picked her own assignments. I'm afraid she got in over her head this time.

SPADE:    How do you mean?

LARKIN:    She called me a couple of nights ago . . . uh . . . the night before she was killed, asked me if I had a half column on Page One I wanted filled with something hot.

SPADE:    What was that?

LARKIN:    Didn't say. Just told me she'd bring the stuff in the next morning.

SPADE:    And she got it that night.

LARKIN:    Yeah . . . poor kid.

SPADE:    You think it was murder?

LARKIN:    Yeah.

SPADE:    Why?

LARKIN:    Checked her room afterwards . . . she lives in one case of those converted mansions on Jackson Street that takes in roomers.

SPADE:    Yeah.

LARKIN:    There was no sign of the story she was working on! Notebooks, papers, everything was gone. She wasn't kidding, Sam. Whatever she found musta been hot, all right.

SPADE:      Okay . . . whatever I find I'll have to report to Homicide.

LARKIN:     Sure- but call me at the same time. If you play it right I've got me a scoop . . .

SPADE:      Okay, Benjamin, I'll see what I can find.

MUSIC:      (BRIDGE)

SOUND:      DOOR OPENED

LANDLADY:   Well?

SPADE:      Uh . . . how do. My name's Spade. I'm . . .

LANDLADY:   Wait a minute now. Didn't you see the sign?

SPADE:      Sign?

LANDLADY:   No peddlers, no agents, no salesmen of any kind.

SPADE:      Wait, now. Don't . . .

LANDLADY:   Get your foot outa the door.

SPADE:      (CHUCKLES) Look . . . look, I'm not here to . . .

LANDLADY:   That's what they all say.

SPADE:      You thought I was a salesman, huh? (CHUCKLES) That's one for the book. I . . .

LANDLADY:   Books, is it? I got all the books I can use . . .

SPADE:      I'm not trying to sell you books. All I want . . .

LANDLADY:   You don't wanta sell me your books. Oh, no. You just wanta place a set of encyclopedias in my home so I can endorse it and . . .

SPADE:      Wait, now.

LANDLADY:    . . . and pay you fifty cents a week from now till . . .

SPADE:    WAIT!

LANDLADY:    . . . Doomsday.

SPADE:    You through?

LANDLADY:    Yep. So are you. Now if you'll git your foot outa . . .

SPADE:    Look . . . see that? It's a private investigator's license. Number 137596. Picture, fingerprints everything.

LANDLADY:    (SUSPICIOUSLY) Oh?   Why you posing as a book salesman?

SPADE:    Makes it easier, getting into places. (DOOR CLOSED) Now, if you're sure everything's all right, I'd like to take a look at the room Chloe Andrews used to live in.

LANDLADY:    She don't live here no more. You see, she . . .

SPADE:    Yes, I know. Uh . . . which way do I go?

LANDLADY:    Upstairs. Come on.

SOUND:    THEY MOUNT STAIRS AS . . .

LANDLADY:    Poor girl was killed two nights ago, you know. Terrible auto crash or something. Her things is still here.

SPADE:    Nobody's been in the room?

LANDLADY:    Well, couple of fellas from her paper, right afterwards. That's all, far's I know.

PHILIPS:    (FADES IN, MUFFLED, SINGING "HOME ON THE RANGE," SHOWER STYLE)

SPADE:    Who's that?

LANDLADY:     Aw, one of the roomers. We get all kinds here. Takin' a shower.

SPADE:     Hmm . . . does he always hang his necktie over the doorknob?

LANDLADY:     Lock's on the blink. Lets the other roomers know he's in there.n

PHILIPS:     (FADES AS THEY MOVE DOWN HALL)

LANDLADY:     This is it, here. (DOOR OPENED)

SPADE:     All the doors left unlocked around here?

LANDLADY:     Bolts on the inside. Gonna have to get 'em fixed up one of these days. (DOOR CLOSED) Well, now if you wanta . . .

SPADE:     Uh . . . if you don't mind, I'd like to spend a little time here alone.

LANDLADY:     Oh, I don't mind stayin', if that's what you . . .

SPADE:     Please, now . . . Mr. Larkin of the San Francisco Post'll vouch for me. And here . . . here's a dollar to tell anyone who happens to ask I'm a real book salesman. (DOOR OPENED: SHOVES HER OUT) There you go now. Thanks . . . thanks so much. (DOOR CLOSED)

MUSIC:     (IN AND UNDER)

SPADE:     It didn't take long to find you were 99 percent right about the room: it had been cased and thoroughly. The only relic of Chloe Andrews' career was the portable typewriter on the corner table and a half ream of blank paper . . . oh, yes, and a copy of the Post. It was three weeks old and folded back to the classified section.

Because I couldn't help wondering what Chloe was doing in the classifieds I gave it a second look, discovering thereby that Chloe had cut a square hole in the "Personals" column. This of course suggested a trip to your file department, otherwise known as the Morgue.

SOUND:    MURMURS OF OFFICE. SAM LEAFING THROUGH PAPER

SPADE:    There it developed the hole and contained an ad telling one and all in bold letters, "You, Too, Can Meet Your Dream," and below it in fine print was a flowery blurb extolling the wonders of an outfit calling itself The Silver Key to Happiness, with an office on Sutter Street.

GIRL:    (TIMIDLY) Uh . . . Mr. Spade . . .

SPADE:    (LOOKS UP, ABSORBED) Mm . . . huh?

GIRL:    Here's the file Miss Andrews took home with her. She brought it back the same day, she . . .

SPADE:    Oh. What is it?

GIRL:    A clipping from last January. Shall I read it?

SPADE:    Yeah. What's it say? If you feel up to it?

GIRL:    (CLEARS THROAT) "Atlanta, Georgia, January 23 AP . . . Heirs of Leora McWilliams, elderly spinster who died last week in a hit-and-run accident today requested the District Attorney's office to conduct further investigation of circumstances surrounding her death. Miss McWilliams, supposedly a wealthy woman, was found to have liquidated her asset some weeks prior to the accident and to have died virtually penniless." Uh ... that's all.

SPADE:    That's enough. Thanks a lot. Ooh, don't fall down.

GIRL:       You're a nice man. You'd be surprised how few really nice men there are. You're going?

SPADE:      Yep. I, Too, Can Meet My Dream . . . at the Silver Key to Happiness.

MUSIC:      (BRIDGE AND SEGUE TO "I LOVE YOU TRULY," VIOLIN, COMING, GOOILY OVER P.A . . . )

MISS L:     (SOFT. SMOOTH. UNCTUOUS: THE $1,000,000 VOICE) Let's see now . . . that's Mr. Samuel Spencer?

SPADE:      Samuel J.

MISS L:     Mm-hm . . . and you live in San Francisco?

SPADE:      That's right.

MISS L:     (WRITING) San Francisco. There we are.

SPADE:      Uh . . . where's the violin?

MISS L:     (LITTLE LAUGH) Oh, that's our mood music. Like it?

SPADE:      Uh-huh

MISS L:     I suppose you'll want to know what the Silver Key is, Mr. Spencer. We just have one job here: bringing people together, unlocking the gates to Happiness, showing them the way to a richer, fuller life. Somewhere, Mr. Spencer . . . somewhere in the city there's a Right Person for you . . . someone you may never meet, engrossed as you are with business problems. Uh . . . you do have a business, don't you?

SPADE:      Oh, yes.

MISS L:     Uh-huh. So that's our aim, Mr. Spencer. All of our facilities here at the Silver Key are yours, too . . . to help you find . . . Her.

SPADE:      Object: companionship.

MISS L:     Beg pardon?

SPADE:      Uh . . . nothing. Where do I fill out this application?

MISS L:     Right behind you . . . the green door, Mr. Spencer. That's our Rendezvous Room. When you've completed it, please return it to me and we'll discuss . . . future plans?

SPADE:      Uh-huh.

MUSIC:      (UP ON "I LOVE YOU TRULY," B.G. FOR . . . )

SPADE:      I now know what the male Black Widow spider feels like when the courtship is over and wifey is ready to eat him. The Rendezvous Room was dark as a Powell Street bar; purple walls hung with dark green velvet drapes and gilt framed prints of Toulouse-Lautrec. I sat down near the one lamp in the room and tried to make out the printing on the application: (PAUSE, READS) Mmm . . . age, address and so on . . . Nature of business . . . income 1939-49 inclusive . . . stocks, bonds, other property? (ASIDE) Object: Companionship. (READS) Net worth?

SOUND:      DOOR OPENS

AURELIA:    (ABOUT 50) Hello.

SPADE:      (JUMPS) Huh? Oh . . . I didn't see you. So dark in here.

AURELIA:    I'm sorry I frightened you.

SPADE:      Guess I'm just jumpy. Uh . . . my name's Spencer.

AURELIA:    And I'm Aurelia Winters. You're . . . uh . . . new here, aren't you?

SPADE:      Well, yes. Matter of fact I was just looking over the financial st . . . uh . . . the application here. How about you?

AURELIA:    Well, I've been a client for almost two weeks now.

SPADE:    How are you doing?

AURELIA:    Mr. Spencer. It's . . . so wonderful I can hardly put it into words. You . . . must know what it means to be lonely.

SPADE:    Sure.

AURELIA:    Since Henry died I just haven't known which way to turn. It wasn't money, of course: there was plenty of that but . . . but . . .

SPADE:    Companionship.

AURELIA:    Yes . . . the . . . the gateway to Happiness. The Silver Key has opened it for me, Mr. Spencer . . . shown me the broad bright way that lies beyond.

SOUND:    DOOR OPENED

PHILLIPS:    (ABOUT 50, SOUTHERN ACCENT. OFF) Aurelia?

AURELIA:    Over here, Robert.

SOUND:    DOOR CLOSED

PHILLIPS:    Darling, I don't know how to apologize for keepin' you waitin' so long.

AURELIA:    Robert. (CLINCH)

PHILLIPS:    Aurelia . . . darlin'. Ev'y minute without you is like a yeah. I . . .

AURELIA:    (WEAKLY) Robert . . . this is . . . Mr . . .

SPADE:    Spencer.

PHILLIPS:    Oh.

SPADE:      Uh . . . I was just going.

PHILLIPS:   Please now . . . don't let us disturb you.

SPADE:      Not at all. Good luck to both of you. 'Bye Aurelia.

AURELIA:    'Bye, Mr. Spencer. (FADING) Robert, my dear, I just don't know how I ever lived without you. (FADES INTO MURMUR AS.)

SOUND:      DOOR OPENED

MUSIC:      (IN WITH P.A. THEME FOR . . . )

SPADE:      I stopped with door half open as something hit me: the cravat Robert was wearing was the same one I noticed slung over the door knob back at the Jackson Street rooming house occupied by the late Chloe Andrews. This, then, was Mr. Home-on-the-Range. (DOOR CLOSED) I closed the door and stood there in the gloom, with my ears out like a pair of tubas. They must have thought I left, because the conversation picked up from there on:

PHILLIPS:   (SLIGHTLY OFF) It's all set, angel: we're gonna leave for South America first of next week.

AURELIA:    So soon?

PHILLIPS:   It just can't wait, dear. Did you talk to the bank?

AURELIA:    Yes. There are still some securities to be sold, but . . .

PHILLIPS:   How long will it take?

AURELIA:    A few days, they said.

PHILLIPS:   That's wonderful, darlin'. Off with the old, on with the new, eh?

AURELIA:    A new life, Robert . . . a new country.

PHILLIPS:    Just you and I . . . no one else.

AURELIA:    You know, dear . . . I never knew what they meant, till now. The Silver Key.

PHILLIPS:    The Gateway to Happiness.

MUSIC:    UNDER

SPADE:    It went on for a minute or two: Robert's soft, syrupy southern tones and Aurelia's eager answers . . . doing her best to follow in the footsteps of her predecessor in Atlanta: the supposedly wealthy Miss McWilliams who strangely penniless after a hit-and-run driver was through with her.

PHILLIPS:    I think we better be goin' now, honey. (DOOR OPENED) After you, ma'am. (CHUCKLES) (DOOR CLOSED)

MUSIC:    (UP MOMENTARILY, THEN UNDER . . . )

SPADE:    I got his full name when I turned in the application: Robert I. Phillips, the initials of which, you will note, have been used on many a tombstone to signify: Rest in Peace.

MUSIC:    (CURTAIN)

MUSIC:    (SECOND OVERTURE)

SPADE:    I backed out of the offices of the Silver Key, trimmed my sails, boxed my compass and set a course back to the rooming house on Jackson Street. This time the landlady, tired of the whole thing by now, seemed happy to admit me without serious challenge and let me have the entire second floor to myself. So I sidled up the stairs and down the hall, this time to the room currently occupied by Mr. Robert I. "Rest in Peace" Phillips. He had the one door in the house that was lockable, so I entered via Chloe's room and the fire escape. Mr. Phillips was all packed up for a long trip with expensive rawhide luggage which I surmised had been purchased indirectly by the late Miss McWilliams of Atlanta. Until I opened up one of the small pieces and found an engraved gold plate mounted inside reading:    "To Robert Enfield, Cashier, in Grateful Appreciation for Twenty-five Years of Service: M a n a g e-ment of the Midvale County Bank." (PAUSE) Bending thus over somebody else's luggage, I was naturally somewhat flustered when a key sounded in the lock.

SOUND:     KEY, DOOR OPENED

MAN:       Oh . . . uh, sorry, pal. Thought you was out.

SPADE:     What can I do for you?

MAN:       Uh . . . got the key from the landlady. She told me you wasn't in, Mr. Phillips. Baggage ready to go?

SPADE:     Huh?

MAN:       I'm from the airline office. Ya bags is supposed to be at the field by seven and it's six-thirty now. Say . . . (CON-FIDENTIALLY) . . . you was smart, doin' what you done.

SPADE:     What'd I do?

MAN:       Not goin' out to the Skyline Club tonight. Landlady said that's where you was going.

SPADE:     Oh, yeah, yeah. Why am I smart?

MAN:       Well, I'll tell you. (LOW) I got a pal named Ryan, see . . . onna force.

SPADE:     Joe Ryan? I know him.

MAN:       Well if you know Joe you oughta know about tonight.

SPADE:      Haven't seen him lately. What's up?

MAN:        Raid.

SPADE:      Yeah?

MAN:        Got it right from the oatbin. Gonna knock over the Sky-line tonight. I been hittin' the wheel out there once in a while and Joe tipped me to lay off. (GUFFAWS) Bo one on you, huh? Sittin' in the can on a gambling rap while ya plane's taking off fer Noo Yawk! (STOPS) Jeez, I better get after them bags.

MUSIC:      (IN AND UNDER)

SPADE:      The Skyline Club was having a big night, and I say that advisedly, since while the Club was doing fine, Mr. Rest In Peace Phillips, with his collar unbuttoned, his hand painted necktie drooping and a tired-looking mint julep at his side, was not. Aurelia Winters was definitely not along, which presented the possibility he had already ushered her through the Gateway to Happiness.

SOUND:      GAMBLING CLUB: THE WHEEL SPINS, AD LIBS: "PLACE YOUR BETS, FOLKS 'ROUND SHE GOES" "TWENTY SEVEN, ODD, RED." FARTHER OFF: DICE RATTLE. "IT'S AN EIGHT THE HARD WAY." JERRY, BE A DEAR AND CASH ME A CHECK, HUH?" ETC.

SPADE:      As near as I can figure, he went down for around three thousand bucks in the two hours I watched him. Then around eleven, he headed for a phone booth at the back which had a nice thin wall on the dark side, where I happened to be standing at the time.

PHILLIPS:   (MUFFLED) Hello? Brockhurst Apartments? Let me speak to Miss Aurelia Winters, if you please, ma'am . . . Hello,

Aurelia, honey. Hope I didn't get you up . . . . . . I'd like ve'y much to talk to you tonight, if it won't be too much trouble. Little business matter . . . .Yes, honey, I went to the bank. Ev'ything's all ready to go . . . . . . Ve'y well, then:        I'll see you in an houah. 'Buy, honey.

SPADE:        (MUSIC:    SNEAK) I followed him into the bar. It couldn't have been his last dollar he put down for chips, because he had one more for a double Bourbon.

SOUND:        GLASS PUT DOWN, LIFTED.

PHILLIPS:        (DRINKS)

SPADE:        Having a rough night, Mr. Phillips?

PHILLIPS:        (JUMPS) Huh? Oh . . . Mr. Spencer. Uh . . . no, let us say I was fo'ced into a strategic retreat. How about you?

SPADE:        I didn't come here to gamble.

PHILLIPS:        Oh?

SPADE:        I came here to talk to you.

PHILLIPS:        Is that so? What can I do for you, suh?

SPADE:        Maybe you'd better finish that drink first.

PHILLIPS:        Oh? Well, if you say so. (LAUGHS) (DRINKS) There . . . how's that?

SPADE:        Good. Now tell me why you killed Chloe Andrews.

PHILLIPS:        Chloe: (SPUTTERS) I killed . . . ? What do you mean, suh?

SPADE:        You heard me. And while you're at it, fill in the details on Miss Leora McWilliams of Atlanta. A batch of her relatives are wondering what happened to her money.

PHILLIPS:    Now wait a minute, Mr. Spencer . . .

SPADE:    Spade's the name. I'm a private detective.

PHILLIPS:    Why, I . . . I haven't the slightest notion what you're refer-
rin' to.

SPADE:    It's a little late for that, Phillips. You know Chloe had
something on you and you killed her, right?

PHILLIPS:    No, I did not. I . . . I have nothin' to hide. I . . .

SPADE:    Then why'd you change your name?

PHILLIPS:    Why, I . . . I . . .

SPADE:    Robert Enfield's the one you were born with, isn't it?

PHILLIPS:    (MENACING) Now, Mr. Spade, I must caution you to
keep your nose out of my . . .

SPADE:    And I must caution you to keep your hands on the bar. I've
got one of those, too. Now, why don't you level with me? I'm
paid by the day and my client's careful with his dough. I . . .

VOICE II:    (OFF) Stay right where you are, everybody!

CAST (AD LIB CRIES AS THE RAID HITS: Raid! RAID! RAID!

SOUND:    MILLING CROWD. A TABLE OVERTURNED.

CAST:    (AD LIB:    The lights! Turn on the lights!

MUSIC:    (IN HARD AND UNDER . . . )

SPADE:    Everything happened at once: people were underfoot,
climbing tables, trying to find doors and windows in the
dark, and to make it even nicer, a thunderstorm moved in
about then and rain was coming down in buckets when I
finally did get outside. Rest In Peace, of course, was gone.

| | |
|---|---|
| MUSIC: | (UP MOMENTARILY AND UNDER . . . ) |
| SPADE: | When I got back to the nickel zone I put in a call to Head-quarters and arranged a reception party for him on the three o'clock plane to New York . . . on the bare chance he'd still try to keep his appointment with Aurelia, since I knew he needed money and it was there waiting for him: thus I arrived around midnight at the Brockhurst Apartments on California Street. |
| SOUND: | DOOR BUZZER. PAUSE, DOOR OPENED. |
| AURELIA: | Oh, Robert, I though you'd . . . oh. It's Mr . . . . .Mr . . . |
| SPADE: | Spencer. |
| AURELIA: | Yes. Good heavens, you're wet to the skin. Won't you come in . . . I have some hot tea all ready. |
| SPADE: | Thanks. (DOOR CLOSED) Uh . . . but before we go any further, Aurelia, my name's not Spencer, it's Spade. |
| AURELIA: | Oh? |
| SPADE: | Yes. I'm a private detective. |
| AURELIA: | A det . . . ! B-but why . . . |
| SPADE: | Now, don't be alarmed, I'm only here to help you. You're still expecting Mr. Phillips? |
| AURELIA: | Why, yes. |
| SPADE: | Good. I hope he shows up. |
| AURELIA: | B-but what's the matter? |
| SPADE: | Look . . . I hate to pull the props out from under that dream castle you were building, but I'm afraid Mr. Phillips isn't all you think he is. |

AURELIA:    Please tell me.

SPADE:    How much do you know about him?

AURELIA:    Well, I . . . I just met him at the Silver Key a few weeks ago and he . . . he seemed to like me . . .

SPADE:    He liked your money.

AURELIA:    B-but why would he . . . ?

SPADE:    It's an old story:    middle-aged man runs low on funds and looks around for a single lady with some object, companionship.

AURELIA:    B-but Robert is independent! He has money, Mr. Spade.

SPADE:    What makes you think so?

AURELIA:    We're buying a business in South America! He's putting up fifty thousand dollars to match mine.

SPADE:    That's what he told you. Right now he's wanted by the police in Atlanta, Georgia for the murder of a lady named Leora McWilliams.

AURELIA:    (PAUSE) How do you know that?

SPADE:    Because a newspaper woman named Chloe Andrews found out about it . . . just before he killed her, then took her body out on Mission Street and ran over it to make it look like hit-and-run.

AURELIA:    (SHUDDERS)

SPADE:    I know it sounds brutal, Aurelia, but it's pretty hard to sugar-coat a set of facts like that.

AURELIA:    You . . . you've been to the police.

SPADE:      They'll get my report in the morning. Now, why don't we just relax here and wait for Mr. Phillips?

AURELIA:    I . . . I'll get you a cup of tea.

MUSIC:      (IN AND UNDER)

SPADE:      I didn't especially feel like tea at the moment, but it gave her something to do, so I let her bring it in.

SOUND:      POURING TEA

AURELIA:    There you are. Oh, dear, I've forgotten the cream and sugar.

SPADE:      Never mind. I'll take mine straight.

AURELIA:    But I'd like some myself. (FADING) Never could take my tea without cream and sugar.

MUSIC:      (UP SLIGHTLY)

SPADE:      It was lousy tea. I took a swallow and poured the rest in a potted palm while she was out of the room, then leaned back to wait for Robert. Aurelia was trying not to show how hard it had hit her; a half hour later she was still making a brave attempt at conversation.

AURELIA:    (ANTICIPATE SLIGHTLY) . . . and I suppose I should have known then, Mr. Spade, when he kept insisting I convert my holdings into cash, but when you get to be my age, and have to face your future alone, you lose your common sense sometimes.

MUSIC:      UNDER

SPADE:      About here I slumped forward, knocking the tea cup off the table. Then my eyeballs rolled up in a most unattached manner. Then my speech became thickened and incoherent. Whassamatter with me? Whatcha put in that . . . that tea?

AURELIA:    Well . . . (LAUGHS) you're beginning to notice it now, Mr. Spade?

SPADE:    (STRUGGLES, BABBLING)

AURELIA:    No use trying to move . . . because you can't.

SPADE:    (PANTING) You . . . you!

AURELIA:    I've always regretted Leora's death . . . it just wasn't too profitable and had such unpleasant consequences. But as I told you, Mr. Spade, it's been a good lesson for me. Next time I'll be more careful.

MUSIC:    (UP TO COVER SPEECH, THEN UNDER:)

SPADE:    She caught me as I fell forward and did the drunk carry. She got me out of the apartment wielding an obviously practiced hand. Within a matter of seconds we were out in the early morning quiet on the side street- I was deposited gently face down in the rain filled gutter.

SOUND:    RUNNING WATER. CAR GUNNING, OFF

SPADE:    I sneaked a look- and saw a pair of headlights backing of . . . there was a clash of gears and they headed straight for me.

SOUND:    FOLLOW ABOVE . . . CAR MOVES IN, GUNNING AS:

SPADE:    I rolled over fast. The wheels missed my head by six inches.

SOUND:    CAR ROARS PAST, SQUEAL OF BREAKS, DOOR OPENED OFF. HURRIED STEPS AS AURELIA RUNS BACK TO SPADE.

SPADE:    (PAUSE) (THEN GRABS HER) Okay, Aurelia.

AURELIA:    Let go! Let go!

SPADE:    Come on in, the water's fine. (THEY STRUGGLE, SPLASHING AROUND, AD LIB)

MUSIC:    (IN AND UNDER)

SPADE:    It's hardly necessary to state it was highly humiliating for a man in my profession to be found by an officer of the law sitting on the head of a middle-aged woman in the gutter, screaming at the top of my lungs for the police, but that's the way I played the scene, knowing it would make a good copy, as we newspapermen say, eh, Mr. Larkin? I am enclosing several photographs of me in attractive poses to be used in connection with your scoop. My personal favorite is the one representing me in a Tee Shirt, tearing a telephone book in half. I think the kids will like it- and it will silence the Doubting Thomases who go about saying that the shoulders in my suit are not my own. Well, that's 30. Period. End of report. Well, Effie.

EFFIE:    Oh, Sam, it was humiliating.

SPADE:    I boneheaded it? Well, Ef, you can't be right all the time. It looked like Phillips from the beginning and . . .

EFFIE:    Oh, not that.

SPADE:    The gutter, huh? Well, I've been there . . .

EFFIE:    It was horrible, Sam. Unthinkable.

SPADE:    (POURS, DRINKS) Excruciating.

EFFIE:    That's the word. Just to think that you, Samuel Spade . . .

SPADE:    (DRINKING) Yeah.

EFFIE:      Drinking tea!

SPADE:      (CHOKES ON DRINK) Go, woman! Type that up!

EFFIE:      Yes, sir.

MUSIC:      PHRASE OF THEME

EFFIE:      (FADES IN) Here it is, Sam. I . . . uh . . . discovered a more or less important omission.

SPADE:      A hole, Ef? An unturned stone?

EFFIE:      Uh-huh.  With Mr. Rest In Peace Phillips under it . . . or uh . . . Mr. Enfield, I mean.

SPADE:      Oh, that. They ran it down this morning: Embezzlement charge, Midvale, Mississippi. The whole caper's a case history of what happens when two crooks swallow each others' line and try to outswindle each other. It was just unfortunate that it had to start among the plush draperies at the Silver Key, but we've promised to keep them out of the publicity, so . . .

SOUND:      PHONE RINGS, RECEIVER UP.

EFFIE:      Hello?

MISS L:     (FILTER) I'd like to speak to Mr. Spade, please, this is Miss Larchmont of the Silver Key.

EFFIE:      Oh . . . uh . . . Sam, it's for you. (WHISPERS) Miss Larchmont.

SPADE:      Thanks. Hel-lo, Miss Larchmont.

MISS L:     Mr. Spade . . . I just wanted to tell you how sweet you've been in keeping this unfortunate affair out of the papers.

SPADE:      Well, thanks, Miss . . .

| | |
|---|---|
| MISS L: | I . . . uh . . . (SUGGESTIVELY) thought you and I might find a nice quiet place to . . . uh . . . |
| SPADE: | Ohhh? Well . . . |
| MISS L: | Just . . . you and I? |
| SPADE: | (GLOWING) Well, Miss Larchmont, it sounds . . . |
| EFFIE: | Give me that! |
| SPADE: | Ef, wait! |
| EFFIE: | Miss Larchmont, I'm very sorry, but Mr. Spade will be tied up until 1959. |
| MISS L: | Who is this? |
| EFFIE: | (SPUTTERS) His . . . his daughter. (HANGS UP) |
| SPADE: | (PAUSE, SIGHS) Well, unhitched the ball and chain, Ef. I'm going home. |
| EFFIE: | Straight home. Goodnight, Sam. |
| SPADE: | Goodnight, daughter. |
| MUSIC: | CURTAIN |

# THE ADVENTURES OF SAM SPADE
## "JURY DUTY"

SUNDAY, MAY 25, 1947   #35
4:00 – 4:30 PM PST
9:00 – 9:00 PM PST

| | |
|---|---|
| ANNCR: | The Adventures of Sam Spade, detective- brought to you by Wildroot Cream-Oil, the non-alcoholic hair tonic that contains Lanolin . . . Wildroot Cream-Oil "again and again the choice of men who put good grooming first." |
| MUSIC: | PUNCTUATION . . . UP INTO TRILL INTO PHONE BELL |
| SOUND: | PHONE BELL |
| SOUND: | TELEPHONE ON FILTER MIKE LIFT RECEIVER |
| EFFIE: | Sam Spade Detective Agency. |
| SPADE: | (FILTER) I'm through with jury duty, Sweetheart . . . through do you hear- |
| EFFIE: | Oh, Sam- Is the trial finished? |
| SPADE: | The trial's been called off, Sweetheart. |

EFFIE:      Something go wrong?

SPADE:      Nothing serious. The D.A. merely discovered he was try-ing the wrong man for the wrong crime.

EFFIE:      Thanks to Juror Spade, no doubt.

SPADE:      Who else? Stay where you are, Sweetheart, I'll be right down with the lowdown on the Jury Duty Caper.

MUSIC:      (UP INTO THEME AND TO B.G.)

ANNCR:      Dashiell Hammett, America's leading detective fiction writer, and creator of Sam Spade, the hard-boiled private eye, and William Spier, radio's outstanding producer-director of mystery and crime drama, join their talents to make your hair stand on end with the Adventures of Sam Spade . . . (MUSIC ACCENTS) . . . Presented by the makers of Wildroot Cream-Oil for the hair. Why is Wildroot Cream-Oil such an outstanding favorite with so many well groomed people? Because it's the outstanding different hair tonic! Among all the leading hair tonics, only Wildroot Cream-Oil contains LANOLIN . . . only Wild-root Cream-Oil gives you that neat, handsome "Wildroot look!" So get the big economy-size bottle of Wildroot Cream-Oil at your drug or toilet goods counter. And ask your barber for Wildroot Cream-Oil . . . "again and again the choice of men who put good grooming first."

(MUSIC:     SNEAK UNDER) And now, Wildroot brings to the air, the greatest private detective of 'em all . . . in the Adven-tures of Sam Spade!

MUSIC:      (UP TO SHOW)

MUSIC:      OVERTURE

SOUND:      DOOR FOOTSTEPS

EFFIE:      (FADING ON) For heaven's sake, Sam, what happened? Your clothes are all torn-your pants!

SPADE:      They're frozen. Bring your book, Effie.

SOUND:      STEPS OPEN DOOR CHAIR DESK DRAWER ETC.

EFFIE:      (FADING ON) The safest place in the world . . . A jury box.–What happened? Did you fall out of it?

SPADE:      Dictation, Miss Perrine . . . when you have the time!

EFFIE:      What kind of a jury were you serving on? Couldn't the judge keep order?

SPADE:      This one goes to the D.A.'s office, Effie.

EFFIE:      Oh they called and said to forget it. What does that mean?

SPADE:      That's justice, Effie. No more than justice. To the D.A.'s office from Samuel Spade, License number 137596. (MUSIC: SNEAK) Gentlemen: I did not ask to serve on your jury. I was summoned. I went down to the Hall, beefed to the court clerk, insisted that I was prejudiced against the defendant, even told about my 100-proof bottle. Still, I became Samuel Spade, Juror number Eleven, and was assigned to criminal court Part Two. I found my way in the jury box along with the other eleven good man and true. (SOUND: COURT ROOM SOUNDS GAVEL ETC.)

PROSECUTOR: ...May it please your Honor, Mr. Foreman, and Gentlemen of the jury. The defendant, Clarence "Rocky" Morrison has been indicted by the San Francisco County Grand Jury of murder in the first degree, in charge of having killed and murdered Albert Fogerty (FADES) with premeditation and deliberation, with malice aforethought . . .

SPADE:              (MUSIC: SIMULTANEOUS) (OVER FADE) The pros-
                    ecutor went on like that for an hour or so. It seemed
                    the defendant, Rocky Morrison, had thrown a couple
                    of slugs into Albert Fogarty in a fit of temper. Fog-
                    arty had been a contractor with a few side interests
                    ranging from sand and gravel to control of the policy
                    racket. Rocky Morrison was a small time gunsel em-
                    ployed by Big Louie Havoc, an ex-Chicago boy who
                    owned a controlling interest in more of the local busi-
                    nesses that didn't pay taxes. After the indictment was
                    read, the State called its first witness. I took one look
                    at her and decided jury duty could be interesting . . .

CLERK:              (ECHO) Do you swear to tell the truth, so help you
                    God?

DORYCE:             I'll surely try . . .

CLERK:              Take the stand.

DORYCE:             Thank you, I'm sure. (COUGHS) "Scuse me. Just got
                    out of the hospital. Pneumonia-double. (SOUND:
                    GAVEL) Sorry, I'm sure. (SOUND:        REGISTER
                    PROSECUTOR'S STEPS)

PROSECUTOR:    Your name?

DORYCE:             Doryce De Soto.

PROSECUTOR:    Is that your real name, or an alias?

DORYCE:             A what?

PROSECUTOR:    An assumed name.

DORYCE:             Oh, an al-y-us. That's my stage name.

PROSECUTOR:    You are an actress by profession?

DORYCE:          I'll thank you to keep your insinuendos to yourself.

JUDGE:           The prosecutor means what do you do for a living,
                 Miss De Soto?

DORYCE:          Well, why didn't he say so? I'm a receptionist. At
                 least I was-I just got out of the hospital and-

PROSECUTOR:      Yes, you mentioned that. You say you are a recep-
                 tionist. By whom are you employed?

DORYCE:          Blue Bottle Bar and Grill, Columbus Avenue. I was
                 the third receptionist from the right as you go in, and
                 I would have been promoted to the first if I hadn't
                 been in the hospital. I had pneumonia-double. Some-
                 times I get those shooting pains-you know-and . . .
                 right about here-and they run all the way down to
                 my vaccination scar-and you know-you can see how
                 much weight I lost-you know.

JUDGE:           The witness will please remember that she is here to
                 give testimony, and is not an exhibit.

DORYCE:          I'm sorry, I'm sure.

PROSECUTOR:      You were acquainted with the defendant, Clarence
                 "Rocky" Morrison?

DORYCE:          Rocky? Sure he used to come in the Blue Bottle all
                 the time. You know to collect and that. You know?

PROSECUTOR:      To collect what?

SNYDER:          Your honor!

JUDGE:           Yes, Mr. Snyder? (SOUND: SLOW DELIBERATE
                 STEPS)

SPADE:           (MUSIC SIMULTANEOUS) And that was when I
                 noticed for the first time who the defense attorney

was. Marty Snyder, Big Louie Havoc's mouthpiece, one of the smartest criminal lawyers in the country. He walked up to the judge's bench, took up a stance facing the jury, and gave the spectators a good view of his profile, before he spoke.

SNYDER: Your honor, as counsel for the defense, I object to the prosecutor's line of questioning as incompetent, irrelevant and immaterial.

JUDGE: Object sustained. You will proceed with more caution, Mr. Prosecutor.

PROSECUTOR: Your honor, it was my hope to obtain testimony from the witness, linking the defendant to certain rackets or financial operations, and thus to prove the motive behind the murder of Albert Fogarty.

SNYDER: That's a lie. He's trying to blacken my client's character!

JUDGE: You may continue your questioning, Mr. Prosecutor. Sit down, Mr. Snyder.

PROSECUTOR: I have only one more question to ask, Miss De Soto. What happened in the Blue Bottle Bar and Grill on the night of February the second?

DORYCE: Well, I was drinking a hot rum toddy at the end of the bar, and Mr. Fogarty came in and asked for Gladys . . .

PROSECUTOR: That is Gladys Raye?

DORYCE: Yes, that's her stage name-Gladys Raye-so Gladys went into a booth and ordered some drinks and like that. And then Rocky came in, straight out of a weed 'patch somewhere, honestly, and he said something in a real low voice to Mr. Fogarty, and then they all went in the office the three of them, and then there were the shots and that, and Gladys screamed, and came running out and said that Rocky had killed Mr. Fogarty.

SNYDER:         Objection! Hearsay evidence!

PROSECUTOR:     Your witness, Mr. Snyder.

SNYDER:         No cross.

PROSECUTOR:     If your honor pleases, I would like to call my next witness-Miss Gladys Raye.

CLERK:          Gladys Raye to the stand. (PAUSE) State's Witness Gladys Raye to the stand, please. (PAUSE)

BIZ:            HUSHED MURMUR IN COURTROOM,

PROSECUTOR:     Your honor.

JUDGE:          Yes.

PROSECUTOR:     The witness, Gladys Raye has disappeared. Under the circumstances, the prosecution is forced to ask for a postponement of the trial until this key witness, the only eye witness to the crime, can be located.

JUDGE:          Postponement denied. The trial will proceed!

SPADE:          (MUSIC: SIMULTANEOUSLY) It proceeded. It might proceed until next Christmas. This was an appalling prospect. At 9 P.M. I was locked into a room until juror number three a gentle little man named R. Crossley Hooper. Mr. R. Crossley Hooper came equipped to battle every germ that science had ever discovered.

HOOPER:         Oh yes, Mr. Spade. One can't be too careful.

SOUND:      SPRAY

HOOPER:     You should use this spray on your throat.

SPADE:      No thanks. I'll just gargle with bourbon. What's that oil-skin sack?

HOOPER:     This? My sleeping bag. Always use it when I travel. The sheets in hotels, you know. See? Climb in like this.

SOUND:      CRACKLE-CRACKLE OF OIL SKIN

SPADE:      But-doesn't that crackling keep you awake?

HOOPER:     (CHEERILY) You get used to it. Besides, I take a sleeping pill. Here-have one.

SPADE:      (MUSIC: SIMULTANEOUS) Mr. Hooper put a sleeping pill in his glass of water. I took two pills-and dropped them into a glass of water-Mr. Hooper's. Ten minutes later R. Crossley Hooper was in what is coyly known as the Land of Nod . . . Fifteen minutes later I was tip-toeing cautiously down the fire escape. (SOUND: LOUD CLATTER ON FIRE ESCAPE) Just as I arrived at the fourth floor landing, (SOUND: WINDOW RAISED STEPS OUT) a window flew up and a nylon-encased leg emerged there from. I recognized the vaccination scar. It was Doryce De Soto, the State's prize exhibit of the day. (MUSIC: ACCENT AND OUT) Going out for a breath of air, Miss De Soto?

DORYCE:     Eek! Hey, who are you?

SPADE:      I'm on the jury, three bucks a day. What are they paying you?
            DORYCE: Listen, you won't tell on me, will you?

SPADE:      We'll make a deal, if you won't tell on me, I won't tell on you.

DORYCE:     Say that's right, you're illegal too. Listen, maybe you can help.

SPADE:      Maybe I can. It's like this. I don't like serving on a jury. The pay is poor, the seats are very hard, and my business will come to a bad end unless I can find that missing witness and get this trial over with.

DORYCE:     All right. Come on. First we'll call on Eloise.

MUSIC:

SPADE:      We lowered ourselves down into the alley back of the hotel via a painter's scaffold which was suspended from the roof in the rear of the building. Twenty-five minutes later we were climbing Russian Hill, and I chimed the half-hour by pushing a doorbell.

SOUND:      (DOOR CHIME OFF: DOOR ELABORATELY UNLOCKED AND OPENED: FASHIONABLE STREET NOISES)

ELOISE:     Good evening.

SPADE:      Hello, Eloise, how's tricks?

DORYCE:     Hello, Eloise.

ELOISE:     If you're from the police, I'd like to see your warrant.

SPADE:      Well, I'm not from the police, so I don't need any. But if you're smart, you'll talk. Hiding out a State's witness in a murder trial is a serious offense.

ELOISE:     Who are you?

SPADE:      My name is Spade. I'm a private detective.

ELOISE:     Who planted you in that jury-Marty Snyder?

SPADE:      Maybe.

ELOISE:     Well, you can tell Marty from me that I'm not hiding Gladys here, and I wish he'd stop sending people around here to snoop. Now get out of here, both of you!

SOUND:      STEPS

DORYCE:     Listen, Eloise, you've got to help me . . .

ELOISE:     Please go. Or I shall call the police and have you both ar-
            rested. Goodnight!

SOUND:      (DOOR CLOSED)

DORYCE:     Now you've spoiled everything. I'll have to go back and
            be looked up with the other witness, and that.

SPADE:      Not if you're smart.

DORYCE:     What do you mean?

SPADE:      Gladys Raye?

DORYCE:     I wish you wouldn't say that name out loud. It makes me ner-
            vous. If Big Louie Havoc found out you were asking for her.

SPADE:      I'll handle Big Louie. Where do we go next?

DORYCE:     Gee, you're not scared of anything, are you? What's your
            given name?

SPADE:      Sam.

DORYCE:     Well, Sam, there's Ruthie's down lower on Leavenworth.
            We might try there.

SPADE:      Leave us not delay. On to Ruthie's!

MUSIC:      BRIDGE

SOUND:      LESS FASHIONABLE STREET SOUNDS

SOUND:      ORDINARY TYPE DOORBELL . . . DOOR CRACKED
            OPEN

RUTHIE:     Hello, you. Hun, Doryce, where'd you come from?
            Thought you was down to the Blue Bottle.

DORYCE:     I been sick. This is Sam Spade.

RUTHIE:     Well come right in. (SOUND: DOOR CLOSED) Now you just tell Ruthie all about it, dearie.

DORYCE:     Well, I was in the hospital. Double pneumonia- and I shouldn't ought to be out now-I got these shooting pains- (SOUND: DRINK POURED)

RUTHIE:     Drink this, dear, it'll help you.

SPADE:      (COUGHS)

RUTHIE:     Oh, pardon me. Say when, Mr. Spade.

SPADE:      Just to the top of the glass.

RUTHIE:     You two meet in the hospital?

DORYCE:     No, he's in the jury, and I'm a witness, isn't that the limit, and we're both AWOL . . .

RUTHIE:     Now, isn't that cunning.

DORYCE:     And we're looking for Gladys- (SOUND: GLASS SLAMMED DOWN ON TABLE) an account of the trial will go on forever, Ruthie-we've just got to find her.

RUTHIE:     Get out!

DORYCE:     Ruthie, did we say anything wrong?

RUTHIE:     Get out! You're trying to ruin me. Who sent you here? Big Louie? I told Marty Snyder she wasn't here, and I was leveling. You come here like this you'll get me knocked off. Now get out.

MUSIC:      BRIDGE AND TO B.G.

SPADE:      The rest of the way was all downhill. Down Leavenworth to Turk Street, across Turk to Mason and back to

Columbus. (SOUND: SNEAK HARBOR SOUNDS) Finally we got somewhere in the neighborhood of North Point.

(SOUND:       VERY UN-CHIC STREET NOISES AND LOUDER HARBOR SOUNDS) (SPADES AND DORYCE'S FOOTSTEPS ALONG THE STREET)

DORYCE:       It was right along in here somewhere, I know it was.

SPADE:        What's the street number?

DORYCE:       Would you mind stopping just a minute? I've got that shooting pain again. I shouldn't ought to have come out like this.

SPADE:        We'll catch a taxi back to the Hall. Here lean on me.

DORYCE:       This is the place. Right here with the brick front.

SPADE:        Sure you feel well enough to go on?

DORYCE:       Sure, sure I'm okay.

SOUND:        TRUCK ROARS PAST BACKFIRE?

DORYCE:       (GASPS) What was that?

SPADE:        It's okay, Truck backfiring.

SOUND:        KNOCKING ON DOOR: DOOR OPENED

LANDLADY:     What you want?

SPADE:        We're looking for Gladys Raye.

LANDLADY:     You the law?

SPADE:        This young lady is her sister. She just came into town and she wants to find Gladys.

LANDLADY:    What's the matter with her? She sick?

DORYCE:    I been in hospital. Double pneumonia. I get these pains. Listen we walked a long way. If Gladys is here, please don't tell us any lies.

LANDLADY:    Up the stairs, Big Louis Havoc's office. First door to your left.

DORYCE:    You mean she's here?

LANDLADY:    Sure. Go on up. She's expecting you. The door's unlocked.

SPADE:    Thanks. Can I have my wallet back now?

LANDLADY:    What's that?

SPADE:    It's in your apron pocket there.

LANDLADY:    Now how'd it get there? Huh-five dollars-take it.

SPADE:    Thanks. Come on, Doryce.

SOUND:    STEPS UPSTAIRS

SPADE:    Can you make it?

DORYCE:    I'm okay.

SPADE:    That's just what I was thinking. Come here.

DORYCE:    (COMING OUT OF CLINCH) Gee, you're nice.

SPADE:    Come on.

SOUND:    STEPS ON LANDING KNOCK ON DOOR DOOR OPENS

MUSIC:    PUNCTUATE AND UNDER

SPADE:      The shabby, rickety looking door swung open, and we walked into another world. Stream-lined office furniture, indirect lighting, no windows, but you could smell the air-conditioning. (SOUND: DOOR CLOSES)

The door clicked shut behind us, and I wheeled around. (MUSIC: ACCENT) The shabby wooden door that opened off the hallway was backed with a layer of steel armor-plate, and covered in green baize. There was no knob or lock on the inside of Big Louie Havoc's office and you couldn't have slipped a razor-blade into the crack around it. No baseboards, no openings but a couple of air-conditioning vents about the size of my head. Then Doryce leaned against me.

DORYCE:     (SOBS) Oh Sam-Sam.

SPADE:      Take it easy, Sweetheart. You're okay, remember?

DORYCE:     Sam-would you kiss me again?

SPADE:      Sure. (PAUSE)

DORYCE:     Don't let go, hold onto me-

SPADE:      (SEES THAT SHE IS WOUNDED) Hey-

DORYCE:     Yeah-I didn't want to say anything- I was afraid you'd take me back to the hospital-I was afraid you'd take me back to the hospital-I was so sure we'd find Gladys here-is it- is it very bad, Sam?

SPADE:      I don't know- it's small caliber . . .

DORYCE:     Oh (GASPS) . . . it is bad . . . it is bad . . .

MUSIC:      KNIFE CHORD AND UNDER

SPADE:      She held on for a split second, her nails digging into my coat sleeve, and then all at once she went as limp as a rag doll there in my arms. I carried her over to the couch and made sure of what I already knew. Poor little Doryce De Soto was a very dead doll. I looked at my hand. There was blood on it. I reached in my overcoat pocket for a handkerchief, my hand closed on cold metal-it was a beautiful little twenty-five caliber automatic known in the trade as a belly-gun. Light enough to be planted in my overcoat pocket by the landlady while she was lifting my wallet, but powerful enough to kill. (MUSIC UP AND DOWN BRIEFLY) . . . I found a bottle of bourbon in the desk drawer, and poured myself a slug of it. An hour later the bottle was empty, but I was still no nearer to the answer. All I know for sure was, that because a man named Big Louie Havoc did or did not want a man named Rocky Morrison to take the rap for the murder of a man named Albert Fogarty, and a girl named Gladys Raye did or did not want to testify Doryce De Soto was dead and I was framed with the murder weapon.

MUSIC:      FIRST ACT CURTAIN

ANNCR:      The makers of Wildroot Cream-Oil are presenting the weekly Sunday adventure of Dashiell Hammett's famous private detective . . . SAM SPADE!

MUSIC:      (UP AND RESOLVES OUT)

ANNCR:      Now! Here's important news on good grooming: Better than four out of five users of Wildroot Cream-Oil to all other hair tonics. Here is news and even more conclusive evidence that Wildroot Cream-Oil is . . . "again and again . . . the choice of men . . . who put good grooming first." So if you want the well-groomed look that helps you get ahead, socially and on the job, listen: Recently, thousands of people from coast to coast who brought Wildroot Cream-Oil for the first time were asked: "How does Wildroot Cream-Oil compare with the hair tonic you previously used?" The results were amazing. Better than four out of five said they preferred Wildroot Cream-Oil. And no wonder. It gives you the advantage that men consider most important: Wildroot Cream-Oil grooms your hair neatly and naturally . . . relieves annoying dryness . . . and removes loose ugly dandruff. What's more, non-alcoholic Wildroot Cream-Oil is the only leading hair tonic that contains LANOLIN, that's like the oil of your skin. So ask for Wildroot Cream-Oil . . . "again and again . . . the choice of men . . . who put good grooming first."

MUSIC:      (ACCENT AND HOLD)

ANNCR:      And now back to "JURY DUTY" . . . .tonight's adventure with SAM SPADE!

MUSIC:      (SECOND OVERTURE AND B.G.)

SPADE:      The more I thought about it the madder I got. I don't like any murder, but a stupid murder makes me boil. And nobody who knew Doryce De Soto well enough to kill her would have anything but a stupid reason for doing it. I put my overcoat over her body and went back to casing Big Louie Havoc's office-type trap. Nothing there but a desk calendar. The month showing on the calendar was January, 1943. If this was Big Louie's hideout there'd be some simple way to unlock the door from the inside. And there was. I ran my hand along the under-edge of the desk. There was a button there.

| | |
|---|---|
| (SOUND: | BUZZER) I pushed it, and naturally the door swung open. (SOUND: STEPS OUT OF ROOM AND DOWN RICKETY STAIRCASE) |
| LANDLADY: | (FADING ON) Who's that? What are you doing up there? |
| SPADE: | I want some answers and I want them fast. I haven't got much time. |
| LANDLADY: | I stand mute. I know my rights. |
| SPADE: | Who told you to slip this gun in my pocket? Where's Big Louie Havoc? |
| LANDLADY: | Don't you yell at me! |
| SPADE: | Why you old hag, I ought to cut your fingers off at the knees . . . secret rooms- gangsters hideouts- a girl murdered on your doorstep- where's your phone, I'm calling the cops. |
| LANDLADY: | It's out of order-and besides we don't have any phone. |
| SPADE: | Where is it? |
| LANDLADY: | Okay, son, you got me bluffed. Can I trust you to keep me out of it? |
| SPADE: | Where's Big Louie? |
| LANDLADY: | I ain't seen him since forty-three. Snyder says he's on ice somewhere. |
| SPADE: | Why did you tell me Gladys Raye was up there? |
| LANDLADY: | Well, ain't she? |
| SPADE: | No, she ain't. Now- tell me where she is, or I'll tear your wig off! |

LANDLADY:    Don't you contradict me, young man-I said she's up there and I mean it. I seen her- she come in with Snyder. He says he wants to keep her on ice for a while. I ain't moved away from the lace curtains since. Lessen she disappeared into woodwork, she's in that room.

SPADE:    Now listen, Granny-

LANDLADY:    Now before you go flyin' off the handle again, go back and take another look.

MUSIC:    PUNCTUATES AND B.G.

SPADE:    So I did. (SOUND: RIPPING UP CARPET) I ripped up the carpet, a strip at a time. Nothing there. But under the desk I did find something. A switchbox, sunk in the concrete. (SOUND: TO SUIT ACTION) I pried it open and looked inside. It was an ordinary-type electric switch, and it said on it in English "On" and "Off"- It was on, so I turned it off. I waited for something to happen. Nothing did, except a kind of a deathly quiet settled over the room. I looked up at the air-conditioning vent-the little ribbon of crepe paper on grill was still fluttering in the breeze. I took another look at that switch. Just under the on-off part of it there was a knob with some numbers around it. I blew some of the dust of. It was a thermostatic control, and the numbers were figured in degrees below freezing. I remembered what the old lady had said about Marty Snyder wanting to keep Gladys on ice for a while, and a rather horrible thought crossed my mind. SOUND: THUMPS AND MUFFLED CRIES Then I heard the thumping on the other side of the wall. I edged along it, my ear flushed with the concrete.

GLADYS:    (OFF MUFFLED) Help-help-let me out of here!

SPADE:    Where are you? Can you hear me?

GLADYS:    (MUFFLED) Help me-I'll freeze to death!

SPADE:    How do I get through the wall?

GLADYS:    The lights! The lights!

SPADE:    Which lights? They're all the way around the room.

GLADYS:    The lights!–right over your head!

SPADE:    (MUSIC: IN AND UNDER) I looked up. The lights were concealed behind a molding that ran near the ceiling. I stood up on a chair to get a better look, lost my balance and grabbed at the molding to steady myself. Instead of steadying me, it carried me with it, all the way to the floor. (SOUND: HEAVY ROLLERS) The whole four-foot section of concrete wall disappeared into the floor, and a blast of refrigerated air roared out at me. The cold room was half the size of Big Louie Havoc's office, and stashed inside it was the reason for Big Louie's elaborate ice-box. Enough nitroglycerin and detonating caps to crack every safe in the city. And huddled up against a pile of crates was a very cold blond. Her face and hands were blue, and her teeth were chattering, but she still seemed afraid to come out.

GLADYS:    Who-who are you?

SPADE:    Never mind that now, we'll talk when we get you thawed out. (SOUND: STEPS)

GLADYS:    But-but-wait-we can't just leave him there.

SPADE:    Here, put this coat around you. Leave who in there?

GLADYS:    It's so terrible, I can't even talk about it . . . go and look for yourself . . . behind that hunch of boxes.

SPADE:      (MUSIC: IN) I went, and I looked. I thought at first at it was a great wax dummy. But it wasn't (MUSIC: PUNC-TUATE) It was Big Louie Havoc. If he had been in there four days or four years, he wouldn't have looked any different, but from what I hadn't heard of him in the past four years, I settled for that. I left him there. Gladys was beginning to show signs of life. She'd found a bottle of whiskey in the desk drawer and held it steady enough to get a drink out of it. (MUSIC OUT)

GLADYS:     (GULPS)

SPADE:      Here, let me help you. You'll break those beautiful white teeth.

GLADYS:     (GULPS) Thanks. Hey, who's that over there on the couch? Looks like Doryce.

SPADE:      Yeah.

GLADYS:     She asleep.

SPADE:      Yeah, let her alone. She's had a hard day.

GLADYS:     Didn't she testify at the trial?

SPADE:      Yeah, she testified.

GLADYS:     What's she doing out?

SPADE:      She was worried about you, Gladys.

GLADYS:     I just couldn't get up there and testify against Rocky Morrison. He didn't kill Fogarty. It was Marty Snyder. Marty told him if he kept his mouth shut, he'd defend him and get him off, and Big Louie would make a big shot out of him as a reward. Big Louie-that's a laugh.

SPADE:      How long has he been dead?

GLADYS:     Four years-since January-forty-three.

SPADE:      Marty knock him off?

GLADYS:     No. He died natural. Heart attack. Sitting right here in this chair. And that was when Marty told me about his big idea. He said with Big Louie dead the organization would fall to pieces-but if we went on pretending that Big Louie was alive-and Marty acted like he was just carrying out his instructions-then everything would go on just the way it did before.

SPADE:      So Marty told the boys that Big Louie was hot, and was going to stay on ice for a while?

GLADYS:     Yeah-but I never knew till now how true that was.

SPADE:      Why are you spilling all this to me?

GLADYS:     Because that Marty Snyder is a rat. He tried to kill me too. Just because I wouldn't say anything to put Rocky Morrison in the gas chamber. Rocky's a right guy. That's why Marty hates him so-because he's a right guy.

SPADE:      Have another drink. You and Rocky Morrison, eh.

GLADYS:     Yeah-me and Rocky-so what. And I'm going to kill that Marty Snyder. (FOUND BOTTLE ON THE DESK) Kill him dead-you hear me? I'm done! (GASPS AND STOPS)

SOUND:      DOOR OPENS

MUSIC:      UNDER

SPADE:      She stopped suddenly. I heard the door open behind me. I didn't turn around, but I knew who it was by the look in her eyes. She walked straight into my arms, put her left arm around my neck and kissed me deliberately. At the same moment, I felt her hand go in my inside coat pocket, when it came out she pushed me out of the way and let him have it.

SOUND:        SHOTS-BODY FALL-SPADE'S STEPS ACROSS

SNYDER:    I heard you were looking for her- word's all up and down the hill. Didn't think you'd find her.

SPADE:     I think you've got it bad, Snyder. Why don't you get it off your chest? Just say yes twice. Did you kill Fogarty, and frame Rocky Morrison for it?

SNYDER:    Well-I-I well, yes.

SPADE:     And did you kill Doryce tonight?

SNYDER:    Yeah-shot her from the truck.

SPADE:     (BREATHS SIGH) Okay, Snyder. I'd like to be able to say I'm sorry for you, but I honestly can't.

MUSIC:     CLIMAX AND UNDER

SPADE:     And these, gentlemen, are the true facts concerning the deaths of Doryce De Soto, about which I feel very bad, and of Marty Snyder, about which I feel nothing in particular. As you know, the next morning, when Gladys Raye was put on the stand, the defense collapsed. I consider that I have discharged my civic duty as pertains to service as juror for the calendar year 1947. Thank you, and good-night Mr. District Attorney, Period. End of report.

EFFIE:     Well of all the- Sam it just gives me goose pimples all over. Imagine that Big Leo Hovic.

SPADE:     Big Louis Havoc, Effie!

EFFIE:     Well, that's what I meant. In that ice box for four years and all that nitroglycerin around.

SPADE:      Yes-that's dangerous, Effie- he could have got killed-

EFFIE:      Well, I suppose I should be glad you got out of jury duty, Sam. But you know the way things are-three dollars a day-it's sure money, Sam. And your meals and . . .

SPADE:      Oh, go home.

EFFIE:      Why goodnight, Sam.

SPADE:      Goodnight, Sweetheart.

MUSIC:      CURTAIN

ANNCR:      It's true, fellows, girls are mighty particular about the way your hair looks. They like to see it groomed the handsome "Wildroot Way" . . . neatly and naturally . . . They like to see that handsome "Wildroot look" . . . casual and well groomed. So get that handsome Wildroot look with Wildroot Cream-Oil! It does a wonderful job of grooming your hair. Remember there's not a drop of alcohol in Wildroot Cream-Oil and it contains soothing LANOLIN. So take Wildroot's Close-Up Test . . . won't you? Yes, stand in front of your mirror and take a good close-up look at your hair and scalp. You may be startled by what you see! Signs of unruly hair, dryness or loose dandruff tell you-you need Wildroot Cream-Oil . . . "again and again . . . the choice of men . . . who put good grooming first."

MUSIC:      THEME

ANNCR:      The Adventures of Sam Spade . . . Dashiell Hammett's famous private detective is produced and directed by William Spier. Sam Spade is played by Howard Duff. Lurene Tuttle is Effie. "The Adventures of Sam Spade" is written for radio by Bob Tallman and Gil Doud, with musical direction by

Lud Gluskin. This is Dick Joy reminding you that next Sunday, author Dashiell Hammett and producer William Spier join forces for another adventure with Sam Spade brought to you by Wildroot Cream-Oil . . . again and again . . . the choice for me who put good grooming first.

MUSIC:       (GOODNIGHT SWEETHEART TO: )

# THE ADVENTURES OF SAM SPADE
## "THE BAY PSALM CAPER" #184

SUNDAY, MARCH 26TH, 1950
5:00 – 5:30 PM PST

ANNCR: Wild Root Cream-Oil Hair Tonic, and new Wildroot Liquid Cream Shampoo present – "The Adventures of Sam Spade"

MUSIC: UP INTO TRILL . . . INTO PHONE RING:

SOUND: PHONE UP . . . SPADE ON FILTER:

EFFIE: Sam Spade Detective Agency.

SPADE: A beautiful woman, Sweetheart, is a booby trap!

EFFIE: Sam! Were you caught?

SPADE: That is hardly respectful to your employer, Effie. You can take your bill for back wages from the top of the pile and place it at the bottom.

EFFIE: Yes sir. Although you haven't been paying either end.

SPADE: That's because I like to play both ends against the middle.

EFFIE:  But Sam, what about the girl? She was such a gorgeous blonde and you're so easily influenced, I was worried about you.

SPADE:  So was I, Sweetheart.

EFFIE:  Was that man really killed?

SPADE:  If not, the morgue should charge him for overtime parking.

EFFIE:  And – is this right – it had something to do with a bookie?

SPADE:  A very old bookie, Ef. Almost unreadable. Stay right on your shelf, little reprint, and I will take you down, put you on my lap, and browse you while I dictate my report on a Collector's Item, which we will call enigmatically, the "Bay Psalm" Caper!

MUSIC:  (THEME AND TO B.G.)

SPADE:  (COMES IN SINGING)

EFFIE:  Hello, Sam . . . Hiya, Sam!

SPADE:  (STOPS SINGING, BRISKLY) Date, March 26, 1950, to –

EFFIE:  No greeting, Sam? No opening remarks?

SPADE:  No opening remarks, Effie.

EFFIE:  But, Sam . . . it isn't usually this way.

SPADE:  You might as well know, I'll give it to you straight. We were twenty second over – and you – were considered expendable.

EFFIE:  Oh, Sam! (WAILS)

SPADE:  Stop it now. You wouldn't have wanted me to give up any of my jokes?

EFFIE:      Oh no, Sam. I wouldn't want to infringe on your time.

SPADE:      All right then.

EFFIE:      (WAILS)

SPADE:      Oh, shut up.

SPADE:      SPADE: Date: Fill it in. To: Detective Lieutenant Dundy, Homicide Detail, San Francisco Police. From: Samuel Spade, license number 137596. Subject: The Bay Psalm Caper. Dear Dundy . . . (MUSIC: SNEAK) The brink business you and yours enjoyed over the weekend began when Karen Rowland floated into my office. I say floated, because how else does a dream travel? She was a honey-blond, a great thing at best . . . and this was at best. She had been taking good care of herself, I noticed as she took off her coat, because she was in wonderful shape.

KAREN:      Mr. Spade, you're the only one I can turn to.

SPADE:      You couldn't have made a wiser choice. It's quality, not quality that counts.

KAREN:      I've heard that you give every case your personal attention.

SPADE:      Yes, I find that close contact between client and detective is very desirable. You can count on my undivided attention.

KAREN:      You're so kind. I'm so worried, I could cry.

SPADE:      I have a clean white handkerchief or a comforting old right shoulder, as you prefer. The shoulder's very nice today.

KAREN:      Thank you. My name's Karen Roland. What do you charge for a case?

SPADE:    My fees are flexible. In your case, so moderate I'm almost working for nothing. Now what's the trouble?

KAREN:    It's my husband.

SPADE:    Oh! Prices have suddenly gone up. Change at two, you know. What about your husband?

KAREN:    He's missing.

SPADE:    He doesn't realize how much.

SPADE:    How long's he been missing?

KAREN:    A week.

SPADE:    And you're just reporting it now? Hasty type, aren't you?

KAREN:    We'd been quarreling. At first I thought he'd left me.

SPADE:    How do you know he hasn't?

KAREN:    I don't. But we've always made up when we've quarreled before. This time I haven't heard from him. He left all his clothes and everything.

SPADE:    I'll grant you, Mrs. Rowland, that you don't look like the kind of woman a man in his right mind would leave. Amnesia's a possibility. But why did you come to me? I love it, of course, but – well, I'll say it – Why can't you go to the police?

KAREN:    Because I think my husband's been doing something illegal.

SPADE:    Aha. And what's that?

KAREN:    I don't know. He wouldn't tell me. He came home one night about two weeks ago and dropped a hundred dollars in my lap and said, "Go buy yourself a new dress." Well,

I asked him where he got the money, because he hasn't made any lately-But he wouldn't say. Acted strange . . . sorta froze up. Well, he came home late every night that week and he was afraid. Finally he burst out with it:  H e said he was on a crooked job. That's all he'd say. Just that.

SPADE: Did you tell him to drop it?

KAREN: Yes, I did. That's why we quarreled. He was in too deep, he said, and we needed the money. Roy's a printer. He's been out of work a lot.

SPADE: This mysterious, new, illegal work he's got into. You have no idea about it?

KAREN: It must have been some kind of printing. His fingers were ink-stained when he came home.

SPADE: Uh huh. Do you know where he worked?

KAREN: I'm not sure. I followed him one day and saw him go into that new Mott Building on Market Street. You know, the one they-

SPADE: Yeah. I know the one. Well, it's a start, anyway. Got a picture of him?

KAREN: Yes, here.

SPADE: Thanks. Anything else?

KAREN: I don't know if it means anything, Mr. Spade, but a couple of nights I heard Roy muttering in his sleep.

SPADE: That so? What was he muttering?

KAREN: Once he said-quite distinctly-"Don't do it, Keller."

SPADE: "Don't do it, Keller." I see. And he said something else?

KAREN:    He said it several times. This other thing. Two words. It sounded like "Bay Sum."

SPADE:    Bay Sum? Bay Sum? You sure it wasn't Bay Rum? Maybe he was dreaming he was having a close shave. (PAUSE) Yes. Okay, Mrs. Rowland, I'll see what I can find out.

KAREN:    (PAUSE) You haven't mentioned money, Mr. Spade.

SPADE:    Haven't I?

KAREN:    That hundred dollars he gave me. Here it is.

SPADE:    You didn't buy the new dress.

KAREN:    A woman dresses to please her husband, Mr. Spade. Until Roy comes home again I won't be very interested in what I'm wearing.

MUSIC:    IN AND B.G.

SPADE:    I spent quite a moment, after she's left, wondering if maybe there wasn't something to marriage. I think about that sort of thing, you know, Dundy, about once or twice a year. And then I think of Mrs. Dundy, and I'm all right again. (MUSIC: CHANGES MOOD) The Mott Building is a newcomer among the veterans on Market Street. A lot of names on the register directory board: a doctor, a civil engineer, eight attorneys, and a Lexington Swazey, rare books, sixth floor. (STEPS) There was a reception room with nobody in it. (SOUND: DOOR KNOCKING) I knocked at the inside door but nobody paid any attention. (OPEN) I opened it and saw why. (VOICES ARGUING) Two guys were busy yelling at each other. One was a smooth, white-haired gent with a pince-nez, who looked familiar from someplace. Bookish type. The other was a chunky, swarthy lad who looked like the only reading he'd ever done was in the Alcatraz library.

MURDO:     You're not dealing with a punk, Swazey. You try any fast ones on me and I stop you colder than a mackerel.

SWAZEY:    Don't threaten me. Nick, if you want to do business, you'll do it my way or not at all.

MURDO:     I made my investment and I'm not getting tapped for any more coin, see? You pay the five grand.

SWAZEY:    We'll split it, that's final.

MURDO:     Why, you two-bit Big Shot! I'll blast you to – (SPADE'S STEPS)

SPADE:     Drop the rod, Junior, or I'll drop you.

MURDO:     (ON, NOW) Huh? Who are you? What's the big idea buttin' in?

SPADE:     I said drop it.

SOUND:     GUN DROPPED TO FLOOR

MURDO:     This ain't a healthy thing for you to do, Mister.

SPADE:     I'll swallow a vitamin pill. Now get going!

MURDO:     I don't care who you are-you're not smart to crowd Nick Murdo, I always pay back a favor.

SPADE:     I'll look for you.

MURDO:     Yeah-and you'll find me.

SOUND:     DOOR SLAMMED

SWAZEY:    Thanks for the assist. These small-time hoodlums are hopeless hot-heads.

SPADE:     Was he angry because you don't have a first edition of "Rebecca of Sunnybrook Farm"?

SWAZEY:     Eh? What's that?

SPADE:      Only a pleasantry, sir. Very small.

SWAZEY:     He was here on quite another matter. But I can take care
            of myself. One meets all types in this business. What can
            I do for you?

SPADE:      My name is Spade. I'm looking for a printer named Roy
            Roland. Does the name mean anything to you?

SWAZEY:     Roy Roland? Roy Roland? No, I don't know anyone by
            that name. Am I supposed to?

SPADE:      He's had dealings with someone in this building. I thought
            it might be you.

SWAZEY:     Oh. What gave you that idea, Mr. Spade?

SPADE:      He's a printer, you deal in rare books. No connection?

SWAZEY:     I'm afraid not. I'm neither a publisher nor a bookseller
            in the retail sense. My specialty is a procurement of rare
            items for collectors. Sort of middleman between the deal-
            ers and the bibliophiles.

SPADE:      I see. If I wanted to pick up a rare book-say a Kipling first
            or a Gutenburg Bible- you could get it for me.

SWAZEY:     Given proper time, yes.

SPADE:      By the way, Mr. Swazey, do you know Chicago pretty well?

SWAZEY:     Chicago? Why no, I've never been there.

SPADE:      Oh? Well, thanks for your time.

SWAZEY:     Not at all. I hope you find your man. Good reading, sir!

MUSIC:      BRIDGE AND B.G.

SPADE:      The face and polished manner of this charming book expert remained with me long enough for me to visit your picture gallery, Lieutenant, and check my memory. Dapper Dan Swan. He'd been indicted as a con man in charming Chicago eight years ago; the indictment didn't stick. Well, maybe Swan or Swazey was playing straight nowadays . . . but he wasn't. Then I thought of another name: Keller: It was just the right kind of company for a rare book man. I just thought of Mission Keller Book Mart. The store was dark when I opened the front door. But a minute later, the alleyway behind it blazed up like a Fourth of July.

SOUND:      FOUR GUN SHOTS: CAR MOTOR UP & ROARS OFF

MUSIC:      PUNCTUATION

SPADE:      A dark sedan, running without lights, roared out of the alleyway as I reached it. (STEPS . . . DOOR PUSHED) Behind the back door of the shop lay a gun with a green eyeshade. He'd been locking the back door; the keys were still in his hand. In his breast pocket was a bankbook, with a bullet through it. It said Account of Carl Keller. (THIN STING) "Don't do it, Keller," that's what Roy Roland had said in his sleep! Well, whatever it was, Keller wouldn't be doing it anymore. I thumbed through the bank-book. The entries were mostly sixty-seven dollars. The last entry, though, made this very day, was a five thousand dollar deposit! In his coat pocket was a slip which was written Coral Book Shop- Bachrach-Bay Psalm. (MUSIC: THIN STING) Bay Psalm! Bay Psalm! If you were muttering in your sleep, that might come out "Bay Sum!" (PAUSE) I looked down at the little dead book-seller and wondered what he had that made him worth dreaming about. I phoned your office for the ambulance and medical examiner. (STEPS AROUND MARBLE STAIRS, AND DOWN HALL) Then I doubled back to Swazey's building to get the answers to a few questions. There was a light in the office. I went in. Swazey was now here in sight- but his debating chum whom I'd relieved of the gun was there-with a friend. The friend had shoulders like an ox. It looked unhealthy in there, but I couldn't just leave. Murdo had gotten hold of another gun and was pointing it at me.

MURDO:     Come in, Come in! It's a pleasure to see you again, Pal.

SPADE:     The pleasure's all yours, Murdo.

MURDO:     Yeah, ain't it, though. This time I got the heater, Buttin-sky, and you'll give me yours-and the one you took off me.

SPADE:     Relax, Murdo.

MURDO:     Let's have 'em.

SPADE:     Okay-here's my gun-and yours.

SOUND:     GUNS DROPPED ON DESK

MURDO:     Thanks, Pal. So you're a private shamus, huh?

SPADE:     Redundant, but I suppose I should get double billing. You're fooling with Sam Spade, Junior.

MURDO:     That's very interesting. Only I ain't fooling. Tiny here ain't fooling, either, are you, Tiny?

TINY:      Naw, I ain't foolin'

SPADE:     He looks like the serious minded type.

MURDO:     Why you been stickin' your nose in here? Come on, whaddys know?

SPADE:      Not very much, Nick. What do you know?

MURDO:      A smart guy. I love smart guys. Come on, let's hear you.

SPADE:      You've got the wrong private eye, Nick. I've never had singing lessons.

MURDO:      You hear that, Tiny? He never took lessons.

TINY:       Yeah, boss, I heard.

MURDO:      Give him a lesson, huh, Tiny?

TINY:       A pleasure, Boss. Hold him.

SOUND:      PUNCH

SPADE:      (GRUNT OF PAIN)

MURDO:      What did you say? I couldn't here that.

SPADE:      Nuts!

MURDO:      He don't learn much from one lesson, Tiny.

SOUND:      PUNCH

SPADE:      (GRUNTS)

MURDO:      You was just a plain Buttinsky, you'd get off with a plain working over. But you're not even the law. You don't work for the taxpayers. We're taxpayers, Tiny.

TINY:       Yeah, sure, Boss. We're taxpayers.

SOUND:      PUNCH

SPADE:      (GRUNTS)

MURDO:      We can't leave a blabbermouth around.

SOUND:      PUNCH

TINY:        Ow! He hit me back!

MURDO:       He's out on his feet and he's still in there punchin'! This
             guy should get a hand, Tiny-full of knuckles!

MUSIC:       SNEAKING UNDER

SOUND:       BEATING AND BODY FALL, PICKED UP AGAIN

MUSIC:       UP TO FIRST ACT CURTAIN

MUSIC:       SECOND OVERTURE, AND B.G.

SPADE:       I lay there for a while. It might have been twenty years,
             but I think it was twenty minutes. When my muscles
             wanted to move again they moved. I was still in Swazey's
             office. Tiny and Murdo were gone. The big clock on the
             building across the street said eight-ten. In a desk drawer
             I found a bottle with a couple of belts of bourbon still left.
             They helped. I had things to figure out before I went to
             bed. I hate to get up in the morning wondering. I was just
             reaching for the door when the handle turned.

SOUND:       DOOR OPENED

SWAZEY:      Well, Mr. Spade, isn't it? To what do I owe this late visit?
             And what happened to your face?

SPADE:       You don't know?

SWAZEY:      Me? How could I?

SPADE:       Your friend Nick Murdo was here to see you. He saw me
             first. An ox called Tiny used me for a punching bag.

SWAZEY:      Well, you must have had a real rough time.

SPADE:       Yes, I must have. Now I want a few answers from you.
             Fast. I'm a little impatient about here.

SWAZEY:     Let's not take that tone, Spade. I'm not responsible for your misfortune.

SPADE:      A bookseller named Cal Keller was shot and killed about an hour ago. What do you know about it?

SWAZEY:     Keller killed? Too bad. A fine chap. A sound scholar with an extraordinary knowledge of books.

SPADE:      And poor knowledge of people-he trusted them. Why was he killed?

SWAZEY:     Me? Why ask me?

SPADE:      There's nobody else to ask – I'm in a hurry.

SWAZEY:     Sorry. I can't help you.

SPADE:      And you still don't know what happened to Roy Roland?

SWAZEY:     I told you that before. Any more questions?

SPADE:      Uh huh-here's one- Why does a con-man like Dapper Dan Swan suddenly show up in the rare book business under the name of Lexington Swazey?

SWAZEY:     Spade, I'm sorry you asked me that. I deeply regret this turn of events, but I'll have to ask you to walk into that closet.

SPADE:      My gun again. Well, that tells me something.

SWAZEY:     Back up. Into the closet.

SPADE:      It might be a little stuffy in there.

SWAZEY:     Will you walk in or will I carry you in? That'll be so noisy-and messy-and final.

SPADE:      These decisions-they're driving me crazy. Okay, okay, I'm walking.

SWAZEY:    There's nobody in the building so you can scream your head off tonight. Get in.

SOUND:    DOOR LOCKED

MUSIC:    AND UNDER

SPADE:    The closet wasn't built for comfort. Small, dark and reeking of camphor. Not a place for a self-respecting moth or man. The key was in the lock on the other side of the door. There was a wire coat-hanger in the closet. (PAUSE) Unwind it, turn it back into a length of wire. Poke through the lock.

SOUND:    KEY DROPPING TO FLOOR

SPADE:    Not much room under the door but enough. Poke around till you find the key on the floor, drag it inside. You see.

SOUND:    DRAGGING KEY ACROSS FLOOR:    KEY UN-LOCKING DOOR:    DOOR OPENED

MUSIC:    UP AND DOWN

SPADE:    One of the things that make San Franciscans better educated than New Yorkers is the fact that our public library is open till 9 P.M. - and the Manhattan Library's been closed three hours by that time. Of course, it's midnight then in New York . . . but that's their own fault. Our public library has a rare books department so I went there. The clock on the wall said eight forty-five. The man in charge looked like he was two hundred years old, but he couldn't have been more than 150 . . . I beg your pardon.

LIBRARIAN:    (ECHO) Oh! You startled me! This is a library, young man, not a stadium. No need to shout, you know.

SPADE:        I didn't realize I was shouting. I'd like some information.

LIBRARIAN:    You can't wish it into your brain, young man.

SPADE:        You are right, Sir. Nevertheless, I would like some information.

LIBRARIAN:    I have much to give. I've read a great many books in my time. Some day I shall write a great memoir of my own telling the world of my astonishing adventures among masterpieces of literature.

SPADE:        I'll buy a copy. Right now I want to know whether Bay Psalm means anything to you. That's B-A-Y, P-S-

LIBRARIAN:    Haste-impetuosity. Signs of a decadent age. Virtually no-one takes time to ponder and reflect and meditate these days. Of course there's such a book. I'm pleased to say we have a copy. Under lock and key of course.

SPADE:        It is valuable?

LIBRARIAN:    Extremely. Why do you realize, young man, that the Bay Psalm Book was the first volume printed in the Anglo-American colonies?

SPADE:        Aha! I didn't realize it, I confess.

LIBRARIAN:    Ah, yes, it was the very first book published in America. It came out of Stephen Daye's printing established at Cambridge, Massachusetts. Of 1700 copies of the work originally published, only eleven are still known to exist. Ergo, any one of these commands a fabulous price.

SPADE:        How high might be fabulous?

LIBRARIAN:  If memory serves, the last sale of a Bay Psalm Book, at an auction a few years ago, brought $151,000.

SPADE:  Wow! That's more than I make in a week!

LIBRARIAN:  In this case, I believe, the buyer was Mr. A.S.W. Rosenbach, the internationally known rare book dealer of New York City.

SPADE:  Any such in San Francisco?

LIBRARIAN:  Offhand, Mr. Felix Bachrach of this city comes to mind as a man who's well known in this field.

SPADE:  Bachrach . . . Bachrach! Ah, now we're getting somewhere. Thank you very much!

LIBRARIAN:  Don't rush off, young man. Do you realize that the Bay Psalm Book originally brought only twenty cents!? I must remember to include that in my memoirs.

SPADE:  I'll buy two copies.

SOUND:  BELL RINGS- NEWSPAPER TYPE

LIBRARIAN:  (SHOUTING) Nine o'clock! Closing time! Everybody out!

MUSIC:  BRIDGE, TRANSITION, UNDER

SPADE:  Funny how money clarifies a picture. A little collection of hymns published 200 years ago by a man who had trouble peddling the book for twenty cents. Now age and scarcity made it worth $150,000. $151,000, even. And for that kind of money guys who couldn't read more than the numbers on a race-track board would think murder was a good risk. On the slip of paper I'd taken from his pocket, I read again the words Bay

Psalm-Bachrach-Coral Book Shop. I found Bachrach's address in the phone book. He lived up on Nob Hill-naturally. Parked on a side street not far from his place was a girl who looked familiar. Karen Roland.

KAREN:     Oh, Mr. Spade! I've had good news.

SPADE:     You have? Your husband's back?

KAREN:     No, but he's all right. I can't tell you more, but I've heard from him. He's been working on a special assignment. I'm on my way to see him now. And I'm grateful for your interest and all your trouble.

SPADE:     Thank you for your gratitude.

KAREN:     Keep the money. And now you can drop the case. Now please go.

SPADE:     I'm afraid not, beautiful.

KAREN:     Oh, please, you must! Roy's life may be in danger if you don't.

SPADE:     I took this case when it was only a matter in your husband's dreams. It's cost one life already-I've taken a beating-no, I stay with this baby till it goes to bed. Who's taking you to see your husband?

KAREN:     I- I'm not at liberty to say, but I'm sure it's all right. Please go, Mr. Spade.

SPADE:     You trust too many guys.

KAREN:     But I trusted you.

SPADE:     That's what I mean. (PAUSE) Okay. I'll go.

MUSIC:     AND UNDER

SPADE:        I left her, but I didn't leave off watching her. I watched her, sitting in the car there, as I went up to Bachrach's door. And when I got inside I watched her through the window while giving Bachrach my other eye. He saw me in his study, a room that had three walls lined with books from ceiling to floor. An affordable little guy in his sixties.

BACHRACH:     Sam Spade? Of a detective agency? Mundane occupation.

SPADE:        Yeah, even on Sundays.

BACHRACH:     You-ah-seem to be dividing your attention. Something fascinating out that window?

SPADE:        Just a blonde I don't want to lose sight of.

BACHRACH:     I see. All very mysterious and detectival. Well. What brings you here, Mr. Spade?

SPADE:        A book you bought today, Mr. Bachrach. The Bay Psalm Book.

BACHRACH:     Oh yes. I made rather a good deal, I thought. I secured it for $130,000. The last copy previously sold brought $151,000.

SPADE:        You bought it from a Lexington Swazey?

BACHRACH:     Why, yes. I paid him this afternoon.

SPADE:        Check or cash?

BACHRACH:     Check, of course. Now what-

SPADE:        Before the banks closed?

BACHRACH:     Yes, as a matter of fact, my bank telephoned to confirm payment of the draft at ten minutes to three.

SPADE:        Don't look now but I think you bought yourself a lemon.

BACHRACH:     I don't understand.

SPADE:        You're stuck with a phony.

BACHRACH:     But that's impossible. I checked the book with a well-known bookseller, Carl Keller. He's an authority. And he phoned that it was genuine.

SPADE:        The money he got for saying so was genuine.

BACHRACH:     But . . . but Keller was honest.

SPADE:        Also hard up. Guys sometimes stop being honest when they're hard up. Keller got five thousand for authenticating this book. Seemed like an easy buck, but it cost him quite a lot. He died of it.

BACHRACH:     What! Why, that's terrible, terrible. I'll call my attorneys and begin suit for recovery of the money from Swazey.

SPADE:        Your attorneys will have to do some fast sprinting to catch him. Swazey's on his way to parts unknown, and- uh uh- I've got to be going.

MUSIC:        AND B.G.

SOUND:        TRAFFIC NOISES

SPADE:        I'd seen Karen Roland come to attention, as if she'd received a signal. Then she released the brake, and rolled down the hill. She rolled one block and pulled up in front of the Coral Book Shop. But before I could get to her, Nick Murdo and Tiny came running out of it and into her car. They pushed her into the back seat and drove away fast. I found a taxi and followed. The trail led across the Golden Gate Bridge to Sausalito. Murdo's car stopped in front of a two-story Spanish package in an eagle's nest setting high above the Bay. I got out of the cab half a block behind and watched Murdo and Tiny take Karen Roland into the house. I saw Tiny come back alone and make for the car. It was very dark, and I got into some shrubbery and made some noise.

| | |
|---|---|
| SOUND: | SHRUBBERY NOISE |
| TINY: | (LITTLE OFF) Huh? Who's that? |
| SOUND: | MORE SHRUBBERY NOISE |
| TINY: | (CAR CLOSED) Who's that making that noise? |
| SPADE: | It's only me-the old caretaker. |
| TINY: | (ON) Oh yeah? Well, old caretaker, you're gonna get taken care of-now, just- |
| SOUND: | POW!! PUNCH |
| TINY: | Ow! Whatsa big idea? |
| SPADE: | I owe you a few, you big ox. This time there's nobody holding a gun on me while you get the exercise. Now talk! |
| SOUND: | FIGHT, CRASHING, THEN DECISIVE WALLOP |
| SPADE: | Talk! |
| TINY: | (GASPS) I don't know anything! |
| SOUND: | PUNCH |
| TINY: | (GASPS) |
| SPADE: | That's for lying. You and Murdo just took Karen Roland in there. What for? |

TINY:        Swazey's orders. He's letting her see her husband.

SPADE:       Who owns the Coral Book Shop?

TINY:        I don't know.

SOUND:       PUNCH

TINY:        Ow!

SPADE:       Who owns it?

TINY:        Nick Murdo. But he don't know nothing about it. Another guy runs it for him.

SOUND:       PUNCH

TINY:        Ow! What's that for?

SPADE:       That's for the lie you're going to tell me when I ask you who killed Carl Keller.

TINY:        I didn't do it, honest. I never use guns.

SOUND:       PUNCH

TINY:        (GRUNTS)

SPADE:       Who did it?

TINY:        Nick.

SPADE:       Why?

TINY:        Nick had to pay him 5 G's. Nick was afraid he'd yap for more.

SOUND:       PUNCH

TINY:        (GRUNTS) What's that for?

SPADE:       Pleasure, pal. It's a real pleasure.

| SOUND: | SERIES OF SOCKS |
|--------|-----------------|
| MUSIC: | STINGER AND B.G. |

SPADE:    I left Tiny cold and tied up in the car, in the glove compartment of which I found my dear very own gun. Then I went toward the light in the house. It came from a basement with barred windows. At the back of the house was a screen door. It's easy to slit a screen and unlatch the door. Find the doorway leading to the cellar.

SOUND:    CREAK OF STAIRS

SPADE:    And not make too much noise. Listen to what's going on.

SWAZEY:   (LITTLE OFF) So now you've seen your husband again, Mrs. Roland. Your anxiety has greatly complicated my difficulties. As a result of your running to this detective, Spade, I find it necessary to leave the country for a while. Very irritating.

ROLAND:   I've done your work, Mr. Swazey, and you've made your money. We won't say anything. You can let us go.

SWAZEY:   My dear, Roland, that's out of the question. I didn't intend to do this, but you leave me no choice. (GUN COCKED)

KAREN:    You can't! You can't shoot us! You'll be caught!

SPADE:    Yes, he will. Drop it, Swazey!

SOUND:    TWO SHOTS:    GUN HITTING FLOOR

SWAZEY:   (GROANS, TOTTERS)

SPADE:    It's just your hand, Dapper Dan. We'll save the rest of you for the state. Uh-uh, Nick! I wouldn't try reaching if I were you. Get hurt.

KAREN:     Mr. Spade!

SPADE:     Always ready to serve the client.

KAREN:     Oh . . . but I was so wrong when I told you to stop the search.

SPADE:     I don't have any will-power. Never could eat just one peanut.

MUSIC:     CLIMAX TO B.G.

SPADE:     And that, Lieutenant, was how I happened to dump Dapper Dan, Nick Murdo and Tiny lad into your care, saving you the toll over Golden Gate Bridge, amounting to one buck round trip which I'll ask you for at your earliest inconvenience. You'll find it difficult to figure out, but nobody else would. Murdo got hold of the stolen copy of the Bay Psalm Book, of course, and called Dapper Dan Swazey in to peddle it. Dapper Dan hired Roy Roland to print up cleverly forged copies, one of which he offered to Bachrach. Keller blackmailed for five thousand to say the book was genuine, Swazey made Murdo pay it and Nick took care of Keller. Period. End of report. (MUSIC OUT)

EFFIE:     Oh, Sam, you've gone through so much! You've been beaten up and shot at and locked in a closet.

SPADE:     That was noting. I'd already had the worst blow. The real suffering came when I found out Karen had a husband.

EFFIE:     Oh, you couldn't go for that sort of woman, could you, Sam?

SPADE:     I could force myself.

EFFIE:     Then-then it was really noble of you to save her husband's life, wasn't it?

SPADE:    That it was. You may address me as Sir Sam. Now be a good girl, Sweetheart, and type that up.

MUSIC:    PHRASE OF THEME

EFFIE:    (FADE ON) (WITH STEPS) Here it is, Sam. But there's something I don't understand.

SPADE:    Well, naturally-unless all precedent is to be shattered. What is it this time?

EFFIE:    That genuine copy of the Bay Psalm Book. Are there really only eleven copies of it?

SPADE:    Only eleven they know about. There may be hundreds. Why, you may have one kicking around your attic.

EFFIE:    But, Sam, I don't have an attic.

SPADE:    Too bad. You've just lost yourself a hundred and fifty thousand dollars. A hundred and fifty one thou-

EFFIE:    Sam?

SPADE:    Yes, Ef. What now?

EFFIE:    If-if my husband were missing would you be eager to find him?

SPADE:    Your husband. (IT FLOORS HIM) You know-such a thought never entered my mind?

EFFIE:    (WAILS) I know it! Oh, Sam-m-m-

SPADE:    Come here . . . what's the matter?

EFFIE:    No, never mind, Sam . . . (STRUGGLING) Oh . . . Mm-mmmmmm . . . (GETS KISSED) Go on, beat it! (WAILS) (MUSIC SNEAK) Goodnight, Sam.

SPADE:      (PUZZLED) Well, all right. Goodnight, Sweetheart.

MUSIC:      UP TO CURTAIN

ANNCR:      The adventures of Sam Spade . . . are produced and directed by William Spier . . . Sam Spade is played by Howard Duff. Lurene Tuttle is Effie.

MUSIC:      THEME 'TIL CUE

ANNCR:      Tonight's Adventure with Sam Spade was written for radio by David Nowinson. Musical direction by Lud Gluskin with score composed by Pierre and Rene Guerregenac. A portion of the program was transcribed. Join us next Sunday, when Producer William Spier, presents another Adventure with Sam Spade, brought to you by Wildroot Cream-Oil . . . again and again the choice of men and women and children, too. This is Dick Joy speaking.

SAM SPADE

THE RADIO ADVENTURES OF SAM SPADE

BY MARTIN GRAMS, JR.

Available from BearManorMedia.com

www.ingramcontent.com/pod-product-compliance
Lightning Source LLC
Chambersburg PA
CBHW060327100426
42812CB00003B/901